Nobody Wrote This Book

The Philosophy, Theology, and Science of Creation and Evolution

2nd Printing

Steven E. Dill, D.V.M.

Nobody Wrote This Book

The Philosophy, Theology, and Science of Creation and Evolution

2nd Printing

By Steven E. Dill, D.V.M.

Copyright 2018, Steven E. Dill

ISBN 978-1-7326258-2-2

All rights reserved.
No part of this book may be reproduced or copied by any means – electronic, mechanical, photocopy, or otherwise – without written permission of the author, except for brief quotations in noncommercial reviews.

Introduction

In this book, I will try to answer a question that has been asked for thousands of years: How did life begin? I say, "try," because I cannot provide an answer that will be proof for everyone. No one can! At least not until Jesus Christ physically returns to earth. When that happens, believers and unbelievers alike will know for certain He is our God, our Master, and our Creator. Believers will know it with unimaginable joy, and unbelievers will know it in utter and eternal despair. On that day, you will stand before the Living Proof, and you will know Jesus Christ is Lord. If you have not yet put your trust in Jesus Christ as your Savior, I pray the Holy Spirit will use my weak words to bring about a powerful change in your heart. I want you to share in that eternal joy, too.

Table of Contents

Introduction 3

Table of Contents 5

Lack of Curiosity Kills the Man 7

Counterfeit Science 15

    The Tale of a Whale Without the Tail of a Whale 15

    Scientific Testing: True or False? 19

    Little Green Apples 24

    The Limits of Science 26

    Epistemology 27

    The Three Systems of Perception 29

    What Constitutes Scientific Proof? 33

The History and Philosophy of Science 35

    What is Science? 36

    What Is Reality? 39

    Philosoraptor vs. *Theologus rex* 39

    Worshiping The Unknown God 46

    Enter Stage Left: The Theory of Relativity 49

    Exit Stage Right: The Theory of Evolution 49

The Modern Definition of Science 89

    The Fathers of Modern Science 92

    20th Century Nobel Laureate Scientists who believed in God 96

    The Chess Grandmaster 98

The Scientific Method 101

    The Domino Universe 104

    Inference to the Best Explanation 106

Evolutionist Errors 109

    False Supposition 1: Life Doesn't Require an Intelligent Cause
....109

        Apparent Design 135

    Apparent Design vs. Actual Design 137

    Intelligent Design 142

    Stanley Miller's Apparatus 147

    Steven Dill's Apparatus 149

    Soup For the Creationist's Soul 150

False Supposition 2: Evolution Happened by Gradual Change 152

    Over The Rainbow 154

    Whale Evolution Family Tree 1 162

    Whale Evolution Family Tree 2 163

False Supposition 3: Natural Selection Caused Evolution 172

    Heredity and Environment 178

    E-Harmony? 185

    Evolution is A Craps Shoot 190

    Terminology Phenomenology 197

False Supposition 4: Evolution Permits Unlimited Change ... 204

False Supposition 5: Randomness Causes Evolution 217

False Supposition 6: Homology Implies Relationship 225

    The Two-Universe Model 230

False Supposition 7: Evolution is Simple 237

False Supposition 8: All It Takes is Infinite Time, Space, Matter, and Energy 251

    Infinite Universes Don't Help 253

False Supposition 9: The Mind is Matter 259

False Supposition 10: The Universe was Caused by Nothing 277

False Supposition 11: The Universe is Nothing 283

Conclusion 291

Index 295

Bible References 297

References 299

Lack of Curiosity Kills the Man

Man has always been curious about his origin, but I think there's more to it than just a question of origin. I think the question of man's origin has always been linked to the question of man's destiny. In fact, I think the question of man's destiny, both individually and collectively, has always been the more important question. As you are aware, the answers to these two questions have arisen from three disciplines of man's studies: Philosophy, Theology, and Science. As you are equally aware, these three disciplines are not necessarily mutually exclusive. There are no universally accepted boundaries dividing them. Their margins tend to blur as their definitions tend to vary. The importance and relevance of each discipline also seems to depend on whether you are a philosopher, a theologian, or a scientist. As we probe deeper into this issue, we will find ourselves facing some tough questions. Some of what I say may be uncomfortable because it might conflict with some of the things you believe. My only request is that you don't let your emotions overrule your intellect. Too often, strong emotions are a thin veneer covering great ignorance. Since these questions have been asked for so many years, and since they have been answered in so many ways, I won't pretend I can answer them in a way that will satisfy you. But, if I can't answer them to your satisfaction, I hope I can approach them in a way that will cause you to take a fresh look at your own answers. Are your answers right? Could your answers be wrong? What is at stake? Is this merely an academic pastime for argumentative debaters, or could your answers determine where you spend eternity?

I believe the answers to these questions are too important to relegate to mere debates. I know some of you will disagree because you love debates. Debates are all well and good, but when a swimmer is drowning, the last thing he needs is three or four lifeguards up on the beach debating over the best technique for saving him. You see, in my lifetime I have attended three university-sponsored evolution-creation debates and have watched several others on video. I am convinced formal debates don't change many minds. In fact, in three of those debates the moderators asked the audience at the end if anyone had changed opinions on the issue. In all three debates, not one person changed sides. Evolutionists coming to the debates left as evolutionists. Creationists coming to the debates left as creationists. I have read about exceptions, but generally I don't think debates save many "drowning swimmers." So, while I'm not sure formal debates will cause many evolutionists to become creationists, I am sure a year or two on a typical college campus will cause the majority of the students who are creationists to become evolutionists, and many of them will become Atheistic Evolutionists. I don't want to win debates; I want to win souls!

So, my plan is to approach this in a way you probably haven't seen in a typical creation vs. evolution book. The road most often traveled, by both sides of this issue, is to throw out questions or problems the other side can't answer, and then assume it proves your point. For example: Creationists often ask evolutionists about Piltdown Man, Archeoraptor, and the English Pepper Moth. They ask about these things because they know they were evolutionary hoaxes. On this basis, creationists claim victory. On the other hand, evolutionists ask creationists about the Paluxy River footprints, the 1977 Japanese Plesiosaur, and starlight traveling through Riemannian Space. These were creationist hoaxes. For evolutionists, this is their measure of victory. This is the kind of thing generally done when creationists and evolutionists clash, and in my opinion, not much is accomplished. Competitive ignorance is not the best way to communicate truth, and communicating truth is what I want to do. I want to present you with the truth, and I want to present it in such a way you will know **WHY** it is true.

Note: The words "creation" and "evolution" mean different things to different people. Not all creationists believe in the same theory of creation. Not all evolutionists believe in the same theory of evolution. As a Gap Theory creationist, I don't agree with some of the things proposed by Young-Earth creationists or with some of the things proposed by Day-Age creationists. Likewise, I know all evolutionists don't agree with some of the things proposed by other evolutionists. Some evolutionists say evolution applies only to the diversification of life, not the origin of life. Other evolutionists disagree; they use the word to include explanations for the origin of life from non-life. Some even include the formation of the stars, galaxies, and planets, *etc.*, and speak of the evolution of the universe. Because there are so many variations and views of creation and evolution, I will not make them a big issue in this book. However, I must point out something about evolution that is a big issue; for Christians, at least. There are two forms of evolution theory: Atheistic Evolution and Theistic Evolution. I reject them both. Why?

Atheistic Evolutionists say there is no God. They say the driving forces of evolution were the fundamental physical forces of nature alone. Theistic Evolutionists can agree with everything Atheistic Evolutionists say about evolution, except they believe God was the driving force. As a Christian Creationist, I totally disagree with Atheistic Evolutionists, but I don't find myself agreeing much with Theistic Evolutionists either. (Even though I used to be one.) I have two fundamental problems with Theistic Evolution.

The first problem is theological. I have a problem with the very concept of it being theistic. It's not that I disagree with the idea there **could be** a truly theistic form of evolution, it's just I don't believe there is any **theological** evidence for it. In spite of all the theologians who say they believe in it, I don't believe there are many (if any) believers in a truly theistic form of evolution. Rather than Theistic Evolution, I find most believers in God who also believe in evolution are Deistic Evolutionists. The difference between theism and deism is that theists believe in a God who is actively and directly involved with His creation. He intervenes from time to time (or continually) to set history moving along the course He wants. Deists believe in a God who created all the fundamental particles and forces, but then let them run on their own. Like a clockmaker who makes a clock, winds it up, and lets it run according to the mechanics he designed into the system, God lets the universe run by the mechanics He built into it. He never (or very rarely) directly intervenes. A theist would point to events such as God parting the Red Sea, providing Manna for the Israelites for forty years, raining fire and brimstone down on Sodom and Gomorrah, killing 185,000 Assyrian soldiers in one night outside of Jerusalem, and Jesus' resurrection as evidence God directly intervenes. Deists must explain these things in terms of naturalistic causes since they don't believe God directly caused them. The reason I don't like Theistic Evolution is because Theistic Evolutionists don't think the mechanics of evolution involved God's direct intervention. Instead, it all played out according to the interworking of the fundamental physical forces and fundamental physical particles He created in the beginning. They believe living organisms evolved, but they say the changes were indirectly caused by God using the mechanics of natural biological mutations and natural environmental changes to "create" new species. Looking at it one layer deeper, we see they also believe the natural biological mutations and the natural environmental changes were caused by the fundamental forces acting on the fundamental particles according to the fundamental properties, qualities, and characteristics God gave them in the beginning. That's Deism! I haven't heard anyone propose a form of evolution that included something like: During the Devonian Period, God came down and directly rewrote (not mutated) the DNA of organisms so Devonian species would exist in the Devonian environment. (Or, that God came down during the Devonian Period and directly changed the Devonian environment, so it would support Devonian species.) I have not heard anyone say God wiped out the dinosaurs by direct, miraculous action. He didn't send an angel down to slay them as He did the Assyrians outside Jerusalem. They all attribute it to the naturalistic process of an asteroid impact, or poisonous volcanic fumes, or disease, or climate change, or some other natural disaster. God used natural forces, not direct intervention. Again, this is Deism.

The problem with Theistic Evolution is it can't be Biblically distinguished from Deistic Evolution. (There are no Biblical passages that speak of evolutionary processes; deistic or theistic.) The problem with Deistic Evolution is it can't be scientifically distinguished from Atheistic Evolution. (There is no direct scientific evidence that God miraculously intervened.) If you are a Theistic Evolutionist, you might become angry as I speak out against evolution. You might object when I place your theory into the same category as the Atheistic Evolutionists' theory. Please hear me out before you toss this book aside. Without evidence that God directly (miraculously) intervened in the process of evolution, how do you know God did it?

1.) Is there a Bible passage telling how God came down and directly wrote genetic instructions in DNA molecules, the same way He came down and directly wrote the Ten Commandments on stone tablets?

2.) Can you point to a geological discovery showing how God miraculously changed a local environment, the same way Jesus miraculously changed the local environment when He calmed a storm at sea?

As we will soon see, changes in DNA instructions and changes in environments are considered to be the two driving forces of evolution. If you can't find a Bible passage or geologic evidence that God directly caused these changes, then your Theistic Evolution Theory is based on your beliefs alone; not on evidence from science or from the Bible. Without evidence that God directly caused evolution, then your Theistic Evolution looks exactly like Atheistic Evolution in terms of what happened, when it happened, where it happened, and how it happened. The fossils are the same, the strata are the same, the transitions are the same, the mechanics are the same, and the time periods are the same. The only difference is that you want to put God into the picture. Now, I commend you for wanting to put God into the picture, but I don't see how Theistic Evolution necessarily puts the God of the Bible into the picture. My warning to Christians is to be careful you aren't swayed by the word "Theistic." Just because someone says, "God did it," it doesn't mean the God of the Bible did it. It could have been Allah, or Zeus, or Odin, or Ra, or some other "supreme god." As Christians, we must make sure we defend the Biblical account of our origin; not just any religious account. Our job is to find the truth from the Bible and find the truth from science, and then share that truth with unbelievers so they will see how the Bible reveals the truth about our origin. This is an important step in removing the so-called "scientific" barriers to the Gospel. **When they see the Bible is 100% correct about our origin, they will be better able to believe it is 100% correct about our destiny.**

The second problem I have with Theistic Evolution is scientific. I believe science disproves evolution (of any kind) as being the process by which life arose and species originated. As I said, Theistic Evolution would look exactly like Atheistic Evolution from a purely scientific (observational) vantage point. If God caused the fundamental physical forces to act on the fundamental physical particles to cause (deistic) evolution, then there ought to be ample evidence from science that evolution happened. As we will see, however, that evidence is sorely lacking. Belief in Theistic Evolution is possible only because some believers in God also believe in evolution. If they didn't believe in evolution, they wouldn't be Theistic Evolutionists; they would be Theistic Creationists. Herein lies the problem: The evidence from science (true science) favors special creation. Why would I believe in Theistic Evolution (based on any religion) if science proves evolution never happened? If you are a Christian and you interpret the Bible as saying God gradually evolved life over long periods of time by a process of, "Survival of the Fittest," (and it takes some pretty powerful interpretive skills to do so) then that's fine with me, provided you realize the scientific evidence disagrees with your interpretation of the Bible. Again, as a former Theistic Evolutionist, I reject Theistic Evolution; however, for the sake of clarity, when I refute evolution in this book, I am generally referring to Atheistic Evolution.

Counterfeit Science

To help you learn to recognize truth, I decided to use the same method the Treasury Department uses to train its agents to recognize counterfeit money. They don't train them by having them study counterfeit bills. They train them by having them study authentic bills. They study the real stuff so thoroughly, and learn what genuine bills look like so well, that anytime they see a counterfeit bill, they instantly recognize it as phony. That's what I want to do in this book. I want you to learn what real science looks like so well, that you will recognize counterfeit science every time you see it. I won't focus so much on individual pieces of evidence. Rather, I want to show you how authentic science works, so you can see how the Theory of Evolution is based on false science. Of course, in doing this I must refute some pieces of evidence, but I don't do it to refute just those pieces of evidence. I do it to show you how evolution-science is faulty from its foundation up.

Let me give an example concerning the discovery of a fossil once used as proof for evolution. I'm not as interested in showing you why this particular fossil doesn't prove evolution. What I want is for you to learn how evolutionists think, how to evaluate their claims, and then to see why fossils don't prove the Theory of Evolution.

The Tale of a Whale Without the Tail of a Whale

I want to begin with the fossils of Rodhocetus, a large sea creature (from about 45 million years ago) discovered in Pakistan in 2001 by Dr. Phil Gingerich of the University of Michigan. Because this creature had some features similar to modern whales, it was declared to be the ancestor of whales. Evolutionists said this was absolute proof of whale evolution. Dr. Gingerich brought the fossils back to the University of Michigan where they were put on public display. Included in the display was a drawing of what Rodhocetus would have looked like in life. The drawing was based on fossil reconstructions, and it looked very whale-like. The drawing of Rodhocetus showed a fluke tail and front and back legs with flippers. Since whales have a fluke tail but not legs with flippers, these fossils allegedly showed how walking land-creatures evolved into swimming whales. For a while, Rodhocetus was the, "best proof ever," that whales evolved from land animals. But, as more and more evidence came to light, it was eventually shown that Rodhocetus didn't exactly prove what the evolutionists first claimed it did.

What typically happens is an evolutionist makes a startling new discovery. Maybe he or she finds a new fossil or a new biochemical that supposedly proves evolution. When that happens, academia and the news media go crazy about it. They use it to "prove" evolution is true, and they use it to "prove" creationists are stupid. Then with more research, the startling new discovery proves to be less startling than originally thought. In time, the claim is shown to be false... but you rarely hear about that in the news. The most interesting thing about these startling new discoveries is in the great majority of cases, other evolutionists are the ones who debunk them. That's right; evolutionists wind up disproving evolutionists. You see, there are so many sub-theories of evolution that scientists can't agree on any one version. Some believe whales evolved from a dog-like animal. Some believe it was from a cat-like animal. Some believe it was from a cow-like animal. Charles Darwin believed it was from a bear. Many evolutionists today believe it was from a hippopotamus-like animal. They all agree on evolution, but they don't want to agree on the other guy's version of evolution.

A video entitled, *Evolution: The Grand Experiment*,[1] tells the Rodhocetus story. (I highly recommend you purchase this video because it reveals much more than just the whale evolution story. It reveals many other errors in evolution's story.) It reveals how Dr. Gingerich's fossils set evolutionists abuzz with excitement. Here are two quotes from that video:

Annalisa Berta: "What's good about these particular fossil whale specimens is that they do show us intermediates in the evolution of the whale. We don't often get fossil intermediates so we can actually trace the development and characters; say for example, the evolution of swimming in whales. We don't often have that opportunity."

Annalisa Berta is a Professor of Biology at San Diego State University.

Kevin Padian: "There's a big exhibit out in Michigan. I was just there. They have all these things just sitting out there. They're all there. I mean you really have to be blind or three days dead to not see the transitions among these. You have to not want to see it."

Kevin Padian is a Professor of Integrative Biology at the University of California—Berkeley and the Curator of Paleontology, University of California Museum of Paleontology.

Hearing these two scientists make such bold statements about whale evolution, you would think these fossils proved evolution beyond question. This would be especially true if you were one of their students. Students don't hear the complete story in the classroom, or see all the evidence in their textbooks. Claims like these tend to make students believe evolution is true, but there was a problem with Rodhocetus. The fossils discovered by Gingerich didn't include bones from the tail or bones from the ends of the legs. He had no idea what these structures looked like. Nevertheless, the University of Michigan's drawing of Rodhocetus clearly depicted legs with flippers and a fluke tail. When it was pointed out to Dr. Gingerich those necessary intermediary structures were missing from his fossil specimen, he acknowledged he had speculated about them. Eventually the fossils of the legs were found, and it was shown that Rodhocetus had feet, not flippers. With that new information, Dr. Gingerich admitted Rodhocetus didn't have legs with flippers or a fluke tail. Since it didn't have the intermediate structures an intermediate species needed, it didn't show how swimming evolved in whales.

Now think back to those two quotes about how these fossils actually showed us the intermediates, and that you had to be blind or three days dead not to see the transitions. Was it because you were blind or three days dead you didn't see the intermediate structures, or was there another reason? There was another reason. You didn't see them because they weren't there, and they never had been! The evolutionists were seeing things that weren't there, yet they criticized creationists for not seeing them too. The only thing this story proves is that it is okay for scientists to use speculation as scientific "proof" if it favors the Theory of Evolution. Don't get me wrong. I'm not accusing Dr. Gingerich of being an evil evolutionist dedicated to corrupting the morals of our youth. I'm not accusing him of academic dishonesty. In fact, he strikes me as a very honest fellow. There is nothing wrong with speculation if it is not presented as fact, and he didn't present the drawing of Rodhocetus as fact. Even before the fossil legs with feet were discovered, he acknowledged he was speculating about Rodhocetus having legs with flippers. Once those fossils were discovered, he openly admitted Rodhocetus did not have legs with flippers or a fluke tail. He let the evidence speak for itself, and you can't get more academically honest than that. It pains me to say this, but in this he is more honest than most creationists. Most creationists have a distorted interpretation of the Bible, and/or a distorted interpretation of science, and they refuse to let the evidence speak for itself. Nor am I accusing Dr. Berta or Dr. Padian of anything diabolical. Like all of us, they tend to think and believe what they think and believe; and like all of us, they tend to agree more with what agrees with them. The point of disagreement I have with these three scientists is even if Rodhocetus had legs with flippers and a fluke tail, it wouldn't prove evolution.

This is a typical story of how evidence for evolution pops up from time to time, only to be later discarded by real science. Creationists are right in investigating these claims, but it always leaves us one-step behind. Yes, we need to show how these specific discoveries don't prove evolution, but when we do that, we only find ourselves facing the next startling new discovery that "proves" evolution. Rather than trying to disprove these individual "proofs" of evolution, I want to show you how the entire foundation of evolutionary thinking, their entire system of logic, is scientifically counterfeit.

Scientific Testing: True or False?

For a scientific statement to be true, it must be proved it isn't false. A proposed statement MUST BE FALSIFIABLE before it can enter the scientific realm. By falsifiable, I do not mean it must be shown to be false. I mean there must be a way of proving it is false if it is false. This applies to all three categories of scientific statements: Hypotheses, Theories, and Laws. We must be mindful that scientists think of these words differently than how the general public thinks of them. Don't think of Laws, Theories, and Hypotheses as purely a hierarchy of truthfulness. It's not that Hypotheses are not true, Theories are sometimes true, and Laws are always true. Often, we say something like, "Speaking hypothetically, if pigs had wings, they could fly." When we speak of hypotheses in this fashion, we are starting from the position that hypotheses are not true.

We also say things like, "Theoretically speaking, if you put a quarter in the slot machine and pull the handle, you could win $1,000." When we speak of theories in this fashion, we are starting from the position that sometimes theories are true and sometimes they are false. Of course, we all know Scientific Laws are facts and never wrong; right? Wrong. If you have studied the history of science, you know many "Scientific Laws" were later proven false when more and better evidence was considered. (Later in the book, I will share with you some of the Laws of Evolution presented as "proofs" for evolution, only to disappear from the realm of science because they were not true.) So, we must not think of Hypotheses, Theories, and Laws in this way. A true Hypothesis is just as true as a true Law. A false Law is just as false as a false Theory. While it is true to a certain extent that Laws imply a greater deal of certainty than Theories, and Theories more certainty than Hypotheses, these three scientific statements try to explain natural phenomena from a slightly different approach. Rather than being ways for declaring truth, they are ways for discovering truth. (This is what science is supposed to be all about.)

Hypotheses

Hypotheses try to discover **IF** something happens. They test to see if what is proposed to happen, truly happens. Thus, if I were to hypothesize an unseen force causes rocks to float upward when released from my hand, I would have to test my hypothesis by releasing rocks to see **IF** they float upward. If they didn't float upward, then my hypothesis would be falsified, and any theory or law based on my hypothesis would be invalid.

Theories

Theories try to discover **HOW** something happens. Theories are not mere expressions of possibilities. This is not how scientists think of theories. Instead, theories provide rules or explanations for the phenomenon in question. One problem with theories is they can be so eloquently expressed, people tend to think they are true just because they sound good. Another problem with theories is they are often assumed to be true just because the "experts" agree they are true. Theories must be subject to tests for falsifiability before they can be accepted as scientifically true. Any Theory of Floating Rocks based on my Hypothesis of Floating Rocks, must be rejected. It wouldn't matter how eloquently I described how rocks could float. No matter how many scientifically-sounding explanations for floating-rocks I gave, and no matter how many scientists agreed with me, my theory is not scientific because I could never prove rocks float when released.

Laws

Laws try to discover **WHAT** happens. The Law of Gravity says all particles of matter have an attraction for/to all other particles of matter. Laws often contain mathematical expressions. For instance, physicists describe gravity in terms of an acceleration at the rate of 32 feet/sec^2 at the surface of the earth. The Law of Gravity describes what the Force of Gravity causes, but not how. This is why the Law of Gravity still falls under the overarching Gravitational Theorem. The Theory of Gravity factors in relativity, quantum physics, curved-space, String Theory, and things like that as it tries to explain **HOW** gravity does **WHAT** gravity does. (No one knows.)

Thus, any Theory of Evolution is a set of rules or explanations for **HOW** living organisms supposedly came to be. (No one knows.) Darwin's explanation was Natural Selection. His theory, while the most well-known theory, was not and is not the only explanation for how evolution was supposed to have worked. There are other theories of evolution that propose different mechanisms explaining how life got here. Sometimes it's easy for creationists to criticize these other theories; they often contradict each other. However, this does not disprove the Theory of Evolution. It takes scientific evidence to do that, not the testimonials of other evolutionists. The Make-or-Break issue for these theories is not providing plausible explanations for how evolution COULD have happened. The Make-or-Break issue for all these theories is providing evidence that evolution DID happen. If it DID NOT happen, then creating an explanation for HOW it was supposed to have happened, is an exercise in futility. I might be able to come up with a theory for HOW the moon came to be made of green cheese, but once you prove the moon is not made of green cheese, my theory explains nothing. We will look at some of Darwin's hypotheses upon which he based his theory. If we can prove his hypotheses are false, then his theory falls apart.

Another thing we need to be mindful of is all three of these scientific statements are descriptions of what we observe happening in nature; they are not forces that cause those things to happen. The Law of Gravity does not cause the Force of Gravity. When someone says, "The Law of Gravity causes rocks to fall," or, "The Second Law of Thermodynamics causes things to wear out," they are not speaking scientifically; they are confused. The Laws of Nature are not the Forces of Nature. Likewise, when someone says they don't believe in evolution because, "it is only a theory and not a law," they are equally confused about science. (And I should know; I said this myself many years ago before I understood science.)

Scientific statements must be shown to be not-false before they can be accepted as true. Thus, false hypotheses must be able to be falsified. False theories must be able to be falsified. False laws must be able to be falsified. Science must provide tests that can prove false statements are false. Our job is to look at evolution's Hypotheses, Theories, and Laws to see if they are scientifically valid. Simply put, we need to determine if evolution's statements are falsifiable. If a proposed statement cannot be tested for falseness, then it cannot be accepted as a scientific truth **NO MATTER HOW MUCH EVIDENCE SEEMS TO SUPPORT IT.** A Test-for-Falseness must exist, or we are not dealing with true science. (This is the very argument atheists use to keep God out of the classroom. God's existence can't be falsified by science, therefore belief in God is unscientific... or at least that's what they argue. When they say this, they aren't speaking scientifically either; they too are confused. I'll explain why later.) The power of science is not in proving true statements are true, but in proving false statements are false. This may seem like a backward way to arrive at the truth, but it is a necessity in science. This concept can be confusing because proving something is true seems more powerful than proving it is not false. But that's not true. Let me prove it.

Little Green Apples

Imagine all the apple trees in the world produce only red apples... with one exception. There is a small orchard, on a small hill, in a small valley, on a small island, somewhere out in the middle of the Pacific Ocean, with apple trees which produce green apples. Further imagine this island has never been discovered. Because of this, the world's foremost apple expert, Dr. Red Appleby, makes this scientific statement: "All the apples in the world are red."

Now, let's ask this question: Is his statement true? No! Why isn't it true? It's because we know there really are green apples. The only problem is no one has ever discovered them. It may seem true, but it is not true. Dr. Appleby and all the Appleologists in the world have observed only red apples, but that does not prove his statement. After millions of observations show that apples are red, it may seem like his statement is true; but you and I know it's not true. **Evidence that apples are red does not eliminate the possibility that apples might be green.** Finding red apples does not prove the statement. No matter how many red apples you find, you haven't eliminated the possibility the statement might be false. An experimental test must be done that could falsify his statement if it is not true. If it is not true, then science requires a test to show it is not true. If there are non-red apples in the world, then scientists must be able to provide a test that proves the existence of non-red apples. Only after the test-for-non-red-apples proved there were no non-red apples, could scientists say with certainty that all the apples in the world are red. What kind of test would be required to satisfy true science? It would require looking at all the apples in the world, including the ones on that small island in the Pacific. No matter how many red apples you have observed in the past, it doesn't prove the statement is true; **but once you observe one green apple, it proves the statement is false.**

If you think about this, you can see what tremendous pressure this puts on the Theory of Evolution. **Finding evidence FOR the Theory of Evolution does not PROVE the Theory of Evolution.** It's like finding red apples. Observing red apples doesn't prove there are no green apples. Observing anatomical similarities, biochemical similarities, genetic similarities, and particular sequences of particular fossils in particular geological strata, is like observing red apples. These things may appear to prove the Theory of Evolution, but they don't. They don't falsify the alternative theory that there was a Creator of life. Atheists must prove there is no Creator before they can say Atheistic Evolution is true. This means they must be able to devise a test that could falsify the existence of a Creator, and then prove a Creator cannot exist. But, since they cannot devise such a test, the Theory of Evolution can never be a scientific truth. It lies outside scientific testability.

"Yes," you say, "That is true for the Atheistic Theory of Evolution, but the Theistic Theory of Evolution, (God created evolution.) and the Directed Panspermia Theory of Evolution, (Aliens from another galaxy created evolution.) and the Multiverse Theory of Evolution (Infinite Universes created evolution.) might be possible even if atheists are wrong about God."

True, those other theories aren't disproved by proving the existence of God. For that reason, this book is not just an attempt to prove God exists. (Even though I pray it does that for you if you don't already believe it.) This book is an attempt to prove that ALL theories of evolution are unscientific. We will explore this in detail later, but for now, let me hint at where we are headed. All Theories of Evolution are founded on suppositions that are not scientifically testable. Since they are not scientifically testable, no Test-for-Falseness can be provided. **Since no Theory of Evolution can be scientifically tested for falseness, none is a scientific statement.** The Theory of Evolution is not science! Rather than science, it is a belief system. For many, it is a religion-substitute. Most evolutionists never think deeply enough about their beliefs to realize their theory is not even scientific.

The Limits of Science

So, if they have to be able to jump backwards through hoops, how do scientists discover the truth about the universe around us? The answer to that depends on whom you ask. Ask a philosopher and you'll be told that scientists can't find truth, or at least what is known as "ultimate truth." The reason philosophers say this is because science is limited to the observations of nature. Anything "outside of" nature, "beyond" nature, or "other than" nature (the supernatural) cannot be studied or tested by natural observations. To be scientifically observed or tested, something must have some kind of natural interaction with nature. If it has no natural interaction with nature, there is no scientific way to test it. Science is limited to the natural realm—natural causes and natural effects. Therefore, scientists can make no valid scientific statements concerning ultimate truths, ultimate causes, or ultimate purposes for nature. Those things, if they exist, exist "outside of" nature. **When a scientist makes the claim that there is no God, he or she is making a claim that cannot be observed, measured, tested, verified, or falsified by true science!**

Epistemology
I Think: Therefore I Am... I Think!

Look at these words: "think," "know," "believe," "accept," "feel," "suppose," "assume," "presume," "assert," and "contend." What do they mean? What does "know" mean? What does "believe" mean? Can you find a universally accepted definition for all these words? Can't do it? I'm not surprised. These words have scores of different meanings and connotations. You might say you believe in something, and mean something vastly different from what I mean by saying I believe in it. Because of their many meanings, these words can wind up being essentially meaningless. So, I prefer to use a different word. I will disregard these words for now, and use the word "perception." When you say you believe, know, or think something, it is in fact, the way you perceive it.

Epistemology is the study of knowledge. It involves the study of the origin and nature of knowledge, as well as its limits. Epistemologists discuss the methods of how we come to know things, and even if we can know anything. (How do epistemologists know epistemology is the study of knowledge?) I'm not an epistemologist, or at least I don't think I am, but epistemology is a branch of philosophy that interests me. Then again, maybe it doesn't interest me; maybe I just believe it interests me. How can I know? Maybe I can't know.

I'm sure you can quickly grasp the dangers lurking in this fuzzy discipline of study. I can visualize the discussion going on when a candidate for a PhD in epistemology defends a doctoral thesis.

Professor: "On what do you base your belief that knowledge is ephemeral and lacks substance?"

Student: "I can't really know why I believe it."

Professor: "Very good. Now, explain why you feel you've earned a PhD in epistemology."

Student: "I don't think I can. I'm not sure it's even possible to explain."

Professor: "Excellent. Now, one final question. Is reality real?"

Student: "I think you must first define reality before I can answer that."

Professor: "Perfect! It gives me great pleasure to award you with your doctorate in epistemology."

Student: "Thank you… I think."

    Don't ask me if reality is real. I don't want to jump into that quagmire. There is no end to the opinions about whether anything is real or true. However, I do want to ask you something. How do we come to "think," "know," "believe," "accept," "feel," "suppose," "assume," "presume," "assert," and "contend" that anything is real or true? Or that anything even exists, for that matter? Again, there are all kinds of conflicting opinions that complicate this issue. With so much disagreement, is there a foundational statement upon which we all could agree? Can we start our search for truth and knowledge from a position that none can deny? I think there is. In fact, I think there are two foundational statements upon which we can all agree. I will give the first foundational statement here at the beginning of our study, and I will give the second foundational statement at the end of our study.

I believe the first step in knowing is perception. Now, we can argue that nothing is real, but it would be difficult to argue that we don't perceive anything. You could argue with me and insist that I don't exist, but it would be futile to argue with me and insist that you don't perceive me. The very act of telling me you don't perceive me would destroy your argument. We all perceive the world around us, and it would be equally futile to insist we don't. Reject perception, and you reject anything perceived from science, philosophy, or theology. Reject perception, and you reject knowledge itself. So, if "knowing" means we truly know something, then the one thing we truly know is that perceptions exist. This is my first foundational statement:

**First Foundational Statement:
We all perceive perceptions.**

Deny it if you want, but by denying it, you prove you perceived the statement. So, while perceptions DO exist, this nagging metaphysical question remains: Is what we perceive the real reality?

The Three Systems of Perception

Well, if the first step in knowing, is knowing we have perceptions, then the second step in knowing is knowing how we perceive. There are three systems of perception; three ways we perceive things: Zero Degree Perception, First Degree Perception, and Second Degree Perception.

Zero Degree Perception

0° perception = The things I perceive as true that are not based on anything other than my own outlook on life. 0° perception is best described as: I believe what I believe because that's what I want to believe. This often can't be evaluated by the other two systems of perception. Nevertheless, it is a valid system of perception even if it doesn't always produce universal agreement. The undeniable truth is that we all have 0° perceptions whether they are true or not. Here are some examples of 0° perception.

Example: I believe I am the only being in the universe. You and everything in the universe are creations of my imagination. This is what I believe, and you can't prove me wrong because you don't exist.

Example: I believe the universe was created only five minutes ago. Everything in it that appears old was created to appear old. Evidence against my belief was also created five minutes ago by a creator who wanted to make the universe appear old.

Example: Nothing is real. Everything that seems real is an illusion produced by a cosmic force that causes all perceptions. When I see and touch a table, I only perceive what the cosmic force produces. The perceptions of seeing and feeling a table are true, but there is no table there. You can't disprove this to me because we don't exist. The cosmic force just makes us think we do.

First Degree Perception

1° perception = The things we perceive with our five senses. (And all the technological enhancements to our senses… telescopes, microscopes, *etc.*) These are the things we see, hear, touch, taste, and smell. We believe/know/feel/think the things we perceive with our senses are real. Now, it's tempting to think this is the best system of perception. We often say, "Seeing is believing," but this isn't provable without first assuming it is true. We believe the things we sense are true representations of reality, but it is by an act of $0°$ perception that we believe $1°$ perceptions are true representations of reality. We assume seeing something means it's real, but we can't prove reality exists without first assuming our senses are real and trustworthy. Assuming our senses truly reveal reality is itself a $0°$ perception.

Example: I can see, feel, taste, and smell an apple as I eat it. I can even hear it crunch as I bite into it. Because I sense the apple with my physical senses, I believe it is a physical reality I am physically eating. (Which means I must be a physical reality, too—I eat, therefore I am.) If the apple is not real, then there must be an explanation for why my five senses elicit five independent but harmonized perceptions that are always present and consistent when I eat apples. When I eat an apple, it always looks, feels, tastes, smells, and sounds like an apple. An apple never looks like a pumpkin, feels like an artichoke, tastes like a turnip, smells like Limburger cheese, or sounds like sipping soup as I eat it. Since we all experience this sort of consistency with everything we perceive, we all tend to believe our experiences are representations of reality. But, this is just because we are so accustomed to them. Because our $1°$ perceptions are 99.9+% consistent, we live our lives 99.9+% of the time believing and responding as though $1°$ Perception reveals reality. However, this doesn't eliminate the possibility that an unknown force might be causing us to have these consistent perceptions. It doesn't eliminate an unknown force that cannot be perceived by the physical senses. It doesn't eliminate an unknown force "outside of" time and space, or one that is "other than" matter and energy. It especially doesn't eliminate an unknown force preventing us from perceiving it.

Second Degree Perception

$2°$ perception = The things we perceive through other people. These are the things we haven't perceived directly by $1°$ perception, but we accept/believe/suppose they are true because other reliable sources have perceived them by $1°$ perception, and have told us so. (And, of course, "reliable" is a $0°$ perception judgment-call.) Many things we know, are known by means of $2°$ perception. We learn things from our parents, our teachers, from books and magazines, from television and videos, and a whole host of other secondary sources.

Example: I have never been to Paris personally, and I have never seen the Eiffel Tower directly with my eyes. However, I know it is there because of what other reliable people tell me.

Example: I have never repeated the research that proves everything is made of atoms. Nevertheless, I believe everything is made of atoms, simply because others who have done this research are reliable enough to believe.

When someone tells us something is true, we know it's true only if we first know they are truthful and knowledgeable sources of truth and knowledge. Current scientific "truths" are built upon the foundation of previous scientific "truths" proposed and presented by the "reliable" scientists who came before us... and the ones before them... and the ones before them.... **The problem with most evolutionists is they have put their faith in the teachings of previous evolutionists without bothering to test their "truths" for**

truthfulness. They criticize Christians for our faith in the Word of God, all the while they have put their faith in the words of men.

What Constitutes Scientific Proof?

1.) Those things perceived by $1°$ perception are considered valid representations of reality. Remember, this statement is itself a $0°$ perception statement. It is the only $0°$ perception assumption allowed in science. With this assumption made, scientists can insist the natural world is the real reality. (However, they can't insist it is the complete reality or the only reality.) The philosophy of the scientist is this: You can stand on the railroad tracks contemplating whether the freight train speeding your way is real or not, but you'd better not stand and contemplate too long.

2.) $1°$ perception is the only valid system of perception that can be used for scientific proof. No portion of a scientific proof relies on $0°$ or $2°$ perception. While $0°$ and $2°$ perceptions cannot be used as scientific proof of something, they can make us aware of what might be true.

3.) Perceptions made in the $1°$ must be observable and verifiable (tested and repeated) before they can be considered valid.

From this point forward, I want you to evaluate the statements made by evolutionists to see if what they say is based on $1°$ perceptions. I think you will discover what I did when I first began to challenge my own belief in evolution: The Theory of Evolution is based almost entirely on the $0°$ perceptions of a small group of biased scientists, and on the $2°$ perceptions of other scientists who believe those $0°$ perceptions are true. Most evolutionists believe evolution is true because they believe the evolutionists who told them it was true.

The History and Philosophy of Science

We will continue by focusing on the history and philosophy of science, but before we do that, we need to define science. You see, here is the first "counterfeit bill." The definition of science has changed over the centuries. As cultures changed and as philosophies changed, the definition of science changed. Scientists of today have a definition of science that scientists of the past would have rejected. Let me repeat this because it is a key issue.

Scientists of today have a definition of science that scientists of the past would have rejected.

Some of the most current definitions of science, held by some of the most outspoken scientists, include exotic concepts such as unseen and uncaused universes popping into existence by the billions every second. (The Multiverse Theory) That's right! Billions of new universes are popping into existence every second, all around us... we just can't see them. (Maybe we are blind or three days dead.) Such an idea would have been considered unscientific by the academic establishment a mere fifty years ago. One hundred years ago, scientists refused to believe the universe had an absolute beginning. Such a notion wasn't scientific by their standards. Today, it is a fundamental concept of cosmology. By looking at the history and philosophy of science, we will see **WHY** the definition of science changed over time. I know this may seem boring to some, but I think it will help answer some important questions.

What is Science?

I will begin answering questions by asking questions. I have two important questions:

1.) What is the definition of science?
2.) Who gets to decide that that is the correct definition?

These questions are so important that if you quit reading this book right now, I would consider my mission accomplished... so long as you went away deeply and honestly motivated to find the answers. So, let me repeat these questions:

1.) What is the definition of science?
2.) Who gets to decide that that is the correct definition?

Where better to find the definition of a word than in a dictionary? And where better to find a good definition of an English word than in the Oxford Dictionary?

OxfordDictionaries.com—Science:
"The intellectual and practical activity encompassing the systematic study of the structure and behaviour of the **physical and natural** world through observation and experiment."[2] (emphasis mine)

Now, that is an excellent definition... except I had to read it four or five times to understand it, and even then, I'm not sure I grasp all of it. Let's look at a simpler definition.

Dictionary.com—Science: "A branch of knowledge or study dealing with a body of facts or truths systematically arranged and showing the operation of general laws."[3]

That's a little better. At least it has some words I understand: "knowledge," "study," "facts," "truths." I'm still a little fuzzy on what "systematically arranged" means or how these "general laws" operate. Let's simplify it even more.

Wiktionary.org—Science: "Knowledge attained through study or practice."[4]

Well, that's certainly easy to understand, especially when you consider the original meaning of the word. The English word "science" comes from the Latin word *scientia*, which means "knowledge." At one time "science" simply meant "knowledge."

But, this reveals a philosophical problem. Does ALL knowledge fall under the category of science, or is there a limit to the knowledge we can learn from science? Is there a boundary beyond which science cannot tread? For example: As I study my Bible, I attain knowledge about God. Is such knowledge considered science? After all, I attained it through study, and the definition said, "Knowledge attained through study." Well, it depends on your philosophy of science. According to the philosophy of science today, the answer is, "no." Before the mid-19th century, the answer would have been, "yes." Here is the definition of "science" from the 1828 edition of Noah Webster's Dictionary:

"Science—In a general sense, knowledge, or certain knowledge; the comprehension or understanding of **truth or facts** by the mind. The science of God must be perfect."[5] (emphasis mine)

As an example, Noah Webster spoke about the science of God. In 1828 the definition of science included the science of God. At that time, the science of God (the knowledge, comprehension, or understanding of God) was considered part of science because it was considered part of what was real/true. Look carefully at Webster's definition and you will notice Webster didn't limit science (knowledge) to just the **physical and natural** as today's Oxford Dictionary does. Instead, he focused on **truth or facts**. Webster considered the knowledge, comprehension, and understanding of God as part of science because he believed God truly existed. Today, atheists are not interested in the truth; they don't care about the facts. All they care about is the physical and natural. They limit "truth" to just the natural and physical. In doing this, however, they reveal they worship the creation rather than the Creator. They presume ($0°$ Perception) the physical and natural things they perceive ($1°$ Perception) are the only things that are true. Atheists using today's definition of "science" automatically exclude the science of God as part of real science. To them, science is the knowledge, comprehension, and understanding of the physical and natural; not the knowledge, comprehension, and understanding of truth or facts.

Should the science of God be part of real science today? To figure out if the science of God is real, we must figure out if the philosophy of God is real. But to do that, we must first figure out if God is real. Is God real? Are we real? Is anything real? These are very uncomfortable philosophical, theological, and scientific questions. So, let's get right to the heart of this issue.

What Is Reality?

The issue we face (individually and collectively) is to determine the make-up of reality. Is reality limited to the physical realm of time, space, matter, and energy? Or, could there be something "outside of," "beyond," or "other than" the physical realm? Is the natural all there is, or is there a supernatural? Are material things the only things that exist, or are there immaterial* things? Is reality composed entirely of the physical, or is there a metaphysical component? Is reality real, or is it only part of something "more real?" As you can see, these questions fall into the realms of philosophy and theology just as much as they fall into the realm of science. This question takes us all the way back to a time before "science" was science; to a time when philosophers and theologians ruled the academic world.

*(Note: Throughout this book, when I use the word "immaterial," I am using it in the sense of something being non-material, not-physical, and incorporeal. I do not use it in the sense of something being unimportant, trivial, or irrelevant.)

Philosoraptor vs. *Theologus rex*

Let's turn the clock back to a time when Biblical Theologians and Pagan Philosophers first began their battle over the question of origins. What did the Greek philosophers think about the origin of the universe? Now, I mention the Greeks only because I think they perfected the arguments so well. They weren't the only ancient people who developed these thoughts. The Babylonians, the Egyptians, the Sumerians, the Chinese, and just about every other culture came up with theological/philosophical explanations for how and why the universe exists. (Man has always been curious about his origin.) We don't need to look at all the different beliefs of man, but I do want to look at how the Bible differs from ALL of man's beliefs. By knowing the truth of the Bible, we can recognize the counterfeit claims of man.

One of the distinctions between the cosmogony of the Bible and the cosmogonies of the ancient pagan religions is the Bible taught that God created everything out of nothing. The Latin term for this is *EX NIHILO*, and it means "out of nothing" or "from nothing." The pagan religions believed in some form of pre-existing matter and energy, out of which the gods formed, but did not create, the universe. This pre-existing "stuff" was sometimes referred to as "chaos." Sometimes it was a part of a god or gods. A god wept, and it became the ocean. A god bled, and the blood became the sun. A god was killed by another god, and the dead god's body became the earth... things like that. In all these cases, the universe was made from something already in existence. In addition, the pagan religions believed in an infinite universe and in an eternal past. In short, they believed time, space, matter, and energy were all infinite. The Bible alone taught that time and space and matter and energy DID NOT EXIST before God created them. In fact, this was a point of ridicule the Greeks had against the Jews. The Greeks were very advanced in science and philosophy, and they realized our universe is a universe of causes-and-effects.

Our Universe is a Universe of Causes-and-Effects

Everything that happens in the universe has a cause... and those causes have causes... and those causes have causes. When it came to explaining the origin of the universe, the Greeks knew they had two choices. The first was an infinite regression of causes and effects. In other words, the universe had no beginning; it was eternal and infinite. It needed no creator because it was never created. The gods (or the inanimate forces) only "tinkered" with the universe to make it what it is. The only other choice was an uncaused-cause. But, the idea of an uncaused-cause was generally rejected. In fact, it was repugnant to them, and you will see why in a moment.

They saw the connection between cause and effect as one of movement. Unless something moves, it cannot cause something else... at least that's how they saw it. A tiny pebble couldn't start an avalanche unless it hit and moved other stones, which hit and moved bigger stones, which hit and moved even bigger stones. The cargo in a ship couldn't move from one port to another port unless the ship moved it. But the ship at sea couldn't move unless the wind hit the sails, which moved the ship, which moved the cargo. Nothing was done unless movement was involved. So, **an uncaused-cause would be an unmoved-mover**. The thing they didn't like about this was the uncaused-cause/unmoved-mover began to look disturbingly like it was SOMEONE rather than SOMETHING. You see, they ascribed an inherent IMPERSONAL principle to their Infinite and Eternal Universe Model. They believed the universe itself tended to produce order. This ordering-principle was why cosmos was the opposite of chaos. They saw it at work all the time. Trees took in chaotic earth, air, fire (sunlight), and water, and fashioned them into orderly fruit, leaves, trunks, and branches. Rotting meat would produce orderly worms and maggots. The movements of the sun and moon and stars were so orderly and precise they could navigate their ships by them. Such an impersonal ordering-principle seemed perfectly rational to them. Order was the First Principle of Nature. (Even though we know today that such a concept violates the Second Law of Thermodynamics.)

It was the Hebrew Creation Model, the Uncaused-Cause Model, that posed the problem for the pagan philosophers. An uncaused-cause would not be part of the universe. It would be "other than" or "outside of" the natural realm. It would be responsible for physical movement without itself being physically moved. Was such a thing possible? Yes, the Greeks recognized there was an IMMATERIAL force that could initiate a MATERIAL movement without itself being MATERIALY moved. That force was the **MIND**. Generally, they believed the mind wasn't material. It didn't have mass and it had no spatial dimensions. Nearly all the pagan cultures believed the mind existed apart from the physical realm. That's why they believed that when you died your soul, mind, essence, spirit, or whatever they called it went to Heaven, or Paradise, or Valhalla, or Nirvana, or Shangri-La, or Hades, or wherever they thought they went after death. Some believed the immaterial part of man became reincarnated. No matter what they believed happened to the mind after death, they believed the mind was "outside of" the physical realm; therefore, the thoughts of the mind could operate "outside of" the rules of physics. You can imagine elephants flying, fish dancing in the desert, or even cows jumping over the moon, but such things are physically impossible. So, in their minds, the mind was not limited by physics. The mind could initiate a chain of physical causes and effects without first being physically caused to do so. A man could decide to start an avalanche by throwing a rock without being caused or moved to do so by some other physical force. He wouldn't have to be hit by a rock in order to throw a rock. His mind alone could make the decision to become the unmoved-mover or the uncaused-cause of a chain of physical events. He could make a choice to start an avalanche.

So, if an uncaused-cause created the universe, it (He) did so by choice. Nothing outside the uncaused-cause caused the uncaused-cause to cause the universe. (Say that six times fast!) The act of causing the universe originated solely from within the uncaused-cause itself and by nothing else. This meant when it came to creating the universe, the unmoved-mover did it by the force of mind, not by the force of nature. Nature wouldn't have existed yet. This meant the uncaused-cause had to be a MIND, not an IMPERSONAL PRINCIPLE, (Impersonal principles can't make choices.) and that was an uncomfortable thought in the minds of the Greek philosophers. You see, they also knew causes and movers must be more powerful than the effects and the movements they create. The wind must be more powerful than the ship to move it; smaller stones must move with more force than the bigger stones to dislodge them. This meant the uncaused-cause of the universe was more powerful than the universe it caused. The uncaused-cause would have been all-powerful. He was OMNIPOTENT. Their gods didn't have such power; they were subject to the forces of nature.

The uncaused-cause was not caused to create the universe, so this meant it chose to do it. Choice was the only way to initiate a finite chain of causes and effects without a previous cause. If an uncaused-cause created the universe, it meant the uncaused-cause could make choices. But as the Creator of nature, it also meant He could make any choice about nature He wanted. He could create a universe with any kind of fundamental particles and forces He desired. He would be SOVEREIGN over the universe. Their gods weren't. The Sovereign God could make choices… but choices require knowledge. This meant the uncaused-cause had all knowledge about the universe. He was OMNISCIENT. Their gods didn't have such knowledge. This ultimate cause was "outside of" or "other than" time and space. This meant He was ETERNAL and OMNIPRESENT. Their gods were limited by time and space. Nothing could move or change this unmoved-mover; so this ultimate cause would have been IMMUTABLE. Their gods changed; they were born, and they could die.

It began to look rather like the uncaused-cause was a personal, powerful, intelligent God, totally unlike any of their gods. This was not an impersonal fundamental principle. It looked a lot like the Hebrew God, and the Greeks didn't like that idea. This God did not need to be given life; He was eternally alive in-and-of-Himself, and therefore the source of life. This God required nothing from humans. He needed no temples built by hands. He required nothing man could provide. He was totally different from man. All their gods were, in essence, human beings on a grand scale. They needed food, followers, servants, armies, and sex-partners, but this God needed nothing. He was "outside of" time and space. He was "other than" matter and energy. It was impossible for humans to interact with Him because we are limited to time and space and we have no access to Him. There was no Mt. Olympus to climb to reach this God. There was no way they could manipulate this God with praise or sacrifice or worship or threats, as their own mythologies revealed they could do with their little gods. In fact, He was so far beyond man, that man could know nothing about Him. **He would have been**

unknown and unknowable. Worst of all, absolutely worst of all, this God would have been the source/cause/agent of an ultimate and absolute morality. Whatever this God considered right or wrong, would have been absolutely right or wrong. If this God existed, they were morally obligated to obey Him and live according to His standards. Above all else, the Greeks didn't want this. They didn't want a God who impinged on their standards of morality. (More accurately phrased: They didn't want a God who impinged on their standards of immorality.) But they weren't dumb. They knew such a God might exist.

Xenophanes, a 6th Century B.C. Greek philosopher and theologian, wrote about this kind of God. Xenophanes taught about one Supreme God who was eternal and uncaused. He had all knowledge, but He was unknowable. He was everywhere at all times, but He could not be seen. He was the mover of all things, but He was immovable. He was unknown from the human perspective, but He knew everything about humans. And again, His morality was unlike the morality of men. Here is a comment about Xenophanes:

"Thus, starting from the notion of omnipotence, Xenophanes derived the concepts of God's unity (that is, unicity or wholeness) and eternity. God, he stated, is present everywhere and acts without intermediary and without displacement or movement, solely by means of His mind's will."[6]

Although Xenophanes wrote about such a God, he didn't like the idea of absolute morality either. So, he added that the Supreme God didn't involve Himself in the affairs of men. Xenophanes was a Deist. The Greeks didn't like the idea of such a God, but they couldn't reject the possibility of such a God, so they worshiped Him...... sort of.

Worshiping The Unknown God

The Apostle Paul knew all about the Unknown God, and he used his knowledge of Greek philosophy, theology, and science as a chance to share the Gospel of Jesus Christ.

Acts 17:22-33
[With my comments in bold print]

"So Paul, standing in the midst of the Areopagus, said: 'Men of Athens, I perceive that in every way you are very religious. {23} For as I passed along and observed the objects of your worship, I found also an altar with this inscription, "To the unknown god." **[TRANSCENDENT]** What therefore you worship as unknown, this I proclaim to you. {24} The God who made **[CREATOR]** the world and everything in it, **[OMNIPOTENT]** being Lord of heaven and earth, **[SOVEREIGN OVER THE UNIVERSE]** does not live in temples made by man, **[OUTSIDE OF SPACE AND TIME]** {25} nor is he served by human hands, as though he needed anything, **[SELF-EXISTENT]** since he himself gives to all mankind life and breath **[SOURCE OF LIFE]** and everything. {26} And he made from one man every nation of mankind to live on all the face of the earth, having determined allotted periods **[CONTROLS TIME]** and the boundaries **[CONTROLS SPACE]** of their dwelling place, {27} that they should seek God, **[CALLS ALL MEN TO HIMSELF]** in the hope **[MERCIFUL]** that they might feel their way toward him and find him. Yet he is actually not far from each one of us, **[OMNIPRESENT]** {28} for 'In him we live and move and have our being'; **[IMMANENT]** as even some of your own poets have said, 'For we are indeed his offspring.' **[HEAVENLY FATHER]** *{29}* Being then God's offspring, we ought not to think that the divine being is like gold or silver or stone, **[OTHER THAN NATURE, *i.e.* SUPERNATURAL]** an image formed by the art and imagination of man. *{30}* The times of ignorance God **[OMNISCIENT]** overlooked, but now he commands all people everywhere **[LORD OVER ALL MEN]** to repent, **[FORGIVING]** *{31}* because he has fixed a day on which he will judge **[JUSTICE]** the world in righteousness **[HOLY]** by a man whom he has appointed; and of this he has given assurance to all **[SALVATION IS AVAILABLE TO ALL WHO TRULY SEEK HIM]** by raising him from the dead.' **[SOVEREIGN OVER THE AFTERLIFE]** *{32}* Now when they heard of the resurrection of the dead, some mocked. But others said, 'We will hear you again about this.' *{33}* So Paul went out from their midst." (ESV)

This was not an altar to some petty god who could be easily overlooked or ignored. Paul equated this God with their supreme God when he quoted the part about man being God's offspring. He quoted the Greek poet Aratus of Soli:

"Let us begin with Zeus, whom we mortals never leave unspoken. For every street, every market-place is full of Zeus. Even the sea and the harbour are full of this deity. Everywhere everyone is indebted to Zeus. For we are indeed his offspring ..."—*Phaenomena* 1–5 (270 B.C.)

Paul knew the philosophy, theology, and science of the Greeks. He knew exactly what the Greeks believed. Today, some people think the Greeks believed this god was a god they knew nothing about, but to whom they made an altar, just so they wouldn't accidentally offend him. Paul knew this wasn't what they believed. Paul knew this was an altar to the **UNKNOWN AND**

UNKNOWABLE GOD. Paul knew this was **THE UNCAUSED-CAUSE; THE UNMOVED-MOVER**. Paul knew this God was the God they knew existed, but didn't want to accept. Paul shattered their belief in an infinite regression of natural causes-and-effects when he revealed to them that this God created the universe. Paul shattered their belief in an Impersonal First Principle of Order when he told them about the resurrection of Jesus Christ. Nothing impersonal can cause a person to come back to life. The First Principle of Order couldn't do that. The best the First Principle of Order could do with a dead body would be to create orderly worms and maggots out of it. Only the Giver-of-Life could restore life. Paul revealed that God was Sovereign over life. Paul also spoke about how God had fixed a day in the future for His appointed man (Jesus) to judge the world—all people; the living and the dead. In this, Paul revealed to them that God was Sovereign over both the natural realm and the supernatural realm. (Life and the Afterlife) In other words, Paul revealed to them their **UNKNOWN** God was the Hebrew God who made Himself **KNOWN** by coming into the world and dying for our sins. Most of the people didn't like Paul's Biblical cosmology. Most people still don't… and for the same reason. **If you accept Biblical cosmology, you have to accept Biblical morality**.

So, for thousands of years people rejected Biblical cosmology. Instead, they chose to believe in an eternal and infinite universe. Time and space and matter and energy were infinite. Every intelligent person "knew" the universe was infinite and eternal. Every educated person "knew" time and space and matter and energy had no limits. Every piece of scientific evidence "proved" the Bible was wrong. People put their trust in an infinite regression of random causes and effects rather than having to obey a God of moral absolutes. **If the universe is infinite and eternal, there is no need**

to believe in absolute morality. For thousands of years people mocked the Bible so they wouldn't have to obey it… but then something unexpected happened.

Enter Stage Left: The Theory of Relativity

In the first few years of the 20th century, Albert Einstein formulated his Theories of Relativity. (The Special Theory in 1905 and the General Theory in 1916.) One of the implications of his theories was that time had an absolute beginning. This meant at one "time" there was no time. Another implication was that space itself came out of nothing and was expanding. Suddenly it seemed very possible that space and time were no longer infinite. The universe could no longer be explained by an infinite chain of causes and effects because such a chain might not be possible. This sent shudders through the world of philosophers and theologians as much as it did through the world of scientists. No one believed it; no one wanted to believe it. It was distasteful to them. Even Albert Einstein couldn't believe all his theories seemed to imply.

Exit Stage Right: The Theory of Evolution

Other scientists began testing Einstein's theories and everything seemed to fit. Then in the 1930's, two astronomers, Edwin Hubble and Milton Humason, made a real, "startling new discovery." The universe was expanding. All the stars and galaxies were moving apart. In fact, space itself was expanding. This meant the universe was smaller at one time, and at a time before that it was smaller, and at a time before that it was even smaller. Suddenly here was scientific evidence Einstein was right. By measuring the movements of the galaxies and the expansion of space, scientists extrapolated backwards until they reached a point at which the entire universe (time, space, matter, and energy) was contained in a dimensionless point; a, "singularity," they called it. It was a point without height, width, depth, or time. Even with that, most scientists didn't accept the possibility the universe began with a, "Big Bang." Then in 1965, two Bell Laboratory scientists, Arno Penzias and Robert Wilson discovered the background microwave energy released by the Big Bang. (It was like hearing the thunder that follows the lightning.) Suddenly, science proved the universe had come out of nothing. Suddenly, science proved time, space, matter, and energy all had an absolute beginning. Suddenly, science destroyed the possibility of an infinite and eternal universe. Suddenly, science proved there couldn't have been an infinite regression of causes and effects. Suddenly, science disproved the philosophies and theologies of ALL the man-made theories and religions. Suddenly, only the Bible's cosmogony remained standing in the light of scientific fact.

    I know what I am about to say will be very uncomfortable for some Christians. I might even lose some friends by saying it. I know a lot of Christians hate the Big Bang Theory. They mock it and argue against it, but in my opinion, they do so out of ignorance. They don't know what it truly reveals, and they don't appreciate how it has become the greatest scientific apologetic for Genesis 1:1 ever discovered. The Big Bang confirms the universe had an *EX NIHILO* beginning, just like the Bible has said for thousands of years. Creationists can rejoice in what science has revealed about the origin of the universe. You see, initially it was the atheists who rejected the Big Bang Theory. Initially theists rejoiced in the Big Bang Theory. It was the atheists who hated it. In fact, the term "Big Bang" was originally used by atheist-astrophysicist Sir Fred Hoyle to mock the idea the universe instantly came out of nothing. Atheists hated it because it meant the universe had an absolute beginning! They hated it because it eliminated the possibility of an infinite regression of natural causes and effects. They hated it because they knew they needed an infinite amount of time, space, matter, and energy to make evolution possible. The Big Bang didn't allow that. According to the Big Bang Theory, only 10^{81} fundamental particles are all that ever came into existence, and only 1.4×10^{10} years is all the time there has ever been. But this meant evolution didn't stand a chance of a chance to begin to begin. Hoyle recognized this when he talked about the odds for Darwinian Evolution creating life in such a short amount of time with such a limited amount of matter:

"The likelihood of the formation of life from inanimate matter is one to a number with 40,000 naughts after it... It is big enough to bury Darwin and the whole theory of evolution. There was no primeval soup, neither on this planet nor any other, and if the beginnings of life were not random, they must therefore have been the product of purposeful intelligence."[7]

You won't find any Darwinian Evolutionists agreeing with Fred Hoyle about this. They can't refute his mathematics, of course, so they dismiss him on the basis he was making comments outside his field of expertise. He was a smart man, they will agree, but he wasn't a trained biologist; therefore, he couldn't possibly understand the finer points of evolution. Is that so? Let's look at what Fred Hoyle knew about evolution. Fred Hoyle was a cosmologist, nuclear astrophysicist, and mathematician. That means he knew a lot about the properties of the universe at both the astronomical scale and the quantum scale. He understood the largest and smallest components of nature. What did he know about evolution? He knew:

Evolution had to be determined by the properties of living organisms.

The properties of living organisms are determined by the properties of organism systems.

The properties of organism systems are determined by the properties of organs.

The properties of organs are determined by the properties of tissues.

The properties of tissues are determined by the properties of cells.

The properties of cells are determined by the properties of organelles.

The properties of organelles are determined by the properties of biochemicals.

The properties of biochemicals are determined by the properties molecules.

The properties of molecules are determined by the properties of atoms.

The properties of atoms are determined by the properties of subatomic particles.

The properties of subatomic particles are determined by the properties of fundamental particles.

The properties of fundamental particles are determined the properties of quantum strings.

The properties of quantum strings are determined by ??????

Well, he didn't know that much, because no human being knows that much—yet. But, he certainly understood fundamental particles and fundamental forces better than the average biologist. For a biologist to say Hoyle didn't understand evolution, would be like me saying automobiles are the results of random physical processes, no intelligence is required to make them, and then denouncing a PhD metallurgist who says I am wrong. The metallurgist knows iron can't become automobiles without the aid of intelligent engineers. The inherent properties of iron could never cause it to self-become engine blocks, frames, pistons, transmissions, gears, drive trains, *etc*. The metallurgist wouldn't need to know a thing about automotive engineering to know iron couldn't spontaneously become a car. Fred Hoyle didn't need to know a thing about biology to know subatomic particles couldn't spontaneously become a cat. Life could not have arisen without a purposeful, intelligence cause. Fred said random evolution was impossible, and Fred was right.

Darwinian Evolutionists complained that Dr. Hoyle doctored his numbers, but Dr. Stephen Meyer answered this complaint in his book *Signature in the Cell*.[8] (If you are interested in truth and facts, you need to read Dr. Meyer's books. He is a Christian and proponent of Intelligent Design, and a brilliant teacher of truth and facts!) He commented on the work of Dr. Douglas Axe, a molecular biologist who earned his doctorate at Caltech and did his post-doctoral work at Cambridge. (*i.e.*, a very smart guy) Dr. Axe calculated the odds for randomly producing a minimally complex cell, and he proved Hoyle was wrong; Hoyle was too lenient… the actual odds were $10^{1,000}$ times worse.

"Axe's experimental findings suggest that Hoyle's guesses were pretty good. If we assume that a minimally complex cell needs at least 250 proteins of, on average,

150 amino acids and that the probability of producing just one such protein is 1 in 10^{164} as calculated above, then the probability of producing all the necessary proteins needed to service a minimally complex cell is 1 in 10^{164} multiplied by itself 250 times, or 1 in $10^{41,000}$."[9]

According to the Big Bang Theory, the universe is limited to 1 x 10^{81} fundamental particles of matter, and has existed for less than 5 x 10^{60} quantum units of Planck time, the smallest possible unit of time; about 10^{-43} seconds. This means if each fundamental particle could become a complete protein molecule (which is physically impossible since each one is only one fundamental particle) every Planck unit of time, then the universe would have created less than 1 x 10^{142} protein molecules since its beginning. Ten of our universes would have created less than 1 x 10^{143} protein molecules. One hundred of our universes would have created less than 1 x 10^{144} protein molecules. One thousand of our universes would have created less than 1 x 10^{145} protein molecules. This means evolution needed 1 x $10^{40,858}$ universes to do what Darwinian Evolutionists say it did. That's not 40,858 universes; that's 1 with 40,858 zeros after it. That's this many universes:

10,000,000,000,000,000,000,000,000,000,000,
000,000,000,000,000,000,000,000,000,000,000,
000,000,000,000,000,000,000,000,000,000,000,
000,000,000,000,000,000,000,000,000,000,000,
000,000,000,000,000,000,000,000,000,000,000,
000,000,000,000,000,000,000,000,000,000,000,
000,000,000,000,000,000,000,000,000,000,000,
000,000,000,000,000,000,000,000,000,000,000,
000,000,000,000,000,000,000,000,000,000,000,
000,000,000,000,000,000,000,000,000,000,000,

000,000,000,000,000,000,000,000,000,000,000,000,
000,000,000,000,000,000,000,000,000,000,000,000,
000,000,000,000,000,000,000,000,000,000,000,000,
000,000,000,000,000,000,000,000,000,000,000,000,
000,000,000,000,000,000,000,000,000,000,000,000,
000,000,000,000,000,000,000,000,000,000,000,000,
000,000,000,000,000,000,000,000,000,000,000,000,
000,000,000,000,000,000,000,000,000,000,000,000,
000,000,000,000,000,000,000,000,000,000,000,000,
000,000,000,000,000,000,000,000,000,000,000,000,
000,000,000,000,000,000,000,000,000,000,000,000,
000,000,000,000,000,000,000,000,000,000,000,000,
000,000,000,000,000,000,000,000,000,000,000,000,
000,000,000,000,000,000,000,000,000,000,000,000,
000,000,000,000,000,000,000,000,000,000,000,000,
000,000,000,000,000,000,000,000,000,000,000,000,
000,000,000,000,000,000,000,000,000,000,000,000,
000,000,000,000,000,000,000,000,000,000,000,000,
000,000,000,000,000,000,000,000,000,000,000,000,
000,000,000,000,000,000,000,000,000,000,000,000,
000,000,000,000,000,000,000,000,000,000,000,000,
000,000,000,000,000,000,000,000,000,000,000,000,
000,000,000,000,000,000,000,000,000,000,000,000,
000,000,000,000,000,000,000,000,000,000,000,000,
000,000,000,000,000,000,000,000,000,000,000,000,
000,000,000,000,000,000,000,000,000,000,000,000,
000,000,000,000,000,000,000,000,000,000,000,000,
000,000,000,000,000,000,000,000,000,000,000,000,
000,000,000,000,000,000,000,000,000,000,000,000,
000,000,000,000,000,000,000,000,000,000,000,000,
000,000,000,000,000,000,000,000,000,000,000,000,
000,000,000,000,000,000,000,000,000,000,000,000,
000,000,000,000,000,000,000,000,000,000,000,000,
000,000,000,000,000,000,000,000,000,000,000,000,
000,000,000,000,000,000,000,000,000,000,000,000,
000,000,000,000,000,000,000,000,000,000,000,000,

000,000,000,000,000,000,000,000,000,000,000,000,
000,000,000,000,000,000,000,000,000,000,000,000,
000,000,000,000,000,000,000,000,000,000,000,000,
000,000,000,000,000,000,000,000,000,000,000,000,
000,000,000,000,000,000,000,000,000,000,000,000,
000,000,000,000,000,000,000,000,000,000,000,000,
000,000,000,000,000,000,000,000,000,000,000,000,
000,000,000,000,000,000,000,000,000,000,000,000,
000,000,000,000,000,000,000,000,000,000,000,000,
000,000,000,000,000,000,000,000,000,000,000,000,
000,000,000,000,000,000,000,000,000,000,000,000,
000,000,000,000,000,000,000,000,000,000,000,000,
000,000,000,000,000,000,000,000,000,000,000,000,
000,000,000,000,000,000,000,000,000,000,000,000,
000,000,000,000,000,000,000,000,000,000,000,000,
000,000,000,000,000,000,000,000,000,000,000,000,
000,000,000,000,000,000,000,000,000,000,000,000,
000,000,000,000,000,000,000,000,000,000,000,000,
000,000,000,000,000,000,000,000,000,000,000,000,
000,000,000,000,000,000,000,000,000,000,000,000,
000,000,000,000,000,000,000,000,000,000,000,000,
000,000,000,000,000,000,000,000,000,000,000,000,
000,000,000,000,000,000,000,000,000,000,000,000,
000,000,000,000,000,000,000,000,000,000,000,000,
000,000,000,000,000,000,000,000,000,000,000,000,
000,000,000,000,000,000,000,000,000,000,000,000,
000,000,000,000,000,000,000,000,000,000,000,000,
000,000,000,000,000,000,000,000,000,000,000,000,
000,000,000,000,000,000,000,000,000,000,000,000,
000,000,000,000,000,000,000,000,000,000,000,000,
000,000,000,000,000,000,000,000,000,000,000,000,
000,000,000,000,000,000,000,000,000,000,000,000,
000,000,000,000,000,000,000,000,000,000,000,000,
000,000,000,000,000,000,000,000,000,000,000,000,
000,000,000,000,000,000,000,000,000,000,000,000,
000,000,000,000,000,000,000,000,000,000,000,000,
000,000,000,000,000,000,000,000,000,000,000,000,

000,000,000,000,000,000,000,000,000,000,000,000,
000,000,000,000,000,000,000,000,000,000,000,000,
000,000,000,000,000,000,000,000,000,000,000,000,
000,000,000,000,000,000,000,000,000,000,000,000,
000,000,000,000,000,000,000,000,000,000,000,000,
000,000,000,000,000,000,000,000,000,000,000,000,
000,000,000,000,000,000,000,000,000,000,000,000,
000,000,000,000,000,000,000,000,000,000,000,000,
000,000,000,000,000,000,000,000,000,000,000,000,
000,000,000,000,000,000,000,000,000,000,000,000,
000,000,000,000,000,000,000,000,000,000,000,000,
000,000,000,000,000,000,000,000,000,000,000,000,
000,000,000,000,000,000,000,000,000,000,000,000,
000,000,000,000,000,000,000,000,000,000,000,000,
000,000,000,000,000,000,000,000,000,000,000,000,
000,000,000,000,000,000,000,000,000,000,000,000,
000,000,000,000,000,000,000,000,000,000,000,000,
000,000,000,000,000,000,000,000,000,000,000,000,
000,000,000,000,000,000,000,000,000,000,000,000,
000,000,000,000,000,000,000,000,000,000,000,000,
000,000,000,000,000,000,000,000,000,000,000,000,
000,000,000,000,000,000,000,000,000,000,000,000,
000,000,000,000,000,000,000,000,000,000,000,000,
000,000,000,000,000,000,000,000,000,000,000,000,
000,000,000,000,000,000,000,000,000,000,000,000,
000,000,000,000,000,000,000,000,000,000,000,000,
000,000,000,000,000,000,000,000,000,000,000,000,
000,000,000,000,000,000,000,000,000,000,000,000,
000,000,000,000,000,000,000,000,000,000,000,000,
000,000,000,000,000,000,000,000,000,000,000,000,
000,000,000,000,000,000,000,000,000,000,000,000,
000,000,000,000,000,000,000,000,000,000,000,000,
000,000,000,000,000,000,000,000,000,000,000,000,
000,000,000,000,000,000,000,000,000,000,000,000,
000,000,000,000,000,000,000,000,000,000,000,000,
000,000,000,000,000,000,000,000,000,000,000,000,

000,000,000,000,000,000,000,000,000,000,000,000,
000,000,000,000,000,000,000,000,000,000,000,000,
000,000,000,000,000,000,000,000,000,000,000,000,
000,000,000,000,000,000,000,000,000,000,000,000,
000,000,000,000,000,000,000,000,000,000,000,000,
000,000,000,000,000,000,000,000,000,000,000,000,
000,000,000,000,000,000,000,000,000,000,000,000,
000,000,000,000,000,000,000,000,000,000,000,000,
000,000,000,000,000,000,000,000,000,000,000,000,
000,000,000,000,000,000,000,000,000,000,000,000,
000,000,000,000,000,000,000,000,000,000,000,000,
000,000,000,000,000,000,000,000,000,000,000,000,
000,000,000,000,000,000,000,000,000,000,000,000,
000,000,000,000,000,000,000,000,000,000,000,000,
000,000,000,000,000,000,000,000,000,000,000,000,
000,000,000,000,000,000,000,000,000,000,000,000,
000,000,000,000,000,000,000,000,000,000,000,000,
000,000,000,000,000,000,000,000,000,000,000,000,
000,000,000,000,000,000,000,000,000,000,000,000,
000,000,000,000,000,000,000,000,000,000,000,000,
000,000,000,000,000,000,000,000,000,000,000,000,
000,000,000,000,000,000,000,000,000,000,000,000,
000,000,000,000,000,000,000,000,000,000,000,000,
000,000,000,000,000,000,000,000,000,000,000,000,
000,000,000,000,000,000,000,000,000,000,000,000,
000,000,000,000,000,000,000,000,000,000,000,000,
000,000,000,000,000,000,000,000,000,000,000,000,
000,000,000,000,000,000,000,000,000,000,000,000,
000,000,000,000,000,000,000,000,000,000,000,000,
000,000,000,000,000,000,000,000,000,000,000,000,
000,000,000,000,000,000,000,000,000,000,000,000,
000,000,000,000,000,000,000,000,000,000,000,000,
000,000,000,000,000,000,000,000,000,000,000,000,
000,000,000,000,000,000,000,000,000,000,000,000,
000,000,000,000,000,000,000,000,000,000,000,000,
000,000,000,000,000,000,000,000,000,000,000,000,

000,000,000,000,000,000,000,000,000,000,000,000,
000,000,000,000,000,000,000,000,000,000,000,000,
000,000,000,000,000,000,000,000,000,000,000,000,
000,000,000,000,000,000,000,000,000,000,000,000,
000,000,000,000,000,000,000,000,000,000,000,000,
000,000,000,000,000,000,000,000,000,000,000,000,
000,000,000,000,000,000,000,000,000,000,000,000,
000,000,000,000,000,000,000,000,000,000,000,000,
000,000,000,000,000,000,000,000,000,000,000,000,
000,000,000,000,000,000,000,000,000,000,000,000,
000,000,000,000,000,000,000,000,000,000,000,000,
000,000,000,000,000,000,000,000,000,000,000,000,
000,000,000,000,000,000,000,000,000,000,000,000,
000,000,000,000,000,000,000,000,000,000,000,000,
000,000,000,000,000,000,000,000,000,000,000,000,
000,000,000,000,000,000,000,000,000,000,000,000,
000,000,000,000,000,000,000,000,000,000,000,000,
000,000,000,000,000,000,000,000,000,000,000,000,
000,000,000,000,000,000,000,000,000,000,000,000,
000,000,000,000,000,000,000,000,000,000,000,000,
000,000,000,000,000,000,000,000,000,000,000,000,
000,000,000,000,000,000,000,000,000,000,000,000,
000,000,000,000,000,000,000,000,000,000,000,000,
000,000,000,000,000,000,000,000,000,000,000,000,
000,000,000,000,000,000,000,000,000,000,000,000,
000,000,000,000,000,000,000,000,000,000,000,000,
000,000,000,000,000,000,000,000,000,000,000,000,
000,000,000,000,000,000,000,000,000,000,000,000,
000,000,000,000,000,000,000,000,000,000,000,000,
000,000,000,000,000,000,000,000,000,000,000,000,
000,000,000,000,000,000,000,000,000,000,000,000,
000,000,000,000,000,000,000,000,000,000,000,000,
000,000,000,000,000,000,000,000,000,000,000,000,
000,000,000,000,000,000,000,000,000,000,000,000,
000,000,000,000,000,000,000,000,000,000,000,000,
000,000,000,000,000,000,000,000,000,000,000,000,
000,000,000,000,000,000,000,000,000,000,000,000,
000,000,000,000,000,000,000,000,000,000,000,000,
000,000,000,000,000,000,000,000,000,000,000,000,
000,000,000,000,000,000,000,000,000,000,000,000,

000,000,000,000,000,000,000,000,000,000,000,000,
000,000,000,000,000,000,000,000,000,000,000,000,
000,000,000,000,000,000,000,000,000,000,000,000,
000,000,000,000,000,000,000,000,000,000,000,000,
000,000,000,000,000,000,000,000,000,000,000,000,
000,000,000,000,000,000,000,000,000,000,000,000,
000,000,000,000,000,000,000,000,000,000,000,000,
000,000,000,000,000,000,000,000,000,000,000,000,
000,000,000,000,000,000,000,000,000,000,000,000,
000,000,000,000,000,000,000,000,000,000,000,000,
000,000,000,000,000,000,000,000,000,000,000,000,
000,000,000,000,000,000,000,000,000,000,000,000,
000,000,000,000,000,000,000,000,000,000,000,000,
000,000,000,000,000,000,000,000,000,000,000,000,
000,000,000,000,000,000,000,000,000,000,000,000,
000,000,000,000,000,000,000,000,000,000,000,000,
000,000,000,000,000,000,000,000,000,000,000,000,
000,000,000,000,000,000,000,000,000,000,000,000,
000,000,000,000,000,000,000,000,000,000,000,000,
000,000,000,000,000,000,000,000,000,000,000,000,
000,000,000,000,000,000,000,000,000,000,000,000,
000,000,000,000,000,000,000,000,000,000,000,000,
000,000,000,000,000,000,000,000,000,000,000,000,
000,000,000,000,000,000,000,000,000,000,000,000,
000,000,000,000,000,000,000,000,000,000,000,000,
000,000,000,000,000,000,000,000,000,000,000,000,
000,000,000,000,000,000,000,000,000,000,000,000,
000,000,000,000,000,000,000,000,000,000,000,000,
000,000,000,000,000,000,000,000,000,000,000,000,
000,000,000,000,000,000,000,000,000,000,000,000,
000,000,000,000,000,000,000,000,000,000,000,000,
000,000,000,000,000,000,000,000,000,000,000,000,
000,000,000,000,000,000,000,000,000,000,000,000,
000,000,000,000,000,000,000,000,000,000,000,000,
000,000,000,000,000,000,000,000,000,000,000,000,
000,000,000,000,000,000,000,000,000,000,000,000,
000,000,000,000,000,000,000,000,000,000,000,000,
000,000,000,000,000,000,000,000,000,000,000,000,
000,000,000,000,000,000,000,000,000,000,000,000,

000,000,000,000,000,000,000,000,000,000,000,000,
000,000,000,000,000,000,000,000,000,000,000,000,
000,000,000,000,000,000,000,000,000,000,000,000,
000,000,000,000,000,000,000,000,000,000,000,000,
000,000,000,000,000,000,000,000,000,000,000,000,
000,000,000,000,000,000,000,000,000,000,000,000,
000,000,000,000,000,000,000,000,000,000,000,000,
000,000,000,000,000,000,000,000,000,000,000,000,
000,000,000,000,000,000,000,000,000,000,000,000,
000,000,000,000,000,000,000,000,000,000,000,000,
000,000,000,000,000,000,000,000,000,000,000,000,
000,000,000,000,000,000,000,000,000,000,000,000,
000,000,000,000,000,000,000,000,000,000,000,000,
000,000,000,000,000,000,000,000,000,000,000,000,
000,000,000,000,000,000,000,000,000,000,000,000,
000,000,000,000,000,000,000,000,000,000,000,000,
000,000,000,000,000,000,000,000,000,000,000,000,
000,000,000,000,000,000,000,000,000,000,000,000,
000,000,000,000,000,000,000,000,000,000,000,000,
000,000,000,000,000,000,000,000,000,000,000,000,
000,000,000,000,000,000,000,000,000,000,000,000,
000,000,000,000,000,000,000,000,000,000,000,000,
000,000,000,000,000,000,000,000,000,000,000,000,
000,000,000,000,000,000,000,000,000,000,000,000,
000,000,000,000,000,000,000,000,000,000,000,000,
000,000,000,000,000,000,000,000,000,000,000,000,
000,000,000,000,000,000,000,000,000,000,000,000,
000,000,000,000,000,000,000,000,000,000,000,000,
000,000,000,000,000,000,000,000,000,000,000,000,
000,000,000,000,000,000,000,000,000,000,000,000,
000,000,000,000,000,000,000,000,000,000,000,000,
000,000,000,000,000,000,000,000,000,000,000,000,
000,000,000,000,000,000,000,000,000,000,000,000,
000,000,000,000,000,000,000,000,000,000,000,000,
000,000,000,000,000,000,000,000,000,000,000,000,
000,000,000,000,000,000,000,000,000,000,000,000,
000,000,000,000,000,000,000,000,000,000,000,000,
000,000,000,000,000,000,000,000,000,000,000,000,
000,000,000,000,000,000,000,000,000,000,000,000,

000,000,000,000,000,000,000,000,000,000,000,000,
000,000,000,000,000,000,000,000,000,000,000,000,
000,000,000,000,000,000,000,000,000,000,000,000,
000,000,000,000,000,000,000,000,000,000,000,000,
000,000,000,000,000,000,000,000,000,000,000,000,
000,000,000,000,000,000,000,000,000,000,000,000,
000,000,000,000,000,000,000,000,000,000,000,000,
000,000,000,000,000,000,000,000,000,000,000,000,
000,000,000,000,000,000,000,000,000,000,000,000,
000,000,000,000,000,000,000,000,000,000,000,000,
000,000,000,000,000,000,000,000,000,000,000,000,
000,000,000,000,000,000,000,000,000,000,000,000,
000,000,000,000,000,000,000,000,000,000,000,000,
000,000,000,000,000,000,000,000,000,000,000,000,
000,000,000,000,000,000,000,000,000,000,000,000,
000,000,000,000,000,000,000,000,000,000,000,000,
000,000,000,000,000,000,000,000,000,000,000,000,
000,000,000,000,000,000,000,000,000,000,000,000,
000,000,000,000,000,000,000,000,000,000,000,000,
000,000,000,000,000,000,000,000,000,000,000,000,
000,000,000,000,000,000,000,000,000,000,000,000,
000,000,000,000,000,000,000,000,000,000,000,000,
000,000,000,000,000,000,000,000,000,000,000,000,
000,000,000,000,000,000,000,000,000,000,000,000,
000,000,000,000,000,000,000,000,000,000,000,000,
000,000,000,000,000,000,000,000,000,000,000,000,
000,000,000,000,000,000,000,000,000,000,000,000,
000,000,000,000,000,000,000,000,000,000,000,000,
000,000,000,000,000,000,000,000,000,000,000,000,
000,000,000,000,000,000,000,000,000,000,000,000,
000,000,000,000,000,000,000,000,000,000,000,000,
000,000,000,000,000,000,000,000,000,000,000,000,
000,000,000,000,000,000,000,000,000,000,000,000,
000,000,000,000,000,000,000,000,000,000,000,000,
000,000,000,000,000,000,000,000,000,000,000,000,
000,000,000,000,000,000,000,000,000,000,000,000,
000,000,000,000,000,000,000,000,000,000,000,000,
000,000,000,000,000,000,000,000,000,000,000,000,
000,000,000,000,000,000,000,000,000,000,000,000,

000,000,000,000,000,000,000,000,000,000,000,000,
000,000,000,000,000,000,000,000,000,000,000,000,
000,000,000,000,000,000,000,000,000,000,000,000,
000,000,000,000,000,000,000,000,000,000,000,000,
000,000,000,000,000,000,000,000,000,000,000,000,
000,000,000,000,000,000,000,000,000,000,000,000,
000,000,000,000,000,000,000,000,000,000,000,000,
000,000,000,000,000,000,000,000,000,000,000,000,
000,000,000,000,000,000,000,000,000,000,000,000,
000,000,000,000,000,000,000,000,000,000,000,000,
000,000,000,000,000,000,000,000,000,000,000,000,
000,000,000,000,000,000,000,000,000,000,000,000,
000,000,000,000,000,000,000,000,000,000,000,000,
000,000,000,000,000,000,000,000,000,000,000,000,
000,000,000,000,000,000,000,000,000,000,000,000,
000,000,000,000,000,000,000,000,000,000,000,000,
000,000,000,000,000,000,000,000,000,000,000,000,
000,000,000,000,000,000,000,000,000,000,000,000,
000,000,000,000,000,000,000,000,000,000,000,000,
000,000,000,000,000,000,000,000,000,000,000,000,
000,000,000,000,000,000,000,000,000,000,000,000,
000,000,000,000,000,000,000,000,000,000,000,000,
000,000,000,000,000,000,000,000,000,000,000,000,
000,000,000,000,000,000,000,000,000,000,000,000,
000,000,000,000,000,000,000,000,000,000,000,000,
000,000,000,000,000,000,000,000,000,000,000,000,
000,000,000,000,000,000,000,000,000,000,000,000,
000,000,000,000,000,000,000,000,000,000,000,000,
000,000,000,000,000,000,000,000,000,000,000,000,
000,000,000,000,000,000,000,000,000,000,000,000,
000,000,000,000,000,000,000,000,000,000,000,000,
000,000,000,000,000,000,000,000,000,000,000,000,
000,000,000,000,000,000,000,000,000,000,000,000,
000,000,000,000,000,000,000,000,000,000,000,000,
000,000,000,000,000,000,000,000,000,000,000,000,
000,000,000,000,000,000,000,000,000,000,000,000,

000,000,000,000,000,000,000,000,000,000,000,000,
000,000,000,000,000,000,000,000,000,000,000,000,
000,000,000,000,000,000,000,000,000,000,000,000,
000,000,000,000,000,000,000,000,000,000,000,000,
000,000,000,000,000,000,000,000,000,000,000,000,
000,000,000,000,000,000,000,000,000,000,000,000,
000,000,000,000,000,000,000,000,000,000,000,000,
000,000,000,000,000,000,000,000,000,000,000,000,
000,000,000,000,000,000,000,000,000,000,000,000,
000,000,000,000,000,000,000,000,000,000,000,000,
000,000,000,000,000,000,000,000,000,000,000,000,
000,000,000,000,000,000,000,000,000,000,000,000,
000,000,000,000,000,000,000,000,000,000,000,000,
000,000,000,000,000,000,000,000,000,000,000,000,
000,000,000,000,000,000,000,000,000,000,000,000,
000,000,000,000,000,000,000,000,000,000,000,000,
000,000,000,000,000,000,000,000,000,000,000,000,
000,000,000,000,000,000,000,000,000,000,000,000,
000,000,000,000,000,000,000,000,000,000,000,000,
000,000,000,000,000,000,000,000,000,000,000,000,
000,000,000,000,000,000,000,000,000,000,000,000,
000,000,000,000,000,000,000,000,000,000,000,000,
000,000,000,000,000,000,000,000,000,000,000,000,
000,000,000,000,000,000,000,000,000,000,000,000,
000,000,000,000,000,000,000,000,000,000,000,000,
000,000,000,000,000,000,000,000,000,000,000,000,
000,000,000,000,000,000,000,000,000,000,000,000,
000,000,000,000,000,000,000,000,000,000,000,000,
000,000,000,000,000,000,000,000,000,000,000,000,
000,000,000,000,000,000,000,000,000,000,000,000,
000,000,000,000,000,000,000,000,000,000,000,000,
000,000,000,000,000,000,000,000,000,000,000,000,
000,000,000,000,000,000,000,000,000,000,000,000,
000,000,000,000,000,000,000,000,000,000,000,000,
000,000,000,000,000,000,000,000,000,000,000,000,
000,000,000,000,000,000,000,000,000,000,000,000,
000,000,000,000,000,000,000,000,000,000,000,000,
000,000,000,000,000,000,000,000,000,000,000,000,

000,000,000,000,000,000,000,000,000,000,000,000,
000,000,000,000,000,000,000,000,000,000,000,000,
000,000,000,000,000,000,000,000,000,000,000,000,
000,000,000,000,000,000,000,000,000,000,000,000,
000,000,000,000,000,000,000,000,000,000,000,000,
000,000,000,000,000,000,000,000,000,000,000,000,
000,000,000,000,000,000,000,000,000,000,000,000,
000,000,000,000,000,000,000,000,000,000,000,000,
000,000,000,000,000,000,000,000,000,000,000,000,
000,000,000,000,000,000,000,000,000,000,000,000,
000,000,000,000,000,000,000,000,000,000,000,000,
000,000,000,000,000,000,000,000,000,000,000,000,
000,000,000,000,000,000,000,000,000,000,000,000,
000,000,000,000,000,000,000,000,000,000,000,000,
000,000,000,000,000,000,000,000,000,000,000,000,
000,000,000,000,000,000,000,000,000,000,000,000,
000,000,000,000,000,000,000,000,000,000,000,000,
000,000,000,000,000,000,000,000,000,000,000,000,
000,000,000,000,000,000,000,000,000,000,000,000,
000,000,000,000,000,000,000,000,000,000,000,000,
000,000,000,000,000,000,000,000,000,000,000,000,
000,000,000,000,000,000,000,000,000,000,000,000,
000,000,000,000,000,000,000,000,000,000,000,000,
000,000,000,000,000,000,000,000,000,000,000,000,
000,000,000,000,000,000,000,000,000,000,000,000,
000,000,000,000,000,000,000,000,000,000,000,000,
000,000,000,000,000,000,000,000,000,000,000,000,
000,000,000,000,000,000,000,000,000,000,000,000,
000,000,000,000,000,000,000,000,000,000,000,000,
000,000,000,000,000,000,000,000,000,000,000,000,
000,000,000,000,000,000,000,000,000,000,000,000,
000,000,000,000,000,000,000,000,000,000,000,000,
000,000,000,000,000,000,000,000,000,000,000,000,
000,000,000,000,000,000,000,000,000,000,000,000,
000,000,000,000,000,000,000,000,000,000,000,000,
000,000,000,000,000,000,000,000,000,000,000,000,
000,000,000,000,000,000,000,000,000,000,000,000,
000,000,000,000,000,000,000,000,000,000,000,000,
000,000,000,000,000,000,000,000,000,000,000,000,
000,000,000,000,000,000,000,000,000,000,000,000,

000,000,000,000,000,000,000,000,000,000,000,000,
000,000,000,000,000,000,000,000,000,000,000,000,
000,000,000,000,000,000,000,000,000,000,000,000,
000,000,000,000,000,000,000,000,000,000,000,000,
000,000,000,000,000,000,000,000,000,000,000,000,
000,000,000,000,000,000,000,000,000,000,000,000,
000,000,000,000,000,000,000,000,000,000,000,000,
000,000,000,000,000,000,000,000,000,000,000,000,
000,000,000,000,000,000,000,000,000,000,000,000,
000,000,000,000,000,000,000,000,000,000,000,000,
000,000,000,000,000,000,000,000,000,000,000,000,
000,000,000,000,000,000,000,000,000,000,000,000,
000,000,000,000,000,000,000,000,000,000,000,000,
000,000,000,000,000,000,000,000,000,000,000,000,
000,000,000,000,000,000,000,000,000,000,000,000,
000,000,000,000,000,000,000,000,000,000,000,000,
000,000,000,000,000,000,000,000,000,000,000,000,
000,000,000,000,000,000,000,000,000,000,000,000,
000,000,000,000,000,000,000,000,000,000,000,000,
000,000,000,000,000,000,000,000,000,000,000,000,
000,000,000,000,000,000,000,000,000,000,000,000,
000,000,000,000,000,000,000,000,000,000,000,000,
000,000,000,000,000,000,000,000,000,000,000,000,
000,000,000,000,000,000,000,000,000,000,000,000,
000,000,000,000,000,000,000,000,000,000,000,000,
000,000,000,000,000,000,000,000,000,000,000,000,
000,000,000,000,000,000,000,000,000,000,000,000,
000,000,000,000,000,000,000,000,000,000,000,000,
000,000,000,000,000,000,000,000,000,000,000,000,
000,000,000,000,000,000,000,000,000,000,000,000,
000,000,000,000,000,000,000,000,000,000,000,000,
000,000,000,000,000,000,000,000,000,000,000,000,
000,000,000,000,000,000,000,000,000,000,000,000,
000,000,000,000,000,000,000,000,000,000,000,000,
000,000,000,000,000,000,000,000,000,000,000,000,
000,000,000,000,000,000,000,000,000,000,000,000,
000,000,000,000,000,000,000,000,000,000,000,000,
000,000,000,000,000,000,000,000,000,000,000,000,
000,000,000,000,000,000,000,000,000,000,000,000,

000,000,000,000,000,000,000,000,000,000,000,000,
000,000,000,000,000,000,000,000,000,000,000,000,
000,000,000,000,000,000,000,000,000,000,000,000,
000,000,000,000,000,000,000,000,000,000,000,000,
000,000,000,000,000,000,000,000,000,000,000,000,
000,000,000,000,000,000,000,000,000,000,000,000,
000,000,000,000,000,000,000,000,000,000,000,000,
000,000,000,000,000,000,000,000,000,000,000,000,
000,000,000,000,000,000,000,000,000,000,000,000,
000,000,000,000,000,000,000,000,000,000,000,000,
000,000,000,000,000,000,000,000,000,000,000,000,
000,000,000,000,000,000,000,000,000,000,000,000,
000,000,000,000,000,000,000,000,000,000,000,000,
000,000,000,000,000,000,000,000,000,000,000,000,
000,000,000,000,000,000,000,000,000,000,000,000,
000,000,000,000,000,000,000,000,000,000,000,000,
000,000,000,000,000,000,000,000,000,000,000,000,
000,000,000,000,000,000,000,000,000,000,000,000,
000,000,000,000,000,000,000,000,000,000,000,000,
000,000,000,000,000,000,000,000,000,000,000,000,
000,000,000,000,000,000,000,000,000,000,000,000,
000,000,000,000,000,000,000,000,000,000,000,000,
000,000,000,000,000,000,000,000,000,000,000,000,
000,000,000,000,000,000,000,000,000,000,000,000,
000,000,000,000,000,000,000,000,000,000,000,000,
000,000,000,000,000,000,000,000,000,000,000,000,
000,000,000,000,000,000,000,000,000,000,000,000,
000,000,000,000,000,000,000,000,000,000,000,000,
000,000,000,000,000,000,000,000,000,000,000,000,
000,000,000,000,000,000,000,000,000,000,000,000,
000,000,000,000,000,000,000,000,000,000,000,000,
000,000,000,000,000,000,000,000,000,000,000,000,
000,000,000,000,000,000,000,000,000,000,000,000,
000,000,000,000,000,000,000,000,000,000,000,000,
000,000,000,000,000,000,000,000,000,000,000,000,
000,000,000,000,000,000,000,000,000,000,000,000,
000,000,000,000,000,000,000,000,000,000,000,000,
000,000,000,000,000,000,000,000,000,000,000,000,
000,000,000,000,000,000,000,000,000,000,000,000,

000,000,000,000,000,000,000,000,000,000,000,000,
000,000,000,000,000,000,000,000,000,000,000,000,
000,000,000,000,000,000,000,000,000,000,000,000,
000,000,000,000,000,000,000,000,000,000,000,000,
000,000,000,000,000,000,000,000,000,000,000,000,
000,000,000,000,000,000,000,000,000,000,000,000,
000,000,000,000,000,000,000,000,000,000,000,000,
000,000,000,000,000,000,000,000,000,000,000,000,
000,000,000,000,000,000,000,000,000,000,000,000,
000,000,000,000,000,000,000,000,000,000,000,000,
000,000,000,000,000,000,000,000,000,000,000,000,
000,000,000,000,000,000,000,000,000,000,000,000,
000,000,000,000,000,000,000,000,000,000,000,000,
000,000,000,000,000,000,000,000,000,000,000,000,
000,000,000,000,000,000,000,000,000,000,000,000,
000,000,000,000,000,000,000,000,000,000,000,000,
000,000,000,000,000,000,000,000,000,000,000,000,
000,000,000,000,000,000,000,000,000,000,000,000,
000,000,000,000,000,000,000,000,000,000,000,000,
000,000,000,000,000,000,000,000,000,000,000,000,
000,000,000,000,000,000,000,000,000,000,000,000,
000,000,000,000,000,000,000,000,000,000,000,000,
000,000,000,000,000,000,000,000,000,000,000,000,
000,000,000,000,000,000,000,000,000,000,000,000,
000,000,000,000,000,000,000,000,000,000,000,000,
000,000,000,000,000,000,000,000,000,000,000,000,
000,000,000,000,000,000,000,000,000,000,000,000,
000,000,000,000,000,000,000,000,000,000,000,000,
000,000,000,000,000,000,000,000,000,000,000,000,
000,000,000,000,000,000,000,000,000,000,000,000,
000,000,000,000,000,000,000,000,000,000,000,000,
000,000,000,000,000,000,000,000,000,000,000,000,
000,000,000,000,000,000,000,000,000,000,000,000,
000,000,000,000,000,000,000,000,000,000,000,000,
000,000,000,000,000,000,000,000,000,000,000,000,
000,000,000,000,000,000,000,000,000,000,000,000,
000,000,000,000,000,000,000,000,000,000,000,000,
000,000,000,000,000,000,000,000,000,000,000,000,
000,000,000,000,000,000,000,000,000,000,000,000,

000,000,000,000,000,000,000,000,000,000,000,000,
000,000,000,000,000,000,000,000,000,000,000,000,
000,000,000,000,000,000,000,000,000,000,000,000,
000,000,000,000,000,000,000,000,000,000,000,000,
000,000,000,000,000,000,000,000,000,000,000,000,
000,000,000,000,000,000,000,000,000,000,000,000,
000,000,000,000,000,000,000,000,000,000,000,000,
000,000,000,000,000,000,000,000,000,000,000,000,
000,000,000,000,000,000,000,000,000,000,000,000,
000,000,000,000,000,000,000,000,000,000,000,000,
000,000,000,000,000,000,000,000,000,000,000,000,
000,000,000,000,000,000,000,000,000,000,000,000,
000,000,000,000,000,000,000,000,000,000,000,000,
000,000,000,000,000,000,000,000,000,000,000,000,
000,000,000,000,000,000,000,000,000,000,000,000,
000,000,000,000,000,000,000,000,000,000,000,000,
000,000,000,000,000,000,000,000,000,000,000,000,
000,000,000,000,000,000,000,000,000,000,000,000,
000,000,000,000,000,000,000,000,000,000,000,000,
000,000,000,000,000,000,000,000,000,000,000,000,
000,000,000,000,000,000,000,000,000,000,000,000,
000,000,000,000,000,000,000,000,000,000,000,000,
000,000,000,000,000,000,000,000,000,000,000,000,
000,000,000,000,000,000,000,000,000,000,000,000,
000,000,000,000,000,000,000,000,000,000,000,000,
000,000,000,000,000,000,000,000,000,000,000,000,
000,000,000,000,000,000,000,000,000,000,000,000,
000,000,000,000,000,000,000,000,000,000,000,000,
000,000,000,000,000,000,000,000,000,000,000,000,
000,000,000,000,000,000,000,000,000,000,000,000,
000,000,000,000,000,000,000,000,000,000,000,000,
000,000,000,000,000,000,000,000,000,000,000,000,
000,000,000,000,000,000,000,000,000,000,000,000,
000,000,000,000,000,000,000,000,000,000,000,000,
000,000,000,000,000,000,000,000,000,000,000,000,

000,000,000,000,000,000,000,000,000,000,000,000,
000,000,000,000,000,000,000,000,000,000,000,000,
000,000,000,000,000,000,000,000,000,000,000,000,
000,000,000,000,000,000,000,000,000,000,000,000,
000,000,000,000,000,000,000,000,000,000,000,000,
000,000,000,000,000,000,000,000,000,000,000,000,
000,000,000,000,000,000,000,000,000,000,000,000,
000,000,000,000,000,000,000,000,000,000,000,000,
000,000,000,000,000,000,000,000,000,000,000,000,
000,000,000,000,000,000,000,000,000,000,000,000,
000,000,000,000,000,000,000,000,000,000,000,000,
000,000,000,000,000,000,000,000,000,000,000,000,
000,000,000,000,000,000,000,000,000,000,000,000,
000,000,000,000,000,000,000,000,000,000,000,000,
000,000,000,000,000,000,000,000,000,000,000,000,
000,000,000,000,000,000,000,000,000,000,000,000,
000,000,000,000,000,000,000,000,000,000,000,000,
000,000,000,000,000,000,000,000,000,000,000,000,
000,000,000,000,000,000,000,000,000,000,000,000,
000,000,000,000,000,000,000,000,000,000,000,000,
000,000,000,000,000,000,000,000,000,000,000,000,
000,000,000,000,000,000,000,000,000,000,000,000,
000,000,000,000,000,000,000,000,000,000,000,000,
000,000,000,000,000,000,000,000,000,000,000,000,
000,000,000,000,000,000,000,000,000,000,000,000,
000,000,000,000,000,000,000,000,000,000,000,000,
000,000,000,000,000,000,000,000,000,000,000,000,
000,000,000,000,000,000,000,000,000,000,000,000,
000,000,000,000,000,000,000,000,000,000,000,000,
000,000,000,000,000,000,000,000,000,000,000,000,
000,000,000,000,000,000,000,000,000,000,000,000,
000,000,000,000,000,000,000,000,000,000,000,000,
000,000,000,000,000,000,000,000,000,000,000,000,
000,000,000,000,000,000,000,000,000,000,000,000,
000,000,000,000,000,000,000,000,000,000,000,000,
000,000,000,000,000,000,000,000,000,000,000,000,

000,000,000,000,000,000,000,000,000,000,000,000,
000,000,000,000,000,000,000,000,000,000,000,000,
000,000,000,000,000,000,000,000,000,000,000,000,
000,000,000,000,000,000,000,000,000,000,000,000,
000,000,000,000,000,000,000,000,000,000,000,000,
000,000,000,000,000,000,000,000,000,000,000,000,
000,000,000,000,000,000,000,000,000,000,000,000,
000,000,000,000,000,000,000,000,000,000,000,000,
000,000,000,000,000,000,000,000,000,000,000,000,
000,000,000,000,000,000,000,000,000,000,000,000,
000,000,000,000,000,000,000,000,000,000,000,000,
000,000,000,000,000,000,000,000,000,000,000,000,
000,000,000,000,000,000,000,000,000,000,000,000,
000,000,000,000,000,000,000,000,000,000,000,000,
000,000,000,000,000,000,000,000,000,000,000,000,
000,000,000,000,000,000,000,000,000,000,000,000,
000,000,000,000,000,000,000,000,000,000,000,000,
000,000,000,000,000,000,000,000,000,000,000,000,
000,000,000,000,000,000,000,000,000,000,000,000,
000,000,000,000,000,000,000,000,000,000,000,000,
000,000,000,000,000,000,000,000,000,000,000,000,
000,000,000,000,000,000,000,000,000,000,000,000,
000,000,000,000,000,000,000,000,000,000,000,000,
000,000,000,000,000,000,000,000,000,000,000,000,
000,000,000,000,000,000,000,000,000,000,000,000,
000,000,000,000,000,000,000,000,000,000,000,000,
000,000,000,000,000,000,000,000,000,000,000,000,
000,000,000,000,000,000,000,000,000,000,000,000,
000,000,000,000,000,000,000,000,000,000,000,000,
000,000,000,000,000,000,000,000,000,000,000,000,
000,000,000,000,000,000,000,000,000,000,000,000,
000,000,000,000,000,000,000,000,000,000,000,000,
000,000,000,000,000,000,000,000,000,000,000,000,
000,000,000,000,000,000,000,000,000,000,000,000,
000,000,000,000,000,000,000,000,000,000,000,000,
000,000,000,000,000,000,000,000,000,000,000,000,
000,000,000,000,000,000,000,000,000,000,000,000,
000,000,000,000,000,000,000,000,000,000,000,000,
000,000,000,000,000,000,000,000,000,000,000,000,

000,000,000,000,000,000,000,000,000,000,000,000,
000,000,000,000,000,000,000,000,000,000,000,000,
000,000,000,000,000,000,000,000,000,000,000,000,
000,000,000,000,000,000,000,000,000,000,000,000,
000,000,000,000,000,000,000,000,000,000,000,000,
000,000,000,000,000,000,000,000,000,000,000,000,
000,000,000,000,000,000,000,000,000,000,000,000,
000,000,000,000,000,000,000,000,000,000,000,000,
000,000,000,000,000,000,000,000,000,000,000,000,
000,000,000,000,000,000,000,000,000,000,000,000,
000,000,000,000,000,000,000,000,000,000,000,000,
000,000,000,000,000,000,000,000,000,000,000,000,
000,000,000,000,000,000,000,000,000,000,000,000,
000,000,000,000,000,000,000,000,000,000,000,000,
000,000,000,000,000,000,000,000,000,000,000,000,
000,000,000,000,000,000,000,000,000,000,000,000,
000,000,000,000,000,000,000,000,000,000,000,000,
000,000,000,000,000,000,000,000,000,000,000,000,
000,000,000,000,000,000,000,000,000,000,000,000,
000,000,000,000,000,000,000,000,000,000,000,000,
000,000,000,000,000,000,000,000,000,000,000,000,
000,000,000,000,000,000,000,000,000,000,000,000,
000,000,000,000,000,000,000,000,000,000,000,000,
000,000,000,000,000,000,000,000,000,000,000,000,
000,000,000,000,000,000,000,000,000,000,000,000,
000,000,000,000,000,000,000,000,000,000,000,000,
000,000,000,000,000,000,000,000,000,000,000,000,
000,000,000,000,000,000,000,000,000,000,000,000,
000,000,000,000,000,000,000,000,000,000,000,000,
000,000,000,000,000,000,000,000,000,000,000,000,
000,000,000,000,000,000,000,000,000,000,000,000,
000,000,000,000,000,000,000,000,000,000,000,000,
000,000,000,000,000,000,000,000,000,000,000,000,
000,000,000,000,000,000,000,000,000,000,000,000,
000,000,000,000,000,000,000,000,000,000,000,000,
000,000,000,000,000,000,000,000,000,000,000,000,
000,000,000,000,000,000,000,000,000,000,000,000,
000,000,000,000,000,000,000,000,000,000,000,000,
000,000,000,000,000,000,000,000,000,000,000,000,
000,000,000,000,000,000,000,000,000,000,000,000,

000,000,000,000,000,000,000,000,000,000,000,000,
000,000,000,000,000,000,000,000,000,000,000,000,
000,000,000,000,000,000,000,000,000,000,000,000,
000,000,000,000,000,000,000,000,000,000,000,000,
000,000,000,000,000,000,000,000,000,000,000,000,
000,000,000,000,000,000,000,000,000,000,000,000,
000,000,000,000,000,000,000,000,000,000,000,000,
000,000,000,000,000,000,000,000,000,000,000,000,
000,000,000,000,000,000,000,000,000,000,000,000,
000,000,000,000,000,000,000,000,000,000,000,000,
000,000,000,000,000,000,000,000,000,000,000,000,
000,000,000,000,000,000,000,000,000,000,000,000,
000,000,000,000,000,000,000,000,000,000,000,000,
000,000,000,000,000,000,000,000,000,000,000,000,
000,000,000,000,000,000,000,000,000,000,000,000,
000,000,000,000,000,000,000,000,000,000,000,000,
000,000,000,000,000,000,000,000,000,000,000,000,
000,000,000,000,000,000,000,000,000,000,000,000,
000,000,000,000,000,000,000,000,000,000,000,000,
000,000,000,000,000,000,000,000,000,000,000,000,
000,000,000,000,000,000,000,000,000,000,000,000,
000,000,000,000,000,000,000,000,000,000,000,000,
000,000,000,000,000,000,000,000,000,000,000,000,
000,000,000,000,000,000,000,000,000,000,000,000,
000,000,000,000,000,000,000,000,000,000,000,000,
000,000,000,000,000,000,000,000,000,000,000,000,
000,000,000,000,000,000,000,000,000,000,000,000,
000,000,000,000,000,000,000,000,000,000,000,000,
000,000,000,000,000,000,000,000,000,000,000,000,
000,000,000,000,000,000,000,000,000,000,000,000,
000,000,000,000,000,000,000,000,000,000,000,000,
000,000,000,000,000,000,000,000,000,000,000,000,
000,000,000,000,000,000,000,000,000,000,000,000,
000,000,000,000,000,000,000,000,000,000,000,000,
000,000,000,000,000,000,000,000,000,000,000,000,
000,000,000,000,000,000,000,000,000,000,000,000,

000,000,000,000,000,000,000,000,000,000,000,000,
000,000,000,000,000,000,000,000,000,000,000,000,
000,000,000,000,000,000,000,000,000,000,000,000,
000,000,000,000,000,000,000,000,000,000,000,000,
000,000,000,000,000,000,000,000,000,000,000,000,
000,000,000,000,000,000,000,000,000,000,000,000,
000,000,000,000,000,000,000,000,000,000,000,000,
000,000,000,000,000,000,000,000,000,000,000,000,
000,000,000,000,000,000,000,000,000,000,000,000,
000,000,000,000,000,000,000,000,000,000,000,000,
000,000,000,000,000,000,000,000,000,000,000,000,
000,000,000,000,000,000,000,000,000,000,000,000,
000,000,000,000,000,000,000,000,000,000,000,000,
000,000,000,000,000,000,000,000,000,000,000,000,
000,000,000,000,000,000,000,000,000,000,000,000,
000,000,000,000,000,000,000,000,000,000,000,000,
000,000,000,000,000,000,000,000,000,000,000,000,
000,000,000,000,000,000,000,000,000,000,000,000,
000,000,000,000,000,000,000,000,000,000,000,000,
000,000,000,000,000,000,000,000,000,000,000,000,
000,000,000,000,000,000,000,000,000,000,000,000,
000,000,000,000,000,000,000,000,000,000,000,000,
000,000,000,000,000,000,000,000,000,000,000,000,
000,000,000,000,000,000,000,000,000,000,000,000,
000,000,000,000,000,000,000,000,000,000,000,000,
000,000,000,000,000,000,000,000,000,000,000,000,
000,000,000,000,000,000,000,000,000,000,000,000,
000,000,000,000,000,000,000,000,000,000,000,000,
000,000,000,000,000,000,000,000,000,000,000,000,
000,000,000,000,000,000,000,000,000,000,000,000,
000,000,000,000,000,000,000,000,000,000,000,000,
000,000,000,000,000,000,000,000,000,000,000,000,
000,000,000,000,000,000,000,000,000,000,000,000,
000,000,000,000,000,000,000,000,000,000,000,000,
000,000,000,000,000,000,000,000,000,000,000,000,
000,000,000,000,000,000,000,000,000,000,000,000,
000,000,000,000,000,000,000,000,000,000,000,000,
000,000,000,000,000,000,000,000,000,000,000,000,
000,000,000,000,000,000,000,000,000,000,000,000,
000,000,000,000,000,000,000,000,000,000,000,000,

000,000,000,000,000,000,000,000,000,000,000,000,
000,000,000,000,000,000,000,000,000,000,000,000,
000,000,000,000,000,000,000,000,000,000,000,000,
000,000,000,000,000,000,000,000,000,000,000,000,
000,000,000,000,000,000,000,000,000,000,000,000,
000,000,000,000,000,000,000,000,000,000,000,000,
000,000,000,000,000,000,000,000,000,000,000,000,
000,000,000,000,000,000,000,000,000,000,000,000,
000,000,000,000,000,000,000,000,000,000,000,000,
000,000,000,000,000,000,000,000,000,000,000,000,
000,000,000,000,000,000,000,000,000,000,000,000,
000,000,000,000,000,000,000,000,000,000,000,000,
000,000,000,000,000,000,000,000,000,000,000,000,
000,000,000,000,000,000,000,000,000,000,000,000,
000,000,000,000,000,000,000,000,000,000,000,000,
000,000,000,000,000,000,000,000,000,000,000,000,
000,000,000,000,000,000,000,000,000,000,000,000,
000,000,000,000,000,000,000,000,000,000,000,000,
000,000,000,000,000,000,000,000,000,000,000,000,
000,000,000,000,000,000,000,000,000,000,000,000,
000,000,000,000,000,000,000,000,000,000,000,000,
000,000,000,000,000,000,000,000,000,000,000,000,
000,000,000,000,000,000,000,000,000,000,000,000,
000,000,000,000,000,000,000,000,000,000,000,000,
000,000,000,000,000,000,000,000,000,000,000,000,
000,000,000,000,000,000,000,000,000,000,000,000,
000,000,000,000,000,000,000,000,000,000,000,000,
000,000,000,000,000,000,000,000,000,000,000,000,
000,000,000,000,000,000,000,000,000,000,000,000,
000,000,000,000,000,000,000,000,000,000,000,000,
000,000,000,000,000,000,000,000,000,000,000,000,
000,000,000,000,000,000,000,000,000,000,000,000,
000,000,000,000,000,000,000,000,000,000,000,000,
000,000,000,000,000,000,000,000,000,000,000,000,
000,000,000,000,000,000,000,000,000,000,000,000,
000,000,000,000,000,000,000,000,000,000,000,000,
000,000,000,000,000,000,000,000,000,000,000,000,
000,000,000,000,000,000,000,000,000,000,000,000,
000,000,000,000,000,000,000,000,000,000,000,000,

000,000,000,000,000,000,000,000,000,000,000,000,
000,000,000,000,000,000,000,000,000,000,000,000,
000,000,000,000,000,000,000,000,000,000,000,000,
000,000,000,000,000,000,000,000,000,000,000,000,
000,000,000,000,000,000,000,000,000,000,000,000,
000,000,000,000,000,000,000,000,000,000,000,000,
000,000,000,000,000,000,000,000,000,000,000,000,
000,000,000,000,000,000,000,000,000,000,000,000,
000,000,000,000,000,000,000,000,000,000,000,000,
000,000,000,000,000,000,000,000,000,000,000,000,
000,000,000,000,000,000,000,000,000,000,000,000,
000,000,000,000,000,000,000,000,000,000,000,000,
000,000,000,000,000,000,000,000,000,000,000,000,
000,000,000,000,000,000,000,000,000,000,000,000,
000,000,000,000,000,000,000,000,000,000,000,000,
000,000,000,000,000,000,000,000,000,000,000,000,
000,000,000,000,000,000,000,000,000,000,000,000,
000,000,000,000,000,000,000,000,000,000,000,000,
000,000,000,000,000,000,000,000,000,000,000,000,
000,000,000,000,000,000,000,000,000,000,000,000,
000,000,000,000,000,000,000,000,000,000,000,000,
000,000,000,000,000,000,000,000,000,000,000,000,
000,000,000,000,000,000,000,000,000,000,000,000,
000,000,000,000,000,000,000,000,000,000,000,000,
000,000,000,000,000,000,000,000,000,000,000,000,
000,000,000,000,000,000,000,000,000,000,000,000,
000,000,000,000,000,000,000,000,000,000,000,000,
000,000,000,000,000,000,000,000,000,000,000,000,
000,000,000,000,000,000,000,000,000,000,000,000,
000,000,000,000,000,000,000,000,000,000,000,000,
000,000,000,000,000,000,000,000,000,000,000,000,
000,000,000,000,000,000,000,000,000,000,000,000,
000,000,000,000,000,000,000,000,000,000,000,000,
000,000,000,000,000,000,000,000,000,000,000,000,
000,000,000,000,000,000,000,000,000,000,000,000,
000,000,000,000,000,000,000,000,000,000,000,000,

000,000,000,000,000,000,000,000,000,000,000,000,
000,000,000,000,000,000,000,000,000,000,000,000,
000,000,000,000,000,000,000,000,000,000,000,000,
000,000,000,000,000,000,000,000,000,000,000,000,
000,000,000,000,000,000,000,000,000,000,000,000,
000,000,000,000,000,000,000,000,000,000,000,000,
000,000,000,000,000,000,000,000,000,000,000,000,
000,000,000,000,000,000,000,000,000,000,000,000,
000,000,000,000,000,000,000,000,000,000,000,000,
000,000,000,000,000,000,000,000,000,000,000,000,
000,000,000,000,000,000,000,000,000,000,000,000,
000,000,000,000,000,000,000,000,000,000,000,000,
000,000,000,000,000,000,000,000,000,000,000,000,
000,000,000,000,000,000,000,000,000,000,000,000,
000,000,000,000,000,000,000,000,000,000,000,000,
000,000,000,000,000,000,000,000,000,000,000,000,
000,000,000,000,000,000,000,000,000,000,000,000,
000,000,000,000,000,000,000,000,000,000,000,000,
000,000,000,000,000,000,000,000,000,000,000,000,
000,000,000,000,000,000,000,000,000,000,000,000,
000,000,000,000,000,000,000,000,000,000,000,000,
000,000,000,000,000,000,000,000,000,000,000,000,
000,000,000,000,000,000,000,000,000,000,000,000,
000,000,000,000,000,000,000,000,000,000,000,000,
000,000,000,000,000,000,000,000,000,000,000,000,
000,000,000,000,000,000,000,000,000,000,000,000,
000,000,000,000,000,000,000,000,000,000,000,000,
000,000,000,000,000,000,000,000,000,000,000,000,
000,000,000,000,000,000,000,000,000,000,000,000,
000,000,000,000,000,000,000,000,000,000,000,000,
000,000,000,000,000,000,000,000,000,000,000,000,
000,000,000,000,000,000,000,000,000,000,000,000,
000,000,000,000,000,000,000,000,000,000,000,000,
000,000,000,000,000,000,000,000,000,000,000,000,
000,000,000,000,000,000,000,000,000,000,000,000,
000,000,000,000,000,000,000,000,000,000,000,000,
000,000,000,000,000,000,000,000,000,000,000,000,
000,000,000,000,000,000,000,000,000,000,000,000,
000,000,000,000,000,000,000,000,000,000,000,000,
000,000,000,000,000,000,000,000,000,000,000,000,

000,000,000,000,000,000,000,000,000,000,000,000,
000,000,000,000,000,000,000,000,000,000,000,000,
000,000,000,000,000,000,000,000,000,000,000,000,
000,000,000,000,000,000,000,000,000,000,000,000,
000,000,000,000,000,000,000,000,000,000,000,000,
000,000,000,000,000,000,000,000,000,000,000,000,
000,000,000,000,000,000,000,000,000,000,000,000,
000,000,000,000,000,000,000,000,000,000,000,000,
000,000,000,000,000,000,000,000,000,000,000,000,
000,000,000,000,000,000,000,000,000,000,000,000,
000,000,000,000,000,000,000,000,000,000,000,000,
000,000,000,000,000,000,000,000,000,000,000,000,
000,000,000,000,000,000,000,000,000,000,000,000,
000,000,000,000,000,000,000,000,000,000,000,000,
000,000,000,000,000,000,000,000,000,000,000,000,
000,000,000,000,000,000,000,000,000,000,000,000,
000,000,000,000,000,000,000,000,000,000,000,000,
000,000,000,000,000,000,000,000,000,000,000,000,
000,000,000,000,000,000,000,000,000,000,000,000,
000,000,000,000,000,000,000,000,000,000,000,000,
000,000,000,000,000,000,000,000,000,000,000,000,
000,000,000,000,000,000,000,000,000,000,000,000,
000,000,000,000,000,000,000,000,000,000,000,000,
000,000,000,000,000,000,000,000,000,000,000,000,
000,000,000,000,000,000,000,000,000,000,000,000,
000,000,000,000,000,000,000,000,000,000,000,000,
000,000,000,000,000,000,000,000,000,000,000,000,
000,000,000,000,000,000,000,000,000,000,000,000,
000,000,000,000,000,000,000,000,000,000,000,000,
000,000,000,000,000,000,000,000,000,000,000,000,
000,000,000,000,000,000,000,000,000,000,000,000,
000,000,000,000,000,000,000,000,000,000,000,000,
000,000,000,000,000,000,000,000,000,000,000,000,
000,000,000,000,000,000,000,000,000,000,000,000,
000,000,000,000,000,000,000,000,000,000,000,000,
000,000,000,000,000,000,000,000,000,000,000,000,
000,000,000,000,000,000,000,000,000,000,000,000,
000,000,000,000,000,000,000,000,000,000,000,000,
000,000,000,000,000,000,000,000,000,000,000,000,
000,000,000,000,000,000,000,000,000,000,000,000,

000,000,000,000,000,000,000,000,000,000,000,000,
000,000,000,000,000,000,000,000,000,000,000,000,
000,000,000,000,000,000,000,000,000,000,000,000,
000,000,000,000,000,000,000,000,000,000,000,000,
000,000,000,000,000,000,000,000,000,000,000,000,
000,000,000,000,000,000,000,000,000,000,000,000,
000,000,000,000,000,000,000,000,000,000,000,000,
000,000,000,000,000,000,000,000,000,000,000,000,
000,000,000,000,000,000,000,000,000,000,000,000,
000,000,000,000,000,000,000,000,000,000,000,000,
000,000,000,000,000,000,000,000,000,000,000,000,
000,000,000,000,000,000,000,000,000,000,000,000,
000,000,000,000,000,000,000,000,000,000,000,000,
000,000,000,000,000,000,000,000,000,000,000,000,
000,000,000,000,000,000,000,000,000,000,000,000,
000,000,000,000,000,000,000,000,000,000,000,000,
000,000,000,000,000,000,000,000,000,000,000,000,
000,000,000,000,000,000,000,000,000,000,000,000,
000,000,000,000,000,000,000,000,000,000,000,000,
000,000,000,000,000,000,000,000,000,000,000,000,
000,000,000,000,000,000,000,000,000,000,000,000,
000,000,000,000,000,000,000,000,000,000,000,000,
000,000,000,000,000,000,000,000,000,000,000,000,
000,000,000,000,000,000,000,000,000,000,000,000,
000,000,000,000,000,000,000,000,000,000,000,000,
000,000,000,000,000,000,000,000,000,000,000,000,
000,000,000,000,000,000,000,000,000,000,000,000,
000,000,000,000,000,000,000,000,000,000,000,000,
000,000,000,000,000,000,000,000,000,000,000,000,
000,000,000,000,000,000,000,000,000,000,000,000,
000,000,000,000,000,000,000,000,000,000,000,000,
000,000,000,000,000,000,000,000,000,000,000,000,
000,000,000,000,000,000,000,000,000,000,000,000,
000,000,000,000,000,000,000,000,000,000,000,000,
000,000,000,000,000,000,000,000,000,000,000,000,
000,000,000,000,000,000,000,000,000,000,000,000,
000,000,000,000,000,000,000,000,000,000,000,000,
000,000,000,000,000,000,000,000,000,000,000,000,
000,000,000,000,000,000,000,000,000,000,000,000,

000,000,000,000,000,000,000,000,000,000,000,000,
000,000,000,000,000,000,000,000,000,000,000,000,
000,000,000,000,000,000,000,000,000,000,000,000,
000,000,000,000,000,000,000,000,000,000,000,000,
000,000,000,000,000,000,000,000,000,000,000,000,
000,000,000,000,000,000,000,000,000,000,000,000,
000,000,000,000,000,000,000,000,000,000,000,000,
000,000,000,000,000,000,000,000,000,000,000,000,
000,000,000,000,000,000,000,000,000,000,000,000,
000,000,000,000,000,000,000,000,000,000,000,000,
000,000,000,000,000,000,000,000,000,000,000,000,
000,000,000,000,000,000,000,000,000,000,000,000,
000,000,000,000,000,000,000,000,000,000,000,000,
000,000,000,000,000,000,000,000,000,000,000,000,
000,000,000,000,000,000,000,000,000,000,000,000,
000,000,000,000,000,000,000,000,000,000,000,000,
000,000,000,000,000,000,000,000,000,000,000,000,
000,000,000,000,000,000,000,000,000,000,000,000,
000,000,000,000,000,000,000,000,000,000,000,000,
000,000,000,000,000,000,000,000,000,000,000,000,
000,000,000,000,000,000,000,000,000,000,000,000,
000,000,000,000,000,000,000,000,000,000,000,000,
000,000,000,000,000,000,000,000,000,000,000,000,
000,000,000,000,000,000,000,000,000,000,000,000,
000,000,000,000,000,000,000,000,000,000,000,000,
000,000,000,000,000,000,000,000,000,000,000,000,
000,000,000,000,000,000,000,000,000,000,000,000,
000,000,000,000,000,000,000,000,000,000,000,000,
000,000,000,000,000,000,000,000,000,000,000,000,
000,000,000,000,000,000,000,000,000,000,000,000,
000,000,000,000,000,000,000,000,000,000,000,000,
000,000,000,000,000,000,000,000,000,000,000,000,
000,000,000,000,000,000,000,000,000,000,000,000,
000,000,000,000,000,000,000,000,000,000,000,000,
000,000,000,000,000,000,000,000,000,000,000,000,
000,000,000,000,000,000,000,000,000,000,000,000,
000,000,000,000,000,000,000,000,000,000,000,000,
000,000,000,000,000,000,000,000,000,000,000,000,
000,000,000,000,000,000,000,000,000,000,000,000,
000,000,000,000,000,000,000,000,000,000,000,000,

000,000,000,000,000,000,000,000,000,000,000,000,
000,000,000,000,000,000,000,000,000,000,000,000,
000,000,000,000,000,000,000,000,000,000,000,000,
000,000,000,000,000,000,000,000,000,000,000,000,
000,000,000,000,000,000,000,000,000,000,000,000,
000,000,000,000,000,000,000,000,000,000,000,000,
000,000,000,000,000,000,000,000,000,000,000,000,
000,000,000,000,000,000,000,000,000,000,000,000,
000,000,000,000,000,000,000,000,000,000,000,000,
000,000,000,000,000,000,000,000,000,000,000,000,
000,000,000,000,000,000,000,000,000,000,000,000,
000,000,000,000,000,000,000,000,000,000,000,000,
000,000,000,000,000,000,000,000,000,000,000,000,
000,000,000,000,000,000,000,000,000,000,000,000,
000,000,000,000,000,000,000,000,000,000,000,000,
000,000,000,000,000,000,000,000,000,000,000,000,
000,000,000,000,000,000,000,000,000,000,000,000,
000,000,000,000,000,000,000,000,000,000,000,000,
000,000,000,000,000,000,000,000,000,000,000,000,
000,000,000,000,000,000,000,000,000,000,000,000,
000,000,000,000,000,000,000,000,000,000,000,000,
000,000,000,000,000,000,000,000,000,000,000,000,
000,000,000,000,000,000,000,000,000,000,000,000,
000,000,000,000,000,000,000,000,000,000,000,000,
000,000,000,000,000,000,000,000,000,000,000,000,
000,000,000,000,000,000,000,000,000,000,000,000,
000,000,000,000,000,000,000,000,000,000,000,000,
000,000,000,000,000,000,000,000,000,000,000,000,
000,000,000,000,000,000,000,000,000,000,000,000,
000,000,000,000,000,000,000,000,000,000,000,000,
000,000,000,000,000,000,000,000,000,000,000,000,
000,000,000,000,000,000,000,000,000,000,000,000,
000,000,000,000,000,000,000,000,000,000,000,000,
000,000,000,000,000,000,000,000,000,000,000,000,
000,000,000,000,000,000,000,000,000,000,000,000,
000,000,000,000,000,000,000,000,000,000,000,000,
000,000,000,000,000,000,000,000,000,000,000,000,
000,000,000,000,000,000,000,000,000,000,000,000,
000,000,000,000,000,000,000,000,000,000,000,000,

000,000,000,000,000,000,000,000,000,000,000,000,
000,000,000,000,000,000,000,000,000,000,000,000,
000,000,000,000,000,000,000,000,000,000,000,000,
000,000,000,000,000,000,000,000,000,000,000,000,
000,000,000,000,000,000,000,000,000,000,000,000,
000,000,000,000,000,000,000,000,000,000,000,000,
000,000,000,000,000,000,000,000,000,000,000,000,
000,000,000,000,000,000,000,000,000,000,000,000,
000,000,000,000,000,000,000,000,000,000,000,000,
000,000,000,000,000,000,000,000,000,000,000,000,
000,000,000,000,000,000,000,000,000,000,000,000,
000,000,000,000,000,000,000,000,000,000,000,000,
000,000,000,000,000,000,000,000,000,000,000,000,
000,000,000,000,000,000,000,000,000,000,000,000,
000,000,000,000,000,000,000,000,000,000,000,000,
000,000,000,000,000,000,000,000,000,000,000,000,
000,000,000,000,000,000,000,000,000,000,000,000,
000,000,000,000,000,000,000,000,000,000,000,000,
000,000,000,000,000,000,000,000,000,000,000,000,
000,000,000,000,000,000,000,000,000,000,000,000,
000,000,000,000,000,000,000,000,000,000,000,000,
000,000,000,000,000,000,000,000,000,000,000,000,
000,000,000,000,000,000,000,000,000,000,000,000,
000,000,000,000,000,000,000,000,000,000,000,000,
000,000,000,000,000,000,000,000,000,000,000,000,
000,000,000,000,000,000,000,000,000,000,000,000,
000,000,000,000,000,000,000,000,000,000,000,000,
000,000,000,000,000,000,000,000,000,000,000,000,
000,000,000,000,000,000,000,000,000,000,000,000,
000,000,000,000,000,000,000,000,000,000,000,000,
000,000,000,000,000,000,000,000,000,000,000,000,
000,000,000,000,000,000,000,000,000,000,000,000,
000,000,000,000,000,000,000,000,000,000,000,000,
000,000,000,000,000,000,000,000,000,000,000,000,
000,000,000,000,000,000,000,000,000,000,000,000,
000,000,000,000,000,000,000,000,000,000,000,000,

000,000,000,000,000,000,000,000,000,000,000,000,
000,000,000,000,000,000,000,000,000,000,000,000,
000,000,000,000,000,000,000,000,000,000,000,000,
000,000,000,000,000,000,000,000,000,000,000,000,
000,000,000,000,000,000,000,000,000,000,000,000,
000,000,000,000,000,000,000,000,000,000,000,000,
000,000,000,000,000,000,000,000,000,000,000,000,
000,000,000,000,000,000,000,000,000,000,000,000,
000,000,000,000,000,000,000,000,000,000,000,000,
000,000,000,000,000,000,000,000,000,000,000,000,
000,000,000,000,000,000,000,000,000,000,000,000,
000,000,000,000,000,000,000,000,000,000,000,000,
000,000,000,000,000,000,000,000,000,000,000,000,
000,000,000,000,000,000,000,000,000,000,000,000,
000,000,000,000,000,000,000,000,000,000,000,000,
000,000,000,000,000,000,000,000,000,000,000,000,
000,000,000,000,000,000,000,000,000,000,000,000,
000,000,000,000,000,000,000,000,000,000,000,000,
000,000,000,000,000,000,000,000,000,000,000,000,
000,000,000,000,000,000,000,000,000,000,000,000,
000,000,000,000,000,000,000,000,000,000,000,000,
000,000,000,000,000,000,000,000,000,000,000,000,
000,000,000,000,000,000,000,000,000,000,000,000,
000,000,000,000,000,000,000,000,000,000,000,000,
000,000,000,000,000,000,000,000,000,000,000,000,
000,000,000,000,000,000,000,000,000,000,000,000,
000,000,000,000,000,000,000,000,000,000,000,000,
000,000,000,000,000,000,000,000,000,000,000,000,
000,000,000,000,000,000,000,000,000,000,000,000,
000,000,000,000,000,000,000,000,000,000,000,000,
000,000,000,000,000,000,000,000,000,000,000,000,
000,000,000,000,000,000,000,000,000,000,000,000,
000,000,000,000,000,000,000,000,000,000,000,000,
000,000,000,000,000,000,000,000,000,000,000,000,
000,000,000,000,000,000,000,000,000,000,000,000,
000,000,000,000,000,000,000,000,000,000,000,000,
000,000,000,000,000,000,000,000,000,000,000,000,

000,000,000,000,000,000,000,000,000,000,000,000,
000,000,000,000,000,000,000,000,000,000,000,000,
000,000,000,000,000,000,000,000,000,000,000,000,
000,000,000,000,000,000,000,000,000,000,000,000,
000,000,000,000,000,000,000,000,000,000,000,000,
000,000,000,000,000,000,000,000,000,000,000,000,
000,000,000,000,000,000,000,000,000,000,000,000,
000,000,000,000,000,000,000,000,000,000,000,000,
000,000,000,000,000,000,000,000,000,000,000,000,
000,000,000,000,000,000,000,000,000,000,000,000,
000,000,000,000,000,000,000,000,000,000,000,000,
000,000,000,000,000,000,000,000,000,000,000,000,
000,000,000,000,000,000,000,000,000,000,000,000,
000,000,000,000,000,000,000,000,000,000,000,000,
000,000,000,000,000,000,000,000,000,000,000,000,
000,000,000,000,000,000,000,000,000,000,000,000,
000,000,000,000,000,000,000,000,000,000,000,000,
000,000,000,000,000,000,000,000,000,000,000,000,
000,000,000,000,000,000,000,000,000,000,000,000,
000,000,000,000,000,000,000,000,000,000,000,000,
000,000,000,000,000,000,000,000,000,000,000,000,
000,000,000,000,000,000,000,000,000,000,000,000,
000,000,000,000,000,000,000,000,000,000,000,000,
000,000,000,000,000,000,000,000,000,000,000,000,
000,000,000,000,000,000,000,000,000,000,000,000,
000,000,000,000,000,000,000,000,000,000,000,000,
000,000,000,000,000,000,000,000,000,000,000,000,
000,000,000,000,000,000,000,000,000,000,000,000,
000,000,000,000,000,000,000,000,000,000,000,000,
000,000,000,000,000,000,000,000,000,000,000,000,
000,000,000,000,000,000,000,000,000,000,000,000,
000,000,000,000,000,000,000,000,000,000,000,000,
000,000,000,000,000,000,000,000,000,000,000,000,
000,000,000,000,000,000,000,000,000,000,000,000,
000,000,000,000,000,000,000,000,000,000,000,000,
000,000,000,000,000,000,000,000,000,000,000,000,
000,000,000,000,000,000,000,000,000,000,000,000,
000,000,000,000,000,000,000,000,000,000,000,000,
000,000,000,000,000,000,000,000,000,000,000,000,
000,000,000,000,000,000,000,000,000,000,000,000,

000,000,000,000,000,000,000,000,000,000,000,000,
000,000,000,000,000,000,000,000,000,000,000,000,
000,000,000,000,000,000,000,000,000,000,000,000,
000,000,000,000,000,000,000,000,000,000,000,000,
000,000,000,000,000,000,000,000,000,000,000,000,
000,000,000,000,000,000,000,000,000,000,000,000,
000,000,000,000,000,000,000,000,000,000,000,000,
000,000,000,000,000,000,000,000,000,000,000,000,
000,000,000,000,000,000,000,000,000,000,000,000,
000,000,000,000,000,000,000,000,000,000,000,000,
000,000,000,000,000,000,000,000,000,000,000,000,
000,000,000,000,000,000,000,000,000,000,000,000,
000,000,000,000,000,000,000,000,000,000,000,000,
000,000,000,000,000,000,000,000,000,000,000,000,
000,000,000,000,000,000,000,000,000,000,000,000

Now, according to cosmologist and Atheistic Evolutionist Carl Sagan, there has been only this many universes:

1

Atheists knew if the Big Bang Theory was true, then the Theory of Evolution was a lie. Ever since the Big Bang was confirmed by science, atheists have been scrambling to find ways to make the universe infinite and eternal again. They haven't been very successful. We will look at that later, but for now, let's get back to how and why the definition of science changed.

The Modern Definition of Science

Let me give you the simplest modern definition of science I can think of: Science is the study of nature. This definition limits science to the natural realm, and this is what atheists demand. They say we can only use natural observations and natural experimentations to explain natural phenomena. Since we cannot observe the supernatural (if it exists) and since we cannot experiment with the supernatural, (if it exists) then we cannot make any scientific statements that appeal to, or depend on anything other than nature. We cannot scientifically observe God; therefore, God cannot be included in science.

Very, very carefully notice how this definition does not disprove (falsify) the possibility of the supernatural. It merely says we can't test it scientifically. No scientist can say God doesn't exist. Such a statement is, by his own definition, beyond his ability to test. Scientists can only make scientific statements about nature. (There is no natural test to test the supernatural.) A scientist must quit being a scientist to make a statement about something "outside of" nature. A scientist must quit being a scientist to say there is no God. Unfortunately, too many scientists have quit being scientists. Modern science is not merely agnostic about God; Modern science is downright atheistic. Atheists adopt the philosophy of Scientific Materialism. Simply put, they believe nothing but the material exists. **The definition of science has changed from, "The physical/material universe exists," to "ONLY the physical/material universe exists."** Because they cannot see it or measure it, they dogmatically believe the supernatural does not exist. Unfortunately for them, their belief cannot be tested by science. How can you use something material to prove something immaterial doesn't exist? You can't! In fact, sometimes it can be virtually impossible to prove that something material doesn't exist. Recall my Little Green Apples story. To prove non-red apples (which are material) didn't exist, it required a physical search of the entire surface of the earth. Even if green apples had never been seen, no scientist could truthfully say green apples didn't exist until every apple tree in the world was observed and tested. So, if proving the nonexistence of material things can be impossible sometimes, how can you prove the nonexistence of immaterial things? To prove that God can't be seen, you would have to observe and test every cubic inch of the universe (and all the Multiverses) to make sure there wasn't a portal, opening, window, doorway, or peephole where one could see or enter the supernatural realm. It is impossible for science to disprove the existence of the immaterial. Scientific Materialism is an idea based on opinion, not on science. **Today's definition of science cannot prove today's definition of science.**

I know atheists will counter my statement by saying a scientist must quit being a scientist to say God exists. Their counter-claim would be valid if God has never interacted with nature. If God has interacted with nature, such as audibly speaking to Moses, revealing Himself in a visible Pillar of Fire, miraculously providing physical food for forty years, miraculously healing people of diseases, and raising Jesus back to life, then God's existence has been naturally (physically/materially) proved. (You really have to be blind or three days dead not to see the evidence Jesus rose from the tomb after being three days dead. You have to not want to see it.) True, those things are not repeatable by scientists today, but not all truths are repeatable. You can't repeat Neil Armstrong walking on the moon in 1969 or the Battle of Hastings in 1066. (You may be able to reenact those events, but you can't repeat those events.) Still, those past events are true. You see, not all truths require **scientific** evidence. (1° Perception) Some truths require **historic** evidence. (2° Perception) A scientist may have to quit being a scientist to say God exists, but then all he or she needs to do is become a historian. Now, it is very important to realize something about this shift from 1° Perception to 2° Perception. 2° Perception may not be used as proof for scientific truth, but it can make us aware of what might be true. This shift from scientist to historian doesn't automatically negate the scientist's statements. It doesn't disqualify him or her from being a scientist. All scientists become historians when they accept the teachings, research, and observations of other scientists. Unless they repeat for themselves all the scientific works, research, experiments, and direct observations of all the scientists in history, they must rely on the historic evidence (2° Perception) from the works and writings of previous scientists. Atheists say they reject Biblical historical evidence because it was written by men. However, they readily accept Academic historical evidence in their journals, studies, reports, *etc.* written by men.

Atheists won't accept the historic evidence about God's existence, but they cannot provide scientific evidence there is no historic evidence for God's existence. Atheists can deny God, but they cannot disprove God. Why? Because God HAS physically interacted with man in the past, and atheists cannot scientifically (1° Perception) prove He hasn't. On the other hand, we can provide historic (2° Perception) evidence He has. Science cannot prove atheists are right, while history proves they are wrong. (And remember, while these evolutionary scientists are smart people, they are not trained historians. They cannot possibly understand the finer points of historical truth.) The past has proved them wrong, and the future will prove them even more wrong. Someday, God will interact with nature again. At that time, He will directly reveal Himself to atheists. The Bible calls that the Judgment Day—only then it will be too late.

Would scientists of the past accept the modern definition of science? Absolutely not! The definition of science from the most ancient of times included the possible existence of a supernatural God or gods as causes of the things around us. Most cultures, especially western cultures, believed many personal gods had played some part in creation. All those ancient philosopher-theologian-scientists would have argued against today's definition of science. If the Fathers of Modern Science were alive today, they would strongly disagree with the modern definition of science. They would call it a counterfeit definition of science.

The Fathers of Modern Science

Nicolaus Copernicus (1473-1543)
Francis Bacon (1561-1626)
Galileo Galilei (1564-1642)
Johannes Kepler (1571-1630)
William Harvey (1578-1657)
Rene Descartes (1596-1650)
Blaise Pascal (1623-1662)
Robert Boyle (1627-1691)
Isaac Newton (1642-1727)
Carolus Linnaeus (1707-1778)
Joseph Priestley (1733-1804)
William Herschel (1738-1822)
Michael Faraday (1791-1867)
Gregor Mendel (1822-1884)
Louis Pasteur (1822-1895)
James C. Maxwell (1831-1879)

All these men viewed science as the study of God's work. They believed God was a God of order; therefore, His creation would be a work of order. It would obey a set of laws established and upheld by His Divine Will and Power. Since God was not a God of randomness and confusion, they believed the laws of nature would not be random and confused. Men could systematically observe and test nature without worrying it might be capricious or random. In fact, this was one of the reasons many of Darwin's contemporaries rejected his Theory of Evolution—it depended on randomness. British astronomer, chemist, mathematician, and philosopher Sir John Herschel called it, "The Law of Higgledy-Piggledy." He didn't reject it because it taught that species changed over time. He believed in that. He objected to Darwin's explanation because it made randomness the cause. Herschel believed God didn't act randomly; therefore, none of His Laws would act randomly. The universe was orderly and non-random because God created it that way. **Since there were no random causes, there would be no random effects.** (And as we will see, Darwin's Theory of Evolution requires random causes and random effects.) These men believed they could learn about God by studying His orderly, non-random handiwork. Their definition of science didn't exclude God. God created science. Science was possible because of two things.

1.) God's creation was orderly and governed by His Fixed Laws.

2.) God created the mind of man in His own image, so we could find Him in His creation.

In short, these Fathers of Science believed Romans 1:20.

Romans 1:20 "For since the creation of the world God's invisible qualities—his eternal power and divine nature—have been clearly seen, being understood from what has been made, so that men are without excuse." (NIV)

Scientists of the past would not have excluded knowledge (*scientia*) of God from the realm of science. At that time, science was still the study of truth and facts, not just the study of the physical and natural. They believed science could reveal knowledge about God. In fact, there is an inscription over the great archway of the Cavendish Laboratory at Cambridge University in England attesting to this. (This one laboratory is responsible for 29 Noble Prizes since its founding. Ironically, this is where Watson and Crick made their discovery of the structure of DNA.) That inscription reads:

Magna opera Domini.
Exquista in omnes voluntates ejus

This is the Latin translation of Psalms 111:2— **"Great are the works of the Lord, sought out by all who take pleasure therein."**

Does it sound like the scientists at Cambridge rejected the Bible? No! In fact, until 1871, students had to pass a test in religion to attend Cambridge University. This was true of many other universities around the world. In our own country, Harvard, Yale, Princeton, in fact over 90 of our first 100 colleges and universities were founded by religious groups or on the religious principle of Romans 1:20. They believed the Works of God could reveal knowledge of God. That's why they were so passionate about studying science; science could reveal knowledge about God. It is hard for me to imagine their definition of science excluded God, since a basic understanding of God was required for a student even to begin studying science. They would have looked at today's definition of "science" and declared it counterfeit! Does it sound like the definition of science has changed? Yes, but does it mean all modern scientists accept that definition? No, there are many scientists who reject the atheistic implications of today's definition of science.

20th Century Nobel Laureate Scientists who believed in God

Ronald Ross (1902 Medicine)
Guglielmo Marconi (1909 Physics)
Alexis Carrel (1912 Medicine)
William H. Bragg (1915 Physics)
Max Planck (1918 Physics)
Robert Millikan (1923 Physics)
Arthur Compton (1927 Physics)
Werner Heisenberg (1932 Physics)
Erwin Schrödinger (1933 Physics)
Isidor Isaac Rabi (1944 Physics)
Ernst Chain (1945 Medicine)
John Eccles (1963 Medicine)
Charles Hard Townes (1964 Physics)
George Wald (1967 Medicine)
Derek Barton (1969 Chemistry)
Christian Anfinsen (1972 Chemistry)
Antony Hewish (1974 Physics)
Neville Mott (1977 Physics)
Arno Penzias (1978 Physics)
Abdus Salam (1979 Physics)
Arthur Schawlow (1981 Physics)
Joseph Murray (1990 Medicine)
Joseph H. Taylor (1993 Physics)
Richard Smalley (1996 Chemistry)
William D. Phillips (1997 Physics)
Walter Kohn (1998 Chemistry)

I know all these scientists didn't believe in God in the same way. I also know that just because these men believed in God, it doesn't prove God exists. Of the all the Nobel Science Prize winners in the 20th century, this list of 26 is less than ten percent. Atheists are quick to point out that greater than ninety percent of Nobel Prize winning scientists aren't on this list. Yes, but that doesn't prove God doesn't exist. The only thing it might prove is that greater than ninety percent of modern scientists are atheists, which I think proves why the definition of science is what it is today. If there are ninety foxes for every ten chickens in the chicken house, the chickens don't have much of a chance. While this doesn't prove God exists, it does prove that scientists who define science in the "old-fashioned way" are still capable of applying their definition of science to discover great things about the universe. When speaking about the scientific evidence confirming the Big Bang Theory, here is what Arno Penzias said:

"The best data we have are exactly what I would have predicted had I nothing to go on but the five books of Moses, the Psalms, and the Bible as a whole." - Arno Penzias, *New York Times*, March 12, 1978

In other words, thousands of years ago, the Bible described a cosmogony that fit perfectly with what modern science eventually proved to be true. I find it hard to believe these Nobel Laureates who believed in God believed science disproves the existence of God. It is very apparent that atheists have cornered the market of academia when it comes to defining science. Not only have they convinced themselves they are right, they have convinced educators, school boards, lawmakers, elected officials, judges, the news media, and the public in general. As long as they can convince others it is "scientific" to reject a Creator, people won't believe in a Creator. They reject God, Creation, and Intelligent Design because according to their definition of science, these things aren't science. But that is their definition of science. That is science according to their rules.

The Chess Grandmaster

Here is a little fact about me you may not know. I am the world's greatest chess grandmaster. That's right! I am the all-time international chess champion. I have never lost a game. No one has ever beaten me. No one can beat me…… **if** we play by MY rules. Ahhh, you see by MY rules, all my pieces have the power and mobility of the queen. By MY rules, all my opponent's pieces are restricted to the moves of pawns. Not only that, but according to MY rules, I can make twelve moves for every move my opponent makes. My opponent makes a move, and then I make the next twelve moves. My opponent makes a second move and I follow with twelve more moves… but it never gets that far. I always checkmate my opponent before he gets a chance to make his second move. Let ME define the rules of chess, and I am the chess champion of the world.

This is what has been done to the rules of science. We are playing by the atheists' rules. For the last one-hundred and fifty years, the definition of science has been the atheists' definition. If we play by their rules, science disproves the existence of God. If we play by their rules, creation cannot be taught in schools. If we play by their rules, only evolution can be taught. If we play by their rules, only evolutionists receive faculty and administrative positions in our colleges and universities. If we play by their rules, creationist students are flunked out and aren't accepted into post-graduate programs. If we play by their rules, teachers and professors who question evolution get fired. But, this is only if we allow their definition to stand. It is time to get a new dictionary.

I will not pretend I can undo WHAT atheists have done to science in the last one-hundred and fifty years, but I think I can show you WHY it needs to be undone. My challenge to Christian students is to go to college. Study hard, and study evolution even harder. Learn it backwards and forwards. Learn it better than any of your atheist classmates. Learn it so well, that no one can accuse you of being ignorant or misguided. Read what your professors require you to read… and then read more. In fact, this is extremely important! **Read much more than what your professors want you to read.** There is an ocean of data they don't want you to swim in. Become familiar with **WHAT** they don't want you to know, and you will see **WHY** they don't want you to know it. If you do that, you will recognize evolution as the counterfeit science it truly is. Do that, and you will know the truth about the origin of life. It may also give you a clue to the destiny of YOUR life.

The Scientific Method

I want to continue our study of science by looking at what is called, "The Scientific Method." The Scientific Method is the systematic way in which scientific information is discovered. It is the way science is done, or at least the way it is supposed to be done. Looking back at my simple definition of science, "science is the study of nature," I can now add a second part to the definition: "Science is the study of nature by using observations and experimentations." This means scientific statements about nature must be based on things that can be observed and tested. I mention this because both evolutionists and creationists sometimes misunderstand and misuse the Scientific Method.

Let me explain the concepts of the Scientific Method by first showing how it is incorrectly understood and applied. I'll start by giving an example of how some creationists misuse the Scientific Method. Now before I get myself into trouble, let me say I don't intend for this to be a criticism of all creationists. After all, I am one. But, I do want this to be a criticism of creationists who misuse or misinterpret science. Sadly, there are some creationists who are more concerned with fame and fortune, than they are with teaching and truth. Most creationists don't operate that way! In most cases when creationists make mistakes, they are either ill-informed or merely repeating something they heard or read from someone else; especially if they think that person is an authority on the subject. Their error is not investigating claims before believing them... or repeating them.

Over the years, I have found it most helpful to hear what one side says about a subject, then find out what the opposite side says about what the first side said, and then find out what the first side says about what the second side said about what the first side said, and then find out what the second side says about what the first side said about what the second side about what… well, you get the picture. By going back and forth, checking claims, counter-claims, and counter-counter-claims, this approach usually results in a better understanding of the issues, and it yields more reliable information. Years ago, this was a tedious process, but now with the Internet and its powerful search-engines, it is easy to investigate people's claims. If you do this, you will quickly discover that sometimes both evolutionists and creationists make false claims. Again, I'm not picking on creationists; evolutionists make many more false claims. However, when I hear atheists make false claims, it doesn't bother me as much as when I hear Christians make false claims. You see, atheists believe they have no absolute moral obligation to tell the truth! Let me repeat that.

Atheists believe they have no absolute moral obligation to tell the truth.

They don't believe they have to answer to God. They believe truth is relative. According to the Doctrine of Evolution, stealing, cheating, and killing are nature's ways of weeding out the competition. Why would lying be wrong? Is lying worse than killing? No! If lying helps evolutionists maintain their control of the halls of academia, and gives them social, political, legal, and financial advantages, then they must believe lying is good—it promotes their survival. Always remember this when you discuss, debate, or argue with evolutionists. They have no allegiance to the truth other than when they can use it to their advantage. Christians, on the other hand, are held to a higher standard. Christians ought to investigate before they believe.

Acts 17:11 "Now the Bereans were of more noble character than the Thessalonians, for they received the message with great eagerness and examined the Scriptures every day to see if what Paul said was true." (NIV)

The Bereans were honored for investigating the teachings of Paul the Apostle before believing them. I think we should apply this same standard to the teachings of lesser men when it comes to the issue of creation. We ought to investigate what creationists tell us, even if it comes from our favorite Bible scholars.

Here is an example of a scientific misunderstanding: Creationists often say the Theory of Evolution is not scientific because evolution was in the past, and the past is not observable. Let me repeat this because it is a very popular, but illogical, argument many creationists believe and use.

Creationists often say the Theory of Evolution is not scientific because evolution was in the past, and the past is not observable.

Using this line of argument, they infer that nothing about the supposed process of evolution can be known. I agree the Theory of Evolution is not scientific, but not for this reason. Where are these creationists going wrong? They are misrepresenting the concept of "observable." Yes, science says natural phenomena must be observable for them to be explained. But, when creationists say the past can't be observed, that's not true science. (Technically, the past is the only thing in nature we can observe. When you look at a star a thousand light years away, you are seeing it as it was in the past; one thousand years ago. When you look at the moon, you are seeing it as it was 1.3 seconds ago. That's how long it takes for the light of the moon to reach us. If you hold a rock in your outstretched hand, you are seeing it as it was about a nanosecond ago. You feel the rock even farther in the past; it takes a few milliseconds for the nerves of you hand to conduct their signals to the brain.) True science says that **some things** about the past can't be observed, but it doesn't say that **nothing** about the past can be observed. The past differs from the present in this way:

We can observe **causes and effects** in the present.

We can observe **only effects** from the past.

In other words, we can't observe past causes, but we can observe past effects. We can then logically use past effects to deduce past causes. Let me give an illustration to clarify this:

The Domino Universe

Imagine I had a line of one hundred dominoes set up on a table in a classroom. I invite a student from the class to come up and knock down the 1st domino. The 1st domino knocks down the 2nd domino, which knocks down the 3rd domino, which knocks down the 4th domino, and on and on until the 99th domino knocks down the 100th. We would be able to observe all one hundred causes and one hundred effects—they are in the present. However, what if you came to class late and didn't see what happened? To you, this would be a past event. You would see the effects of the past, all one hundred dominoes in their present position and arrangement, but you wouldn't be able to see the causes in the past. You might hypothesize from the way the dominoes are arranged that the 100th domino was knocked down by the 99th, which was knocked down by the 98th, which was knocked down by the 97th, all the way back to the 1st domino knocking down the 2nd. You might be able to experiment with other dominoes to provide a Theory of Falling Dominoes. Still, this wouldn't prove my dominoes were arranged according to your theory. Plus, you wouldn't be able to tell who knocked down the 1st domino. You weren't there to observe the 1st cause. You wouldn't know the identity of the "unmoved-mover" of my "domino universe." Whoever moved the 1st domino was outside of the "domino universe." Not only couldn't you observe the first cause, you couldn't observe the other ninety-nine causes. You didn't observe each falling-domino cause the next domino to fall. Those causes are in the past and are finished; they aren't still happening; they no longer exist. By using your Falling Domino Theory, you could assume one domino falling was the cause of the next domino falling, but you didn't observe my dominoes doing that. Having not been a direct observer of how my one hundred dominoes got to be the way they are, you couldn't rule out (falsify) the possibility I came in and intentionally placed all one hundred dominoes in their exact "fallen down" positions and arrangements. Falling and hitting each other isn't the only explanation for how they could be arranged as they are. "In the beginning," I could have created my "domino universe" exactly as it is, by directly placing the dominoes in their seemingly fallen down positions and arrangements. Since you didn't observe a cause, you couldn't prove a cause. All you could observe of this past event would be the effects. While the causes are in the past, the effects continue into the present. The effects of the past are still observable even if the causes aren't. The lesson is this: **Past effects** are observable in the present, but **past causes** are not. Whatever the cause of my "domino universe" (either me intentionally arranging the "fallen" dominoes, or letting one domino knock down the next) it would produce the exact same effect; the exact same "domino universe." You cannot know how my dominoes got arranged in my "domino universe" if you weren't an eyewitness to its creation. You cannot know how the galaxies, stars, and planets were created if you weren't an eyewitness to their creation. You cannot know how life was created if you weren't an eyewitness to the creation of life. Only an eyewitness of these things can truly know how they were created; and since God was the only eyewitness to the creation of all things, only He truly knows how they were created.

Inference to the Best Explanation

Does this mean science can't determine the causes of past events? No! Even though the causes of past phenomena may not be observable, it doesn't mean science can't determine past causes. If science couldn't do that, there would be no forensic science, no geology, no archaeology, and no paleontology because these sciences deal exclusively with past events. Scientists look at the **effects of the past** and try to determine the best explanatory cause based on the known possible **causes in the present.**

For instance, let's say a geologist discovered a layer of pyroclastic ash in a ten-million-year-old geologic stratum. Obviously, no scientists were there to observe what caused this layer. The geologist must infer to the best explanation from all known possible causes. He has some choices. He asks himself, "How do geologic layers form?" He answers himself, "Some layers are water borne, some are wind borne, some are caused by rockslides, some by mudslides, and of course, some are caused by volcanic eruptions." After making his observations he tells himself, "The most obvious cause for this layer of pyroclastic ash is a volcanic eruption."

The reason the geologist selects this cause is because this layer contains all the features found in layers known to be caused by volcanoes in the present. The geologist knows floods, wind, rockslides, mudslides, and other events don't create layers of pyroclastic ash. In other words, the geologist looks at the effects of known present-day causes, and matches those with the effects of the layer in question. **Because the effects match, the geologist proposes the causes match.** The geologist properly uses the Scientific Method in that he is comparing past **observable effects** with present **observable causes**. His science IS based on observation. Thus, he properly concludes this layer of pyroclastic ash was deposited by a volcanic eruption.

So, this kind of attack against evolution, an attack made by many creationists, turns out to be a misapplication of science. In the present, we CAN observe some things about the supposed process of evolution. We CAN observe the supposed effects of the supposed causes of evolution. Again, I agree the Theory of Evolution is false, but it isn't because we can't observe the past. My argument is exactly opposite of what these creationists say. It is because we CAN observe the effects of the past, that we can show how the Theory of Evolution is false. We can use the Scientific Method. **We can determine the causes of effects in the past by observing the causes of those same effects in the present.** And when we do this, we creationists win every time!

Evolutionist Errors

False Supposition 1: Life Doesn't Require an Intelligent Cause

Okay, so much for bashing creationists. Let's turn our attention to some errors made by evolutionists. We need to ask two questions:

1.) WHAT do evolutionists say happened? (What is the supposed **effect** of evolution?)

2.) HOW do evolutionists say it happened? (What is the supposed **cause** of evolution?)

The supposed effect of evolution is this: At some time in the past, inanimate matter became animate. Life sprang from non-life. That's called, "abiogenesis." Then, over long periods of time it gradually developed into the millions of different complex and beautiful species inhabiting our planet today. The supposed effect of evolution includes the increased complexity of living organisms and the increased complexity of the DNA instructions which code for that complexity. In fact, evolution requires tremendous increases in the complexity of the DNA instructions.

The supposed cause of evolution is this: The Theory of Evolution says random physical forces acted on random matter to create life, including the non-random DNA instructions needed for life. Then, the random physical forces increased the complexity of those non-random instructions over time.

Now, I know evolutionists will instantly object. They will say evolution is not random because of the Force of Natural Selection. Well, they are wrong, and we will see why later. For now, let me focus on the issue of DNA instructions. No one, not even the most devoted atheist, denies DNA contains instructions. I typed, "DNA instructions," into an Internet search engine, and got back 112,000,000 hits. That's a lot of people who equate DNA with instructions. Atheistic Evolutionists don't deny DNA contains instructions; they just deny those instructions were created by an intelligent cause. Okay, let's use the Scientific Method to see what we can discover about the CAUSE of DNA instructions. Let's make an inference to the best possible cause. To do that, I first must clarify a very important point. We need to investigate two separate but related phenomena:

1.) We need to investigate the cause of DNA.

2.) We need to investigate the cause of the instructions carried by DNA.

This is a critical distinction: DNA is not the instructions; DNA is the carrier of the instructions!

DNA is not the instructions; DNA is the carrier of the instructions!

It is not the mere PRESENCE of nucleotides in DNA that determines the instructions; it is the ARRANGEMENT of the nucleotides. An analogy is the difference between books (paper and ink) and the specific stories (novels, histories, documentaries, *etc*.) written in those books. Applying ink to paper doesn't tell a story unless there are specific instructions directing how the ink is applied. The ink molecules must be arranged to form specific letters, which must be arranged to form specific words, which must be arranged to form specific sentences, which must be arranged to form specific paragraphs, which must be arranged to form specific chapters, until a specific book is created. The DNA MOLECULE is "the book," but the

DNA INSTRUCTIONS are the "stories." We need to see if the Theory of Evolution has a scientific explanation for how the DNA molecule, "the book," was unintelligently created, but more importantly, we need to see if the Theory of Evolution has a scientific explanation for how the instructions, "the stories," were unintelligently written.

What caused the first DNA molecule(s) needed for life? Scientists don't know. There have been many conflicting chemical evolution theories proposed, but none has been proved true. Despite all their chemical experiments, no one has yet made a living DNA molecule from raw chemicals alone, **without the aid of human intelligence**. If the Scientific Method is applied to this problem, the solution proves how **intelligence is necessary** for the creation of living DNA molecules. If it takes intelligent scientists to make living DNA, why does anyone suspect random physical forces could do it? It has never been seen; it has never been repeated. But let's not focus on just the DNA MOLECULE. That's not the hard part. Let's focus on the DNA INSTRUCTIONS.

What caused the DNA INSTRUCTIONS needed for life? Since this happened in the past, how can we find an answer? We can't observe the past cause of instructions, but we can observe the present cause of instructions. If the Scientific Method is reliable, we can make an inference to the best explanation by discovering the known, observable, and testable cause of instructions in the present, and then applying that to the past. Here is the big question:

What causes instructions in the present?

Here is the even bigger answer:

Instructions are caused only by intelligent agents!

There may be random forces that cause seemingly non-random effects, but there are no random forces that cause instructions. Instructions, by the very definition of the word, contain intelligence, and intelligence cannot arise from randomness. Ultimately, it takes intelligence to generate intelligence. At this point, atheists like to cite an exception.

They say if you give enough monkeys enough time, enough typewriters and ink, and enough paper, they will eventually type the complete works of William Shakespeare. I'm sure you have heard this claim before, and if you have, I hope you deposited it in the waste bin of gobbledygook where it belongs. It is not an appeal to scientific facts or observations. No one has ever seen monkeys type sonnets. There was one experiment a few years ago where some monkeys were given a keyboard with a wireless connection to a computer screen they could view. (Described in *The Monkey Shakespeare Simulator Project*; I'll tell you more about it shortly.) Over a few days, they typed nothing but gibberish. Eventually, the monkeys smashed the keyboard, and then urinated and defecated on it. I don't know if it was because they wanted to watch Animal Planet® instead, or if monkeys just don't like Shakespeare... I suspect the latter. However, now that the idea has been expressed as a hypothesis, it should be tested to see if it CAN happen. After all, this is what real scientists do with hypotheses. The problem with this hypothesis is no one has ever shown it CAN happen. Atheists make an appeal to one unproven hypothesis (Monkeys can type Shakespeare.) as "proof" for another unproven hypothesis, (DNA instructions can be generated by randomness.) hoping you won't realize the credulity it would take to believe it. This is counterfeit science—two unproven hypotheticals don't make a certainty. Furthermore, even though they are strict materialists, they never mention the material requirements for it to happen. It might happen in a supernatural universe, but it can't happen in this universe. How many monkeys are needed? It would take more monkeys than have ever lived on this planet. The monkeys need to eat. How is their food supplied since they're too busy typing sonnets to go forage for food? (And, who is going to clean up all the monkey poop?) In addition, since there are no immortal monkeys, new monkeys must be born to replace the dead monkeys. How do they reproduce since they're too busy typing sonnets to... well, you know what? The typewriters also need to be repaired or replaced as they wear out. It takes sunlight to make the trees that make the paper, and it takes hydrocarbons to make the ink. How is all this matter and energy supplied?

I won't go into the calculation of the mathematical improbability of this because there are several Internet sites that calculate the odds, and you can search them at your leisure. Different sites give different probabilities, but the odds are generally calculated in the neighborhood of one chance in $10^{10,000,000}$. (And that's a whole lot worse odds than the 1 in $10^{40,000}$ odds Fred Hoyle gave Darwin—don't worry, I'm not going to print out ten million zeros.) All the atoms in the universe would be consumed, and all the energy from all the stars in the universe would be depleted long before they could finish. There is not enough matter and energy in our universe to accomplish the task. Since the entire universe would be cold and dead long before the monkeys could do it, this is an UNTESTABLE hypothesis. Claiming intelligent instructions in DNA could be created without an intelligent agent is valid only if scientists agree that untestable hypotheses constitute scientific proof.

Of course, I know they aren't talking about literal monkeys on literal typewriters. With the coming of the computer age, atheists like to "prove" their claims by citing examples of computers "randomly" generating sequences of letters and spaces until they produce all the works of Shakespeare. This eliminates the need for paper, ink, bananas, and all the rest. (And you don't have to clean up the monkey poop.)

Yes, there have been many computer programmers who have written computer programs that recreate the works of Shakespeare. However, none of them is random. The programs were written by intelligent agents, the computers were built by intelligent agents, and the criteria by which the results were deemed successful were determined by intelligent agents.

So, "How can computers generate Shakespeare's works," you ask? I will explain, and then let you decide if it duplicates the actual mechanism by which evolution was supposed to have happened. (Quiz Time: Can-You-Spot-the-Counterfeit?)

They start by programming their computers to generate sequences of random letters and spaces. (Already we're off to a non-random start.) Computer circuitry can only produce binary numbers. These numbers are then non-randomly programmed to be non-randomly converted to English letters. Why, for example, if a computer randomly generates 101 (the decimal number five) is it always converted to the letter "e?" Why not randomly convert it to a "w," or a "q," or an "m?" Why not Chinese letters, or Hebrew letters, or mathematical symbols? Or, why not have the numbers represent attempts to recreate Leonardo da Vinci's *Mona Lisa* with pixels on a computer screen? Since these computers are programmed to accomplish a pre-specified task, there is nothing random about what they accomplish. Besides, the computers are running a non-random operating system that makes generating random numbers possible. The equivalent system in the supposed evolutionary scheme of things would have been intact, fully functional, DNA-based cells (the "computers") generating random strings of DNA that might possibly contain the code for something living. Each sequence of random numbers generated by their computers is considered a "word." That means a "word" can be one-letter long, two-letters long, three-letters long, four-letters long, *etc.*, up to whatever length the longest Shakespearian word was. (That number is pre-programmed into the system.) They let the computers generate several thousand pages of "words" before they analyze the results to see if Shakespeare's words were created. (Again, why are they looking only for English words? Why not Italian words, or French words, or why words at all?) Up to this point, I might concede the process was random, even though the computers and the programs were created by intelligent agents. But, here is the counterfeit science: It is the way they determine "success" that is most certainly non-random. They program their computers to select the "randomly-created-Shakespearian-words," and designate them as "successes." The "successes" even include sequential letters not contained in the same "word." Here is the kind of "sentence" a monkey-simulator might generate:

bfogw henrilt hers hallzsq ouugetw ej nvthre emowr bondsme etopal iaga inncdee pkqyt

(Note: This is merely my simulation of their simulation; their "monkeys" didn't actually type this.)

Does it look like any of Shakespeare's works? If you don't see the first line of *Macbeth*, then you aren't looking hard enough. What is the first line in *Macbeth*?

"When shall we three meet again"

Where are those words found in my simulated computer-generated "sentence?"

bfog**W HEN**rilt her**S HALL**zsq ouuget**W E**j nv**THRE E**mowr bonds**ME ET**opal i**AGA IN**ncdee pkqyt

To be a "success," the sequences of letters don't have to spell the actual words. (In fact, they very rarely do.) Any time a sequence contains a string of letters that match a word from Shakespeare's works, it is considered a "success." It's even considered a "success" if the "words" are found in the wrong order. So, if the computer generated, "ouugetw ej iaga inncdee nvthre emowr bfogw henrilt bondsme etopal pkqyt hers hallzsq," it would still be considered a "success" because it contains words that Shakespeare used; just not in the right order. Here is how this "sentence" is a "success."

ouugetw ej iaga inncdee nvthre emowr bfogw henrilt bondsme etopal pkqyt hers hallzsq

ouuget**W E**j i**AGA IN**ncdee nv**THRE E**mowr bfog**W HEN**rilt bonds**ME ET**opal pkqyt her**S HALL**zsq

This sequence of letters generates the words "we," "again," "three," "when," "meet," and "shall." Since those words are found in the first line of *Macbeth*, but in a different order, the computer designates it as "successfully" generating a line of Shakespeare. (In fact, they are considered "successes" even if the "words" are several pages apart.) I know you can see the dishonesty contained in this claim. First, it doesn't recreate the same requirements for the sequences of nucleotides in living DNA. The nucleotides ("letters") must be copied and processed **in the correct order**, or else the correct proteins won't be made. Even worse for their theory, these computer simulation models focus on Target Words (words used by Shakespeare) while ignoring all the nonsense sequences. The nonsense sequences are equivalent to bad DNA instructions in the evolutionary process, but the computer programs simply ignore them. They affect nothing. This means the computers suffer no bad consequences for generating bad DNA. In real life, all the DNA must be correctly written and correctly ordered, or else it results in death. (And if you haven't heard of Steven Dill's Law of Evolution, here it is: Dead things don't evolve very well.) If they wanted to create a more accurate evolution-simulator, they need to develop a computer system that simulates the needs of real living organisms. The one thing real living organisms can't do, is create thousands and thousands of bad DNA sequences while waiting for a few good ones to pop up. These evolution-simulation computers don't have to get it right 99+% of the time; living organisms do. In their simulations, if the first one-hundred pages of sequences don't generate any Shakespeare, it doesn't matter. Their computers just keep plugging along generating new random sequences. In real life, any organism that did this would die. **To simulate evolution, they must simulate the consequences of generating bad DNA sequences.**

Once a computer generated even a few nonsense sequences, (Non-Shakespearian words) the computer would die. And I don't mean die in the sense of just needing to be restarted or rebooted. I mean die, like in going back to dust—no more computer. To be more accurate, their evolution-simulator would have to factor in the ability to replace dead computers with new computers created randomly from raw materials. Then they would need to generate new computer programs (also randomly) that simulate evolution. In all the different monkey-simulator programs, none of them factor in the "death" of the monkey-simulator. All their computers keep "living" and "living," no matter how much nonsense "DNA" is generated. Life doesn't work that way.

Nevertheless, atheists claim this kind of computer simulation is science because they find what they are looking for. Yes, they find what they are looking for, but it's because they are only looking for what they want to find. If you look hard enough in these same pages of random sequences, you can find all kinds of words. In my first sequence of letters above, I can find "fog," "hen," "hers," "all," "get," "mow," "bond," "me," "opal," "inn," and "deep."

b**fog**w **hen**rilt **hers** h**all**zsq ouu**get**w ej nvthre e**mow**r **bond**s**me** et**opal** iaga **inn**c**dee** pkqyt

I'm sure if I did a computer search, I could find authors who used these eleven words somewhere in their writings. By that standard, I could say this same program, with these same random sequences, created the works of Mark Twain, Agatha Christie, Louis L'Amour, C. S. Lewis, and many others.

Their process of generating words doesn't simulate DNA mutations. Worse yet, their process for selecting "successes" doesn't simulate Natural Selection. The computer has Target Words by which it measures "success." This means the computer must be preprogrammed with all the words Shakespeare ever used, so it can find the correct matches. The program is intelligently searching for preselected sequences supplied by intelligent agents; that's why this process isn't random. In the supposed process of evolution, there could be no Target Words. That would require the organisms to contain the information for preselected sequences of DNA before they had them or needed them. For this to happen, the organisms would need to know what kind of structures they would require in the future to survive. In turn, that would require the organisms to know what kind of environments they would inhabit in the future. If this hypothetical experiment is true, then it implies the entire course of evolution was pre-programmed into the first living organism, and that it had the ability to know how to mutate in just the right ways, at just the right times, in just the right order, for just the right length of time, in just the right geographical locations, millions of years before the "successful" mutations were ever needed. (Have you spotted the counterfeit yet?) This experiment proves there are no non-intelligent causes of instructions in the present. This means there were no non-intelligent causes of instructions in the past. At least, that's what it means if you believe in the Scientific Method.

Now, I gave you an example of a "sentence" a monkey-simulator might type. Remember, I told you my "sentence" wasn't typed by a real monkey-simulator. It was only the product of my simulated monkey-simulator. From this, you might say my simulated monkey-simulator doesn't simulate the real monkey-simulator; therefore, my conclusion is false. So, let's see what a real monkey-simulator truly accomplished.

The Monkey Shakespeare Simulator Project

The details for this project can be found at:

http://www.dailymail.co.uk/sciencetech/article-2042312/Shakespeares-works-finally-reproduced-team-computerised-monkeys.html

The article said the project used, "a huge virtual monkey population," but they didn't say how huge, "huge," was. The article also explained how the desired matches were, "plucked out and formed into his plays, poems or sonnets." They didn't explain that this was an example of intelligently searching for pre-programmed intelligent information. However, they did explain why it was done this way. They did it to, "make the task easier, otherwise it would be nearly impossible." To show how easy it was, they cited the "random" generation of the first line in *Henry IV, Part 2*:

"rumour open your ears"

How long did it take them to generate those four words? It took only 2,737,850 million, billion, billion, billion simulated monkey-years to do it; and this was with the task being made easier. Evolutionists consider this proof? Could this be done in the fourteen billion years since the Big Bang? Sure; all you need are 200,000,000,000,000,000,000,000,000,000 monkeys... for just these four words. (That's twice as many monkeys as there are stars in the universe.) The complete works of Shakespeare contain 884,647 words. Evolutionists are delighted with this kind of "proof." They got four words right! Now they have only 884,643 more to go. If my estimate is correct, those 2×10^{29} monkeys would need over 200,000 times the age of the universe to complete all of Shakespeare's works. (This kind of "science" really is monkey poop.) Disregarding the real-life results to the negative, multitudes of atheists herald the Infinite Monkey Theorem as proof for evolution. They think themselves so brilliant when they come up with a way to explain how intelligent instructions in DNA could be generated without an Intelligent Designer. Personally, if I believed it, I would be embarrassed to reveal I had such little understanding of scientific logic and the scientific method. I certainly wouldn't want my friends and family to know I spent time, money, and effort on proving something that proves nothing.

Atheists are constantly saying we creationists don't understand science, but this kind of monkey business reveals how little they know about science. Remember, I said this was an attempt to use one unproven hypothesis (Monkeys can type Shakespeare.) as proof for another unproven hypothesis. (DNA instructions can be generated by randomness.) Is this the way science works? Does proving one hypothesis, prove another hypothesis? No! This is especially not true if the phenomena in question are totally unrelated in terms of the mechanics involved. But, that's what you must believe if you believe randomly computer-generated Shakespearian sonnets prove DNA instructions can be randomly generated. The two phenomena are unrelated. The first hypothesis involves nothing but virtual "words." (Virtual "words" are nothing more than electric charges inside the manmade environment of computer switching circuitry designed and built by intelligent humans. They are "words" only by virtue of being so-designated by human beings. They are "words" only because someone wants them to be "words.") This system doesn't simulate the inner workings of a living cell. The physical movement of atoms and molecules is not required. Only electric charges need to be changed. The second hypothesis involves the actual movement of atoms and molecules inside living cells. Carbon, hydrogen, nitrogen, and oxygen atoms must be physically arranged in time and space. All the atoms must be in their exactly correct three-dimensional positions, with their exactly correct orientations, with their exactly correct interactions, at exactly the correct time. Otherwise, the cell dies.

Even if computers could randomly generate virtual Shakespeare, would it prove that carbon atoms, hydrogen atoms, nitrogen atoms, and oxygen atoms could randomly form DNA instructions without the aid of an Intelligent Designer? Do you think so? Well, if computers could randomly generate Shakespeare's works, would it prove that iron atoms, copper atoms, magnesium atoms, and chromium atoms could form automobiles without the aid of an intelligent designer? Do you think not? What's the difference? It's the same flight of the imagination. Making automobiles is an unrelated phenomenon too. That process also involves the movement of atoms and molecules. Are carbon atoms smarter than iron atoms? The possibility of spontaneously generating virtual Shakespearian sonnets is not proof for the possibility of spontaneously generating either living organisms or automobiles.

Of course, they don't even prove the hypothesis is true. Evolution doesn't get past the Confirmed Hypothesis Stage. Hypotheses are statements used to test if something DOES happen. Not just if something COULD happen. In real science, if the hypothesis is not confirmed, the statement cannot be considered scientifically true. Proof for hypotheses depends on actual success. **A simulated success is not the same thing as an actual success.** Yes, evolutionists can formulate the hypothesis that Shakespeare can be generated by a random process, but they never have confirmed it. Their "2,737,850 million, billion, billion, billion Monkey-Year Simulator" was not a random process. Remember, they did everything needed to make the task easier, so it wouldn't be impossible. That means they added intelligence into their simulated "random" process. Without adding intelligence, it would be impossible in a real universe only fourteen billion years old.

I can write a computer program that simulates picking millions of sequences of lottery numbers randomly. With enough time and enough picks, I am sure to pick the correct numbers of a winning ticket. Would I win the million-dollar prize? No? Why not? My simulation proved I COULD do it. Even if I simulated it, the Lottery Commission wouldn't pay me the money because my simulated success was not an actual success. My simulator didn't simulate reality. I generated millions of bad numbers without risk—I paid nothing for them. I didn't have to spend any time, money, or effort going to the convenient store to purchase the physical tickets. No Pain—No Gain! Now, if this is true for picking lottery tickets, it's a million times more true for a process that supposedly created all the living organisms on earth. Evolutionists want you to think only about what the very, very, very few "good mutations" MIGHT do for evolution. They don't want you to think about what the very, very, very many bad mutations WOULD do to evolution. Their simulators don't simulate reality, and science is supposed to be the study of reality, or at least it used to.

But setting that aside, let's go one level deeper into the scientific process. Is scientific proof based on what possibly COULD happen, or on what truly DOES happen? Proving that something COULD happen doesn't prove it DID happen, and it's not scientific to claim that it does. Even if you prove Shakespeare's works COULD be randomly generated by a computer, would it prove William Shakespeare DIDN'T write them? Would it prove Shakespeare didn't exist? Ahhh, here you begin to see the Evolutionist's New Clothes. Atheist Evolutionists don't want to admit they can't disprove (falsify) the existence of God, so they parade their arguments around, elegantly dressed-up in nothing at all. They want you to think that as long life COULD have arisen by means of randomly generated DNA instructions, then life DID arise by means of randomly generated DNA instructions. They think it proves God DOESN'T exist. But again, that is the same as saying Shakespeare DIDN'T exist simply because his works can be generated randomly by monkeys. We know this isn't true because of the historical evidence for Shakespeare. We know the same thing about God from the historical evidence for God. Their arguments aren't real science, because their arguments aren't concerned with what truly happened in the past. They aren't concerned with the truth. Concern about truth is so... pre-19th century. They aren't concerned with how real science truly operates. Conclusion: The Hypothesis of Randomly Generated DNA Instructions is falsified!

How does this show us evolution is false? No one has ever proved the hypothesis that complex instructions ARE generated by random processes. (Hypotheses are used to test IF something happens.) This is equivalent to me making a hypothesis that rocks will fly upward when let go. I may present an elegant hypothesis, but if rocks always fall when released, my hypothesis fails. What I believe SHOULD happen, DOESN'T happen. We will test some more of evolution's hypotheses later, along with some of its theories, but before we do that, let's see if the Laws of Evolution can be falsified. (Remember, a Law is a statement expressing/explaining WHAT happens.) Oh yes, there have been attempts at formulating Laws of Evolution, such as the "Law of Abiogenesis," the "Law of Use and Disuse," the "Law of Natural Selection," the "Law of Irreversibility," and the "Law of

Recapitulation," but every time someone says, "This is WHAT happened," other scientists shoot them down because they have no evidence it happened that way. (Evolutionists disproving evolutionists.) Since a great portion of the rest of this book is focused on disproving these ideas, I won't go into detail here. You'll have to wait until you finish the book. I will, however, provide a quick description of each.

1.) The Law of Abiogenesis: Life arose from non-life. This idea has been around for thousands of years in the form of myths, legends, fables, fairy tales, and false religions, but as a Scientific Law, it fails. It has never been seen to happen.

2.) The Law of Use and Disuse: The structures and features of organisms evolved according to their need. If an organism needed wings, it evolved wings. If an organism needed lungs, it evolved lungs. If an organism no longer needed a tail, the tail disappeared. This "Law" was proposed by Jean-Baptiste Lamarck (1744-1829). According to Lamarck, evolution happened because organisms strived to make it happen—giraffes have long necks because their supposed short-necked ancestors stretched to reach the tops of trees for the leaves they wanted. This "Law" was popular before the discovery that DNA carried the instructions for neck-length, as well as all other physical features. No one has ever explained how using a feature creates new DNA instructions. The DNA evidence and the fossil evidence proved this "Law" was not true, and most evolutionists have rejected it. However, it is still believed by some. I think it is an example of evolutionists stretching the truth to reach the conclusion they want.

3.) The Law of Natural Selection: Organisms and the features they possess are the products of "Survival-of-The-Fittest," competition. If an organism has a feature that aids its survival, it survives. If another organism doesn't have that feature, it perishes. This is the mechanism for how good traits supposedly replaced bad traits. It too, has been disproved by science, but you'll have to wait to see the details.

4.) The Law of Irreversibility (Dollo's Law): According to this "Law," evolution happens only in one direction. Organisms go from smaller-and-simpler, to larger-and-more complex. Once a new form/trait evolves, it replaces the old form/trait and the old form/trait is never seen again in evolution. It has also been solidly discredited.

5.) The Law of Recapitulation: Simply put, this "Law" said the embryological stages of an organism replays its evolutionary history. Ernst Haeckel (1834-1919) popularized this "Law" with his famous illustrations comparing the embryonic development of fish, salamanders, reptiles, birds, lower mammals, and humans. His drawings supposedly revealed how these different organisms shared the same embryologic structures as they passed through the same "stages of evolution." This "Law" was shown to be false. It has also been shown that Haeckel's illustrations were fraudulent. They didn't show the true embryological stages of these organisms. Instead, he drew what he wanted people to believe. He wasn't concerned about what was true, only about what he could use to defend the Theory of Evolution.

Evolution's Laws all fail to explain the origin of the intelligent instructions found in DNA. The issue boils down to this: **Either the instructions in DNA were caused by the random forces of nature, or else they were caused by an Intelligent Agent.** The Scientific Method can help us determine which cause is correct. While we cannot observe the cause of instructions in the past, we can observe the cause of instructions in the present. Since the Scientific Method requires us to reject all unobservable and untestable causes, we can reject any theory that proposes unobservable and untestable causes for instructions in the past. Let me illustrate how this works:

Is A the cause of Z in the past?

IF:

1.) Countless observations show that A causes Z in the present.

2.) Countless experiments show that Z is caused only by A in the present.

3.) Both A and Z are knowable, observable, and testable in the present.

THEN:

It is scientifically logical to believe A is the only cause of Z in the past.

Since A is the only known, observable, and testable cause of Z in the present, it is not scientific to claim B caused Z in the past. Why not? Because B is unknown, B is unobserved, and B is untested. If no one has ever seen B, and if B has never been tested, and if B has never been shown to cause Z, then it violates the Scientific Method to insist B caused Z in the past.

Let's apply this to our geologist friend who proposed that a volcanic eruption caused the layer of pyroclastic ash in the geologic strata he observed.

IF:

1.) Countless observations show volcanic eruptions cause layers of pyroclastic ash in the present.

2.) Countless experiments show pyroclastic ash is caused only by volcanic eruptions in the present.

3.) Both pyroclastic ash and volcanic eruptions are knowable, observable, and testable in the present.

THEN:

It is scientifically logical to believe volcanic eruptions are the only cause of pyroclastic layers in the past.

Since volcanic eruptions are the only known, observable, and testable cause of layers of pyroclastic ash in the present, it is not scientific to claim The Flying Spaghetti Monster caused layers of pyroclastic ash in the past. Why not? The Flying Spaghetti Monster is unknown, unobserved, and untested. If no one has ever seen The Flying Spaghetti Monster, and if The Flying Spaghetti Monster has never been tested, and if The Flying Spaghetti Monster has never been shown to cause layers of pyroclastic ash in the present, then it violates the Scientific Method to insist The Flying Spaghetti Monster caused layers of pyroclastic ash in the past.

Atheists will instantly recognize The Flying Spaghetti Monster. It's their own creation. (Created in January 2005 by Bobby Henderson, an Oregon State University Physics graduate.) For more information... and favorite recipes, see *The Church of the Flying Spaghetti Monster* Website at: http://www.venganza.org

They use it as a philosophical illustration to mock our belief in God. They use The-Flying-Spaghetti-Monster-Argument to show why God should be kept out of the classroom. They equate God with The Flying Spaghetti Monster. Oh, they agree The Flying Spaghetti Monster is unobservable and unknowable, but they say God is also unobservable and unknowable. (Just like the ancient Greeks said in Paul's day.) I'm sure there will be a few Flying Spaghetti Monster advocates who claim they have seen or heard The Flying Spaghetti Monster. My challenge to them is: Are they willing to die for their belief like Christian martyrs have died for their belief? Are they willing to face prison, floggings, starvation, or being fed to the lions? When enough of them have done that, I will consider their claims as sincere.

In truth, there is no comparison between evidence for The Flying Spaghetti Monster and evidence for God. God hasn't limited Himself to mere philosophical illustrations. He has provided historical, tangible, real, time-and-space, visible, audible, touchable, testable, and tastable evidence. (Manna, fish, bread, wine, *etc*.) The Flying Spaghetti Monster absolutely fears someone demanding tastable evidence. We aren't going to talk about that. Instead, I am going to use their own argument against them. You see, they claim they can't believe in God because no one has ever seen God. As I mentioned before, they say God's existence can't be scientifically observed, therefore belief in God is not scientific. I also mentioned how this is an example of confused thinking. What they say would be true if God never interacts with nature. Their error stems from their refusal to believe God HAS revealed Himself to people in time and space by interacting with nature. In the past, God HAS interacted with nature in ways it was possible to observe Him. God physically walked with Adam and

Eve in the Garden. God audibly spoke to Noah. God sat down and had lunch with Abram. Moses spent forty days with God on top of Mt. Sinai. Paul saw the risen and glorified Jesus with his own eyes, and Christ's light was so physically bright it physically blinded him. The fact atheists can't see God today is not proof He doesn't exist. Such a claim is not scientific because it assumes God must always be seen. This is a rather childish view of things, something like: "If I can't see you, you don't exist." Think of it this way:

Halley's Comet orbits the sun about every 75 years. Imagine you lived in a time before telescopes and cameras, and there were no photographs or videos of Halley's Comet from previous visits. Also imagine it had been 65 years since its last visit. If you were twenty years old, the only evidence you would have for Halley's Comet's existence would be the historical claims of older people who say they saw it. (Your belief or disbelief in Halley's Comet would depend on $2°$ Perception.) You would not be able to go outside and look up in the night sky and see Halley's Comet; at least not for another ten years. However, when those ten years were up, you would be able to see Halley's Comet with your own eyes. When that happened, you would have the scientific evidence. ($1°$ Perception) Halley's Comet would be physically revealed to you once it returned. Halley's Comet was outside your ability to visualize before the 75 years were up, but that didn't prove Halley's Comet didn't exist. The same is true of God. He has made Himself physically visible in the past. At the current time, He is not making Himself physically visible. In the future, He will return and make Himself physically visible again. God has told us He has appointed a day in the future when He will return and judge the earth. There won't be any problems seeing God on that day. He will be seen by the whole world. God will be observable in the natural realm once again.

(1º Perception) On that day, He will be interacting with the natural realm, and if atheists want to monitor Him and measure Him, they will be able to use all the scientific instruments and gadgetry they want... only they won't want to do that. Rather than enjoying His presence, they will want to flee His presence. But, they won't be allowed to flee. On that day, God will force them to their knees before Him. On that day, they will scream out in forced admission that Jesus Christ is their God, their Creator, and their Judge. It will be their last words before God banishes them from His presence into a fire of absolute darkness, forever in torment, and forever hating the God they will never see again. The only way you can escape that terrible and eternal judgement is by believing/trusting/accepting Jesus Christ as your Savior. If you haven't read the Gospel of John, read it. And if you have read it but didn't believe it, read it again and believe it, believe it, believe it. Do that, and you will be saved.

Atheists say they can't believe in God because no one has ever seen God. Well, I can't believe in randomly created instructions because no one has ever seen randomly created instructions. Any theory that invokes randomly created instructions is non-scientific and shouldn't be allowed in the classroom. It's the exact same argument!

I know some people will say a random-letter generator can create instructions, such as the word "jump." True, the letter sequence "J," "U," "M," and "P" can be generated randomly by a computer programmed by humans, but that doesn't qualify as instructions unless we have some additional instructions on how the sequence of letters is to be interpreted and applied. (Instructions need to be interpreted and applied to cause an effect.) Is it the noun, the adjective, or the verb? If it is the verb, then it might be an instruction. If it is the noun or the adjective, it is not an instruction. Is it English or Spanish? If it is Spanish, then it is just a string on nonsense letters. Even if it is the English verb, it doesn't say jump vertically or jump horizontally. It doesn't specify who is to jump, when to jump, how high to jump, how far to jump, in which direction to jump, how many times to jump, *etc*. In other words, we need instructions to determine if "J U M P" constitutes an instruction. Plus, such a simple instruction would have no evolutionary effect because it doesn't contain the instructions for the replication of the instructions—this is an absolute necessity for evolution. **IN FACT, THE INSTRUCTIONS FOR REPLICATING THE INSTRCTIONS WOULD HAVE BEEN THE VERY FIRST SET OF INSTRUCTIONS CAPABLE OF EVOLVING.** No matter what instructions there where for other biological components, if the instructions for replicating the instructions weren't there, there would be no replication, and evolution couldn't happen. This means the common ancestor from which we all supposedly evolved had to have:

1.) The biochemical machinery necessary to live.

2.) The instructions necessary to create and control the biochemical machinery necessary to live.

3.) The biochemical machinery necessary to replicate.

4.) The instructions necessary to create and control the biochemical machinery necessary to replicate.

Having just the first two components may allow something to live, but it wouldn't allow for evolution. Having the machinery and the instructions that control the machinery are necessary for evolution, but they would not be sufficient for evolution. Today, we have driverless automobiles operated by computers with instructions capable of driving the machinery. (Of course, both the machinery and the instructions were created by intelligent designers.) None of these automobiles has the machinery and the instructions required for self-replication. Driverless automobiles can never evolve without intelligent creators. As far as the creation of living organisms is concerned, both the machinery for replication and the instructions for replication had to be present and fully functional **in the very first organism**, or evolution couldn't start. The first living organism had to have these four FUNCTIONS:

1.) The ability to create the instructions

2.) The ability to interpret the instructions

3.) The ability to implement the instructions

4.) The ability to replicate the instructions

All four of these abilities are found in all truly living organisms today. (Viruses and prions don't have all four of these abilities, but viruses and prions aren't truly living organisms.) All four of these abilities are caused by the preexisting intelligent instructions found in their DNA. This cannot happen by chance; it requires intelligence.

IF:

1.) Countless observations show intelligent agents cause instructions in the present.

2.) Countless experiments show instructions are caused only by intelligent agents in the present.

3.) Both instructions and intelligent agents are knowable, observable, and testable in the present.

THEN:

It is scientifically logical to believe intelligent agents were the only cause of instructions in the past.

This is the very same argument with a different set of variables plugged into it. Since intelligent agents are the only known, observable, and testable cause of instructions in the present, it is not scientific to believe random forces caused instructions in the past.

IT IS NOT SCIENTIFIC TO BELIEVE RANDOM FORCES CAUSED DNA INTRUCTIONS IN THE PAST

If their argument is proof the theory of divinely generated instructions can't be taught in the classroom, then this very same argument is proof the theory of randomly generated instructions can't be taught in the classroom. Darwin's Theory of Evolution should not be taught in the science class. It is as scientific as The Flying Spaghetti Monster. If, "the key to the past is the present," as many evolutionists say they believe, then they have no right to reject the only known cause of instructions in the present. They have no right to appeal to an unknown cause in the past. Proposing that DNA instructions were caused by non-intelligent forces in the past is not science because there are no non-intelligent forces that can do that in the present. The evolutionists' explanation relies on unobserved and untested forces. Because it is unobservable and untestable, the Theory of Evolution is rejected when we properly apply the Scientific Method. Rather than trying to misinterpret, misuse, or deny science, we creationists should be using science to prove our case. That requires us to learn, understand, and embrace science rather than reject it, fear it, and mock it. Sadly, I am ashamed to say far too many Christian Creationists fear, mock, and reject science.

Let's take a closer look into how evolutionists misuse the Scientific Method. They know they can't allow DNA instructions to have been designed by an Intelligent Agent. That would enable us to put the Science of God back in the science class. Yet, they also know they can't let evolution be totally random. Randomness can't create instructions. So, what they propose is a method by which random forces act non-randomly in such a way that the increasingly complex instructions necessary for life could evolve over long periods of time. This proposed method was the crowning achievement of Charles Darwin, and it is called, "Natural Selection." Atheists say Natural Selection is the force that turns random evolution into directed evolution. (Although not directed by intelligence.) They say the Force of Natural Selection is what makes evolution no longer random. Before I talk about Natural Selection, I want to point out the reason they need a non-random but unintelligent force to create life.

Apparent Design

Because design seems to be so observable in living organisms, atheists need something to explain how design could be generated without a Designer. So, they say life isn't actually designed; it only appears that way. They say nature created "Apparent Design."

Francis Crick: "Biologists must constantly keep in mind that what they see was not designed, but rather evolved."[10]

Richard Dawkins: "Biology is the study of complicated things that give the appearance of having been designed for a purpose."[11]

Robert Jastrow: "For the scientist who has lived by his faith in the power of reason, the story ends like a bad dream. He has scaled the mountains of ignorance; he is about to conquer the highest peak; as he pulls himself over the final rock, he is greeted by a band of theologians who have been sitting there for centuries."[12]

Fred Hoyle: "A common sense interpretation of the facts suggests that a superintellect has monkeyed with physics, as well as with chemistry and biology, and that there are no blind forces worth speaking about in nature."[13]

It looks like a superintellect created everything. Everything looks like what theologians have been saying for centuries. Things appear to have a purpose. The universe seems designed. Evolutionists can't let these things be true. So, they came up with their own belief system; their own religion. They praise themselves for the belief that Natural Selection could create Apparent Design, yet they mock the belief that Supernatural Selection could create Actual Design. Actual Design requires an Actual Designer, whereas Apparent Design requires only a force that mimics design. They insist their belief is science but ours is myth. Before we examine their beliefs about Natural Selection, we must investigate their beliefs about Apparent Design. Let me show you how their belief fails from the very start. Let's see how well Apparent Design fares when tested by the Scientific Method.

Apparent Design vs. Actual Design

What are the differences between Apparent Design and Actual Design? What experiment can we perform to tell them apart if we can't observe past causes? If Apparent Design is a scientific phenomenon, then it must be based on observations and experimentations; that's the Scientific Method. Apparent Design is a scientific phenomenon if and only if scientific observations and tests prove it happens. That's the way true science works. So, here is the gauntlet I throw down: Give me an example of an Apparent Design, and show me the experiment that proves it can't be an Actual Design. (In other words, falsify Actual Design.)

I know at this point many evolutionists will eagerly pick up this gauntlet and give examples of Apparent Design from nature that require no Actual Designer. Don't be misled. Before we move forward, we need to take a step back. Even before we can talk about Apparent Design vs. Actual Design, we must define the word "design." Sometimes people mistakenly use the word "design" when they describe something that merely exhibits a pattern. For instance, evolutionists point to snowflakes and say, "See the design. Look at the intricate detail, the order, the symmetry, and the beauty. Snowflakes don't need an Intelligent Designer. The random forces of nature create them. You, creationists are wrong when you say life needs an Intelligent Designer."

Well, snowflakes are certainly beautiful, but beauty is a judgment call (0° Perception) and not a scientific value. And yes, they have very intricate patterns, but they are not designs. **For anything to be a design, it must be designed.** Snowflakes are not designs because no one designed them. (Unless you believe as I do: Every individual snowflake is subject to the Eternal

Sovereignty of God. Each snowflake was planned before the beginning of time to be what it is, where it is, and when it is… but that theological subject requires many, many, many, many more books to explain, and we aren't going to do that.)

Sugar crystals are another example often mentioned by evolutionists. Here is a perfect example of an actual biochemical capable of creating intricate "designs" without the need for a designer. You can dissolve sugar in water and then let the solution evaporate. Sugar crystals will form on their own every time. The sugar molecules don't need instructions from an intelligent agent to form crystals. They fall into those "designs" by the random forces of nature alone. Yes, but again, sugar crystals are patterns, not designs. We must constantly remind evolutionists that patterns are not necessarily designs; we must constantly remind them of this difference:

If a structure is a pattern, it doesn't necessarily need instructions to create it.

If a structure doesn't need instructions to create it, it doesn't contain instructions.

If a structure contains instructions, it needs instructions to create it.

DNA contains instructions; therefore, instructions are needed to create them. No one has ever seen DNA instructions in nature that weren't created by previous DNA instructions. (Which were created by previous DNA instructions, which were created by previous DNA instructions, which were created by DNA instructions, which… We'll, I would say *ad infinitum*, but that wouldn't be possible in a finite universe, would it?) Despite this, evolutionists want us to believe DNA is only an Apparent Design caused by random, unguided forces. This is where evolutionists try to pass off one of their most deceptive counterfeits.

They want you to think randomly created patterns are the same as intelligently created designs.

This is why chemical-abiogenesis "simulation" experiments such as Stanley Miller's Apparatus are hailed as "proof" for evolution. They aren't! They all fail to produce everything needed for life; including the instructions for life. THEY ALL FAIL TO PRODUCE ACTUAL LIFE. Miller only created some very simple biomolecular patterns: amino acids. He didn't create life because he didn't create the instructions for life. **Life requires instructions!** All he created was a tiny, itsy-bitsy, minuscule piece of the puzzle. They want you to think all you need to do is come up with a way to create a few pieces randomly, and it's the same as solving the whole puzzle. It's not! That would be the same as if you came up with a random process for creating paper and ink, and then claiming it is the same as creating all of Shakespeare's writings, the Oxford Unabridged Dictionary, every set of encyclopedias ever printed, the complete instructions for building the Space Shuttle, and every other piece of literature ever written. Even if you randomly created paper and ink, someone must provide the instructions, information, and intelligence required to write and print those books. In fact, randomly creating paper, ink, and even the printing press would be the easy part.

They want you to look at the **order** and **symmetry** in DNA, and think it's the same as seeing **instructions** and **intelligence** in DNA. They don't want you to look too closely, however. Order and symmetry may be nothing more than Apparent Design, but instructions and intelligence can only be by Actual Design. Just as a counterfeiter doesn't want you to compare his $100 bills to real $100 bills, evolutionists don't want you to compare Apparent Design to Actual Design. If you look closely, you will see their deception. They want you to believe that instructions don't require intelligence. This is the crux of the matter: Biomolecular patterns aren't the same as biomolecular instructions. Biomolecules patterns might carry the instructions, but they are not the instructions. The carrier **is material**, but the instructions **are immaterial**. This is where evolutionists run and hide. It's not just a matter of randomly creating **Apparent Designs**. What must be created are **Actual Instructions**. Why? Because there are no such things as **Apparent Instructions**. Instructions either instruct something or they don't. If they instruct something, they are not apparent; they are actual. If they don't instruct anything, they are not instructions. Instructions are instructions no matter what form they take. Instructions can be written as symbols on paper. Instructions can be carried by the vibrating air molecules of spoken words. Instructions can be pressed onto clay tablets as cuneiform symbols. Instructions can be stored on magnetic computer discs. Instructions can be transmitted over long distances like ELF (Extremely-Low Frequency) radio waves that penetrate the ocean depths to communicate with submarines below the surface. Instructions can be communicated visually like the smoke signals of the American Plains Indians, or audibly like the drum beats of the African Zulu warriors. In all these cases, the instructions are immaterial. **Instructions are not made of matter or energy.** Instructions are a subset of information, and information has no mass, no energy, and occupies no space. The medium that carries the instructions is material, and the medium may use energy to convey the instructions, but the instructions themselves are immaterial. This is hard for strict-materialists to explain.

The existence of instructions poses a problem for evolutionists because we are not dealing with instructions isolated in a vacuum. We are dealing with entire Instructional Systems, and Instructional Systems require three components:

1.) Instruction origin: Something must create the instructions.

2.) Instruction medium: Something must store and transmit the instructions.

3.) Instruction destiny: Something must interpret and act upon the instructions.

Cells are living Instructional Systems; therefore, any theory for the origin of life must be able to explain how living cells acquired these three components. Life requires:

1.) Instruction origin: Something must create the instructions for life.

2.) Instruction medium: Something must store and transmit the instructions for life.

3.) Instruction destiny: Something must interpret and act upon the instructions for life.

We know what the last two components are in autonomous living organisms:

2.) DNA and Messenger RNA are the molecules that store and transmit the instructions.

3.) Transfer RNA and Ribosomes are the components that interpret and act upon the instructions.

But what is the origin of the instructions? Evolutionists haven't explained how random forces could create the DNA, the RNA, and the ribosomes. But again, they are the easy parts; they are just the "printing press, ink, and paper." The question before us is this: What created (caused) the Actual Instructions carried by DNA? They might argue that DNA is an Apparent Design, but they can't deny that DNA conveys Actual Instructions. They are not Apparent Instructions. There is nothing apparent about them. They actually, truly, honestly, really, literally, sure-enough, by golly INSTRUCT the biochemical machinery in the cells to produce and reproduce everything needed for life and reproduction. Even if the medium was an Apparent Design, the message in the medium is an Actual Design. Who was the Designer?

Intelligent Design

It has often been repeated by evolutionists that you can't teach Intelligent Design in the classroom because Intelligent Design is not testable. (Oh, they are trying so hard to sound scientific!) My response is this: **Which part of Intelligent Design is not testable; the Intelligence or the Design?** If design cannot be tested, then we need to eliminate all engineers and all the schools of engineering—engineering is the science of design. (Ask an engineer if he or she thinks design can't be tested. Of course, it can be tested—engineers test design a thousand times a day.) On the other hand, if intelligence cannot be tested, then schools, colleges, and universities must quit giving examinations. Examinations test for intelligence. They also must get rid of textbooks—textbooks are designed to contain intelligence. If they don't think intelligent design is testable, how would they know, and why would they care, whether a medical student read the chapter on the microanatomy of the brain stem or a comic book about space pirates? (And if you ever need brain surgery, you'd better pray your surgeon read the right material.) Design is scientifically testable. Intelligence is scientifically testable. It is the Theory of Evolution that is not scientifically testable. We will see why later. For now, let's continue looking at why life requires an Intelligent Designer.

Evolutionists still insist DNA doesn't need an intelligent Creator. Scientists say they can create DNA in the laboratory; and they can. They can disassemble the chemical units of DNA and then reassemble them. But this would be like me taking my first car when I was a teenager, an old 1953 Chevrolet^{tm}, (Licensed Trademark: General Motors Corporation, and one heck of a great car.) and completely disassembling it, every nut and bolt, and then putting it all back together again and claim I created the 1953 Chevy. Now, it's not just having the parts that matters; it is having the parts in the exact right arrangement. If I didn't intelligently put all the parts back in their proper arrangement, my 1953 Chevy wouldn't work. It is not just the presence of nitrogenous base pairs along the DNA core that creates life; **it is the specific sequence of those nitrogenous base pairs that provide the instructions necessary for life**. It is the specific sequence of nitrogenous base pairs that provide the instructions for YOU! Your DNA was designed. Your DNA has a purpose; it carries the instructions designed to create you. Since your instructions have a purpose, it is obvious the Designer has a purpose for YOU. (Surely, you don't think He would plan the existence of every snowflake, but not plan your existence? You're much more valuable to Him than snowflakes.)

Yes, scientists can remove the nitrogenous bases along the deoxyribose-phosphate strands and then reattach them. However, if they let the parts reattach themselves randomly, without the aid of their intelligence, their Apparent DNA is functionless. If they let the parts reattach themselves randomly, without the aid of their intelligence, they do not create Actual DNA. Their Apparent DNA may look just as patterned as living/functional DNA, but without their intelligence, it is dead. The difference is this: Randomly-assembled DNA contains no instructions. (If instructions are not required, instructions are not created.) They want you to think the mere presence of the pieces is more important than the arrangement of the pieces. This is counterfeit science. It would be the same as if I took John 3:16 and cut out all the letters and spaces and then reassembled them randomly.

"For God so loved the world that he gave his only begotten Son that whosoever believeth in him should not perish but have everlasting life."

"hserl moroh hibtnh gwg vdsl eitev sF nevte wnol tduat hlaar hveis oleoey aveGs leun tveh endlh ngdot oeo ebioht poios hiht etrao bf rSeti."

The second sentence contains the exact same letters and the exact same number of spaces. It has all the pieces of the puzzle. If your Bible translation has the first sentence for John 3:16, and you believe it, you will enjoy eternity with Jesus. If your Bible translation has the second sentence for John 3:16, and you believe it, you've got a counterfeit Bible, and you aren't going to be so happy where you wind up. The second sentence doesn't contain the instructions for being saved. It has all the letters and it has all the spaces, but it doesn't contain the instructions. The arrangement of the letters, not just the presence of the letters, is what creates the instructions. (The instructions are immaterial.) The specific sequence of letters is necessary. It is not merely having nitrogenous bases along the central core of the DNA double helix that creates life. It is the specific sequence of those nitrogenous bases that creates life. **Evolution must randomly create the right parts, AND evolution must randomly put them in the right order.** But randomness cannot create order. Chaos cannot produce Cosmos. There is no First Principle of Nature that causes order. The Laws of Thermodynamics prove the opposite: Cosmos produces Chaos. Evolutionists don't want you to think about this: They don't know how the parts were created, but even worse, they don't know how the parts were put in the right order.

Evolutionists believe life was caused by chemical evolution, but they argue over which theory of chemical evolution is true. Some, like Stanley Miller, say amino acids came first. Others say it was DNA. Still others argue that RNA was the molecule that started it all. Not only do they disagree on WHAT came first, they disagree on WHERE it happened. Darwin said abiogenesis began in a warm pond laden with precursor chemicals. Some think it was in shallow tidal pools along rocky beaches. Many believe it happened in superheated thermal vents on the ocean floor. One very popular theory is that abiogenesis happened in the gases of nebulae deep in outer space, and then later these "seeds" drifted to earth. (Or were brought here by space-aliens.) The reason they can't agree on the WHAT and the WHERE, is because no one has every observed WHAT they claim happened, WHERE they claim it happened. It's all based on non-observed science... which means it isn't science. It doesn't matter which theory you want to believe. None of their theories can account for how all the different biochemicals came to be, how they came to be in the same place at the same time, how they came to be in the exact right forms, concentrations, and proportions, how they eliminated contaminates, or how they assembled themselves in the correct order. No one has ever observed this being done. This means the idea is unscientific. None of their theories can account for how intelligent instructions were created. This means the idea is meaningless. No one has ever observed random forces create intelligent instructions in the present. This means they cannot appeal to random forces as the cause of DNA instructions in the past.

Stanley Miller's apparatus was okay for making a few amino acids; but the lipids, carbohydrates, and nucleic acids necessary for life couldn't be made under those same conditions. Nucleic acids would need a different environment and a different set of chemical precursors to form spontaneously. The same is true for all the other essential biomolecules. In the sixty years since Stanley Miller's famous experiment, no one has yet discovered or observed a mixture of nonliving chemicals randomly produce amino acids, nucleic acids, sugars, fats, carbohydrates, and all the other biochemicals of life. Even if they had, and even if all the proper chemicals for life could be produced in the same space at the same time, it still wouldn't generate life unless life-generating instructions were created in the process. Let's compare a couple of "Abiogenesis-Simulators" to see what we can learn about the idea of life arising from non-life.

Stanley Miller's Apparatus

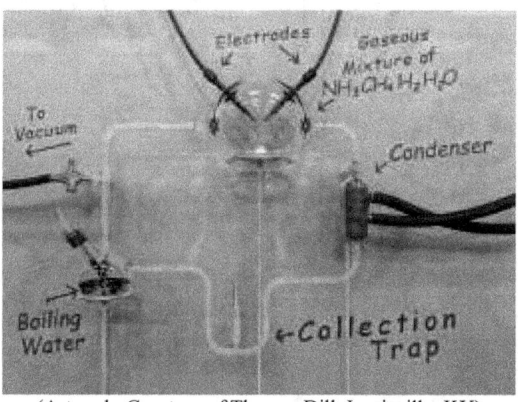

(Artwork: Courtesy of Thomas Dill, Louisville, KY)

Dr. Miller made a very famous apparatus that randomly produced a thin soup of tainted, imperfect amino acids. Miller added water, methane, ammonia, and hydrogen to his apparatus and subjected them to electric sparks in an oxygen-free atmosphere. The sparks supposedly simulated lightning, the "soup" supposedly simulated the primordial ocean, and the gases supposedly simulated the primordial atmosphere. He also subjected the contents to a vacuum, so he could cool-boil the "ocean" without heat destroying the amino acids. As you can see, his apparent primordial earth was not the same as the actual primordial earth. His apparent primordial ocean did not contain the same ingredients as the actual primordial ocean. (The actual primordial ocean contained chlorine, fluorine, sodium, iron, arsenic, and other chemicals that would have destroyed life the instant it was created.) His apparent primordial atmosphere did not contain the same ingredients or the same conditions as the actual primordial atmosphere. (The actual primordial atmosphere was not a vacuum, and it contained oxygen which would have oxidized and destroyed the life as well.) Since his ingredients and conditions weren't the same as the ingredients and conditions of the primordial earth, his apparatus did not prove anything about how life was created on the primordial earth.

In contrast to Miller's apparatus, I have made an apparatus that goes far beyond what Miller could imagine. My apparatus produces a rich soup containing the perfect amino acids, proteins, carbohydrates, lipids, nucleic acids, enzymes, sugars, and all the other biochemicals necessary for life. More than that, my apparatus produces them in the exact right forms, concentrations, and proportions, and without contaminates.

Steven Dill's Apparatus

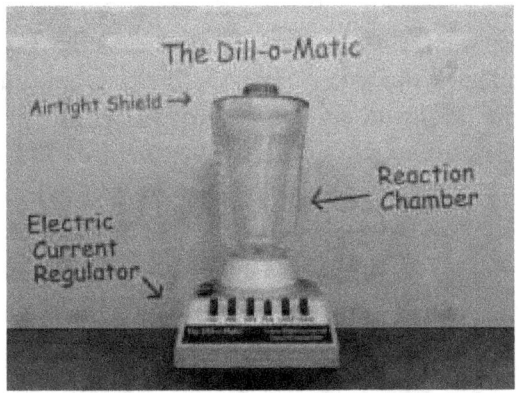

(Artwork: Courtesy of Thomas Dill, Louisville, KY)

To get this thing to work, perform Step One:

Step One:

Pour one cup H_2O into the Reaction Chamber.
Add one medium potato.
Firmly secure the Airtight Shield.
Push the Electric Current Regulator Button that says, "Puree."

Voila! You have just created a better primordial soup than Dr. Miller's. This soup contains not only the right amino acids, but all the nucleic acids, carbohydrates, lipids, vitamins, and minerals required to generate life.

Now, to prove evolution is possible, simply complete Step Two.

Step Two:

Using only the random forces of nature, make it a potato again.

I'm not picking on Stanley Miller. (Yeah, I am!) Actually, his apparatus and my apparatus have something in common—we never won a Noble Prize for them... and for the same reason. What I want you to see is that no one's theory of chemical evolution works. They are all unscientific because they are all based on the unknown, unobserved, and untested belief (faith) that life can arise from chemicals without the need of a Life-Giver. Evolutionists think a mixture of nonliving chemicals will eventually give rise to something living.

This is their hypothesis:

Life **CAN** spontaneously arise from a sterile nutrient broth under the right conditions.

Creationists think otherwise. This is our hypothesis:

Life **CANNOT** spontaneously arise from a sterile nutrient broth under any conditions.

Whose claim is more scientific? Which side has more observable and repeatable data to back its claim? Which side has more experimental evidence? Evolutionists have absolutely no data or evidence. They have never observed life spontaneously arise from nonlife. Abiogenesis has never been observed or repeated. There has not been a single experiment that randomly generates life from nonlife, except in horror stories and monster movies. Creationists, however, can point to billions of experiments proving life cannot arise from non-life.

Soup For the Creationist's Soul

Every can of food is a miniature laboratory. Every can of soup, every can of beans, every can of creamed corn, or spinach, or peas, or beef stock, or carrots...

every item of canned food ever produced is an observable, testable, and repeatable experiment in placing the perfect organic biochemicals in a life-free environment. Every item of canned food ever produced has remained life-free, providing the container wasn't punctured or damaged so as to allow living organisms to enter. The combined shelf-life of all the canned foods ever produced would add up to billions of years, yet in one hundred percent of those abiotic soups, abiogenesis has never happened. Abiogenesis has never been observed, even with perfect ingredients!

So, which side has more scientific evidence to back its claim? Creationists can point to billions of observable, testable, and repeatable scientific experiments (canned foods) as proof life cannot spontaneously arise from any kind of chemical soup even when all the pure and perfect chemicals are present. Evolutionists can only point to a failed experiment that shouldn't have passed peer-review. It didn't contain the same ingredients as the primordial ocean. It didn't replicate the primordial atmosphere. It didn't create the pure forms of amino acids necessary for functional proteins. It didn't produce the instructions needed for life. And above all else, it relied on the addition of Miller's intelligence to make the thing work. **An outside intelligent agent was required!** Even if Miller had created life, it would have proved life can only be created by intelligence. He would have proved life requires a Creator. Miller's apparatus was a classic case of counterfeit science. Yet, it is still published in scientific textbooks and hailed as proof for evolution. The only thing Miller's experiment proves is if you close your eyes, forget scientific principles, and repeatedly reject observable data, you can convince yourself the Theory of Evolution is true.

False Supposition 2: Evolution Happened by Gradual Change

Darwin believed biological changes occurred very gradually over very long periods of time. He believed new species developed very slowly and gradually from previous species; species by species, organism by organism, system by system, organ by organ, tissue by tissue, cell by cell. Since species changed so slowly, he expected the fossil record would reveal billions of intermediate fossils. However, he admitted the fossil record did not support his supposition.

"Firstly, why, if species have descended from other species by **insensibly** fine gradations, do we not everywhere see **innumerable** transitional forms? Why is not all nature **in confusion** instead of the species being, as we see them, well defined?"[14] (emphasis mine)

I am going to make some assumptions about Charles Darwin. First, I am going to assume Charles Darwin was a very intelligent man, in fact, I truly believe he was a genius. Next, I am going to assume he believed he was right, and that he wrote what he believed. Thirdly, I am going to assume he knew his views would be opposed by many theologians and scientists, as well as the public. Because of these three assumptions, I am going to make a fourth assumption about Charles Darwin. I assume he was very careful in his choice of words and in how he expressed his beliefs. I don't think he wanted people to misunderstand him. When he said there should be **innumerable** transitional forms, I am going to take him at his word. I think he thought the fossil record would reveal so many transitional forms, they would be too numerous to count; not dozens, not hundreds, not thousands, but literally millions. (And not just innumerable fossils, but innumerable **transitional** fossils.) Furthermore, when he spoke about **insensibly** fine gradations between species, I think he believed evolution was so slow and gradual, we wouldn't be able to sense (see, feel, detect, *etc.*) the changes from one species to the next. It would only be by comparing great numbers of insensibly fine gradations that we would be able to detect a change. In other words, evolution couldn't be detected by looking at one generation to the next. It would take many generations before we could detect (sense) even the smallest of changes. He believed the gradations ought to be so fine, and the transitions so numerous, that taxonomy would end up in **confusion**. (unable to detect order) Darwin believed as more and more fossils were discover, it would become more and more confusing to place the transitional fossils in their exact and proper chronological order. The differences between them would be too small to tell which fossil came before another. At least, that's what you must believe if you believe Darwin when he used the terms, **"insensibly fine gradations," "innumerable transitional forms,"** and nature, **"in confusion,"** to describe the process of evolution.

Now, I don't have to assume Charles Darwin knew his theory was in trouble from the very beginning. I don't have to assume this, because he admitted it himself. Darwin knew his theory predicted the presence of too many transitional fossils to number, but he also knew his theory didn't fit the scientific facts. The links were missing. He simply believed the "missing links" hadn't been found yet. With enough time and enough geologists, he was sure those fossils would be discovered... someday. That day hasn't arrived yet, but many evolutionists still believe it will. They still believe that over very long periods of time, species very gradually changed according to their ability to survive in the very gradually changing environmental niches.

Those organisms with traits that helped promote survivability very gradually replaced those organisms that didn't have those traits. If what they assert is true, then the fossil record would show very gradually changing biological TRAITS (not just species) as time passed. In fact, the changes in traits would be so gradual, even the Linnaean Classification System would eventually break down. The traits of one Species would gradually blur into the traits of another Species. One Genus would have traits that imperceptibly changed into the traits of another Genus. One Family's traits would change in such small gradations, it would be impossible to draw a definitive line where it changed into another Family. The same would be true for Order, Class, Phylum, and even Kingdom. Alas, the fossil record didn't reveal what they wanted.

Over The Rainbow[15]

I like explaining things with illustrations because sometimes it makes difficult concepts easier to grasp. Imagine you were an artist and you wanted to paint a picture of the visible color spectrum; a rainbow mural. You would start on the left edge of your canvass with red and work your way to the right with orange, then yellow, then green, then blue, then purple, and finally back to red. Let's also imagine your canvass was one hundred miles long. It's a big project. You would start with a can of paint that had 1,000,000 parts of pure red paint and nothing else. With that paint, you would paint a one-inch wide line from the top of the canvass to the bottom of the canvass. Next, you would get a new brush and a can of paint with 999,999 parts of red paint and one part of orange paint. With that paint, you would draw another one-inch line. This line would be touching the first line and be parallel to it for its entire length.

Then you would get a new brush and a can of paint with 999,998 parts of red paint and two parts of orange. You would use this to paint your third one-inch line. For your fourth line, you would use paint that was 999,997 parts red and three parts orange. This process would continue until you painted one million one-inch lines. At that point, you would have a can of paint with 1,000,000 parts of orange paint and no red paint. Once you drew the pure orange line, you would go to your next can of paint. It would contain 999,999 parts of orange paint and one part of yellow paint. Very gradually, line by line, you would have one more part of yellow paint and one less part of orange paint in your paint cans. Once you completed the next million lines, you would have a can of pure yellow paint. Then you would use paint that was one part green and 999,999 parts yellow. You would continue this process color by color. You would add more and more green to your yellow, then more and more blue to your green, then more and more purple to your blue, and finally more and more red to your purple. Each can of paint would differ from its predecessor by one part per million. The total transition through all six colors (red, orange, yellow, green, blue, and purple) would require six million one-inch lines. Your color spectrum would evolve through six million transitions in the space of about a hundred miles.

Once you rested from your work, what would you expect to see? You would expect to see a rainbow with millions of insensibly fine gradations. You wouldn't be able to tell where red ended, and orange began. You wouldn't be able to distinguish the 100% blue line from the 99.9999% blue/0.0001% purple line. You would be able to classify the colors into two "kingdoms," the warm colors (red, orange, and yellow) and the cool colors, (blue, green, and purple) but you wouldn't be able to tell when one "kingdom" ended and the other "kingdom" began. You would be able to see all six "phyla," (red, orange, yellow, green, blue, and purple) but you would find it difficult to see the lines of demarcation. You could create an entire classification scheme by labeling the colors as blue-green, bluish green, greenish blue, or greenish blue-green, but it would be too confusing to decide when something was blue enough to be called bluish blue-green instead of greenish blue-green. In the end, your classification system would be inadequate because there would be too many insensibly fine transitions from one color to the next.

This is the kind of results you would expect from Darwinian Evolution, except it would be even harder to define species. In our rainbow painting example, we have six million steps in one hundred miles. In the case of living organisms, we are dealing with billions of DNA changes over hundreds of millions of years. Changes would have been much, much more gradual! Darwinists insisted the fossil record would eventually reveal this kind of evolution. They believed so many fossils would be discovered, it would be plain for all to see how Darwinian Evolution explained the origins of species. So, if Darwinian Evolution is true, they should have found millions of insensibly finely gradated transitional fossils by now.

Is this what they found? No! A century and a half of intense searching passed, and they kept finding the same kind of fossils, of the same kind of organisms, with the same kind of traits, in the same kind of strata. In fact, this is how the Fossil Index System was made possible. The Fossil Index System was a way of determining when an organism lived, based on its features and its position in the fossil record. Because they kept finding the same kind of organisms, with the same kind of features, in the same geological strata all over the world, they assumed the fossil record was a chronological record of worldwide evolution. When they discovered particular fossils with particular traits, they were able to place them into a particular chronology. Each stratum had its own characteristic fossils with their own characteristic traits. But, if Darwinian evolution was true, then one would not expect to keep finding the same kind of organisms with the same kind of traits in the same kind of strata all over the world. Different species with different traits in different environments would show such gradual transitions that you wouldn't be able to tell when an index fossil started and when it ended. **The Fossil Index System seemed to indicate there had been abrupt changes in biologic traits as well as abrupt changes in environments.** Evolutionists knew if Darwinian Evolution was true, then the changes from one species to the next would be so gradual there would be nothing but transitional fossils in the strata. It began to appear as if biological traits weren't gradually changing. Either that or the ecological niches weren't gradually changing. Darwinian Evolution requires both, but the fossil record provided neither. They kept finding Devonian strata with Devonian fossils, Permian strata with Permian fossils, Jurassic strata with Jurassic fossils, *etc.* The very fact these groupings kept appearing all over the world seemed to prove evolution happened in large, recognizable stages. This was a great discovery for the Fossil Index System, but it was a bad discovery for Darwinian Evolution. Evolutionists couldn't find the innumerable, insensibly fine gradations in the fossil record. They couldn't find the "missing links."

Of course, many evolutionists claimed they have found the "missing links" but those discoveries always proved to be insufficient evidence because no one could unquestionably prove they were very gradual transitions from one group to another. Oh, they might find an organism with a trait that appeared similar to the traits in other groups, but the transitions were still too large and still too abrupt to be universally accepted as proof, even by other evolutionists. You see, it wasn't just creationists who began refuting Darwinism. By the mid-twentieth century, many well-known evolutionists also began doubting Darwin's model. Why did they doubt? For two reasons. First, it was discovered that biologic traits were the products of genetic instructions stored in strands of DNA. The only way to change biologic traits was to change DNA instructions. The only way to change DNA instructions was by random mutations. Because random mutations constantly occur and because environmental niches are constantly changing, there should be no fixity of species. To remain fixed, a species must experience no DNA change and no environmental change. Since these factors are supposedly constantly and gradually changing, nothing should stay the same for very long. **Finding species that remained constant should be the exception and not the rule.** Finding the same kind of fossils, with the same kind of traits, in the same geological strata all over the world was an awkward situation for insensibly fine gradualism. There were large gaps between the different organisms, and they couldn't find many (if any) truly transitional fossils. If Darwin was right, the geological strata ought to show an uncountable number of transitional fossils with imperceptibly small changes. Unfortunately, they couldn't find that. These anti-Darwinian Evolution evolutionists realized paleontology was disproving Darwin's insensibly fine gradualism theory. Every time an evolutionist made a "startling new discovery" in the fossil record, it didn't reveal transitions so gradual they couldn't be perceived. Yes, they looked something-like something before them, and they looked something-like something after them, but the differences were always too great to be considered insensibly fine. Look at the fossils in any Evolutionary Family Tree for any organism and you will see there are quite-noticeable differences from one fossil to the next. They couldn't find any fossils with insensibly fine transitions. That's what Darwinian Evolution demanded, but paleontology kept revealing the opposite. This eventually became such an embarrassment for evolutionists, they quietly laid Darwin's theory to rest. Here was a case of evolutionists disproving evolutionists.

They dumped Darwin's theory and created another Theory of Evolution. That theory is called, "Punctuated Equilibria." Simply stated, evolutionists now claim evolution didn't happen very gradually over very long periods of time. Instead, it happened in very short periods of very rapid changes, with very long quiet periods of time in between. Very rapid bursts of evolution are separated by very long interludes of no evolution. Because the changes were so rapid, and the time periods were so short, there would be very few transitional organisms. That means there would be even fewer transitional fossils. Fish evolved to amphibians so quickly, it was unlikely any transitional forms would be found in the fossil record. Reptiles evolved to birds just as quickly. In fact, one evolutionist said a reptile laid an egg and a bird hatched out. Not much chance of finding transitional fossils in that case. This new theory could now be "proved" because it was based on the lack of evidence. The more transitional fossils you didn't find, the more "true" this theory became. Of course, real science is never strengthened by relying on the idea that the less evidence there is, the more scientific it becomes. Yet, this is exactly what evolutionists have done.

What was the second reason evolutionists began to doubt Darwin's version of evolution? It was because you can fool all the scientists some of the time, but you can't fool all the scientists all the time... not even evolutionary scientists. Some evolutionary scientists knew the claim about "seeing" the transitional fossils wasn't exactly what the science showed. They took notice of what wasn't noticed by the public; most of the "transitions" were **indirectly** connected, not **directly** connected. Where is this clever piece of trickery seen? It is seen in many of the "Evolutionary Family Trees" on the walls of our universities and museums and in the textbooks of our students.

This kind of subtle deception was seen in the Family Tree of whale evolution. As you remember, Rodhocetus was said to be the transition that supposedly showed the evolution of modern whales from land mammals. The Whale Family Tree displayed it as an intermediate between what came before and what came after. (Remember, we often don't get to see real intermediates.) The progression went something like this: The Indohyrus bones were connected to the Pakicetus bones. The Pakicetus bones were connected to the Ambulocetus bones. The Ambulocetus bones were connected to the Kutchicetus bones. The Kutchicetus bones were connected to the Rodhocetus bones. The Rodhocetus bones were connected to the Dorudon bones. The Dorudon bones were connected to modern whale bones. And they were all connected to a hippopotamus-like ancestor... unless you believed they were all connected to a cat-like ancestor... or a dog-like ancestor... or a cow-like ancestor... or a bear. Once the Whale Family Tree was drawn, everybody was happy... except those who don't like deception. They noticed a problem. The "intermediates" were not actual intermediates. (We must constantly remind evolutionists that what they see are not Actual Intermediates; only Apparent Intermediates.) They don't directly connect one species to the next when you look at the real evidence. One species is not truly a transition between the species before it and the species after it. They are depicted that way in many of the simpler drawings, but when you look at the more detailed drawings based on the actual fossils, drawings meant more for scientists than for the public, you see something entirely different. Let me show you how this works by showing you a typical Family Tree of whale evolution.

Whale Evolution Family Tree 1

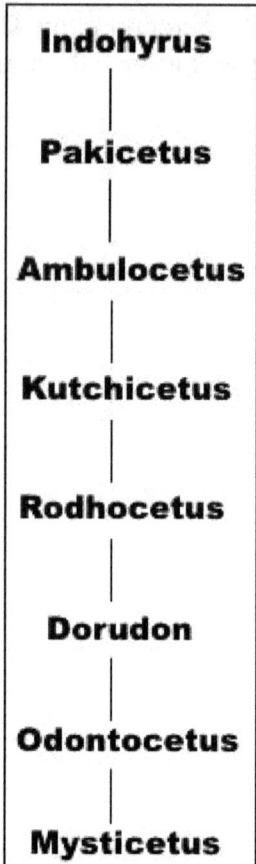

(Source of Chart Information: University of California—Berkeley, and my wild imagination.)

This doesn't give any details, but it "proves" modern whales (Odontocetus, the Toothed-Whales and Mysticetus, the Baleen-Whales) evolved from some small land animal many millions of years ago. Now let's look at a more detailed Family Tree.

Whale Evolution Family Tree 2

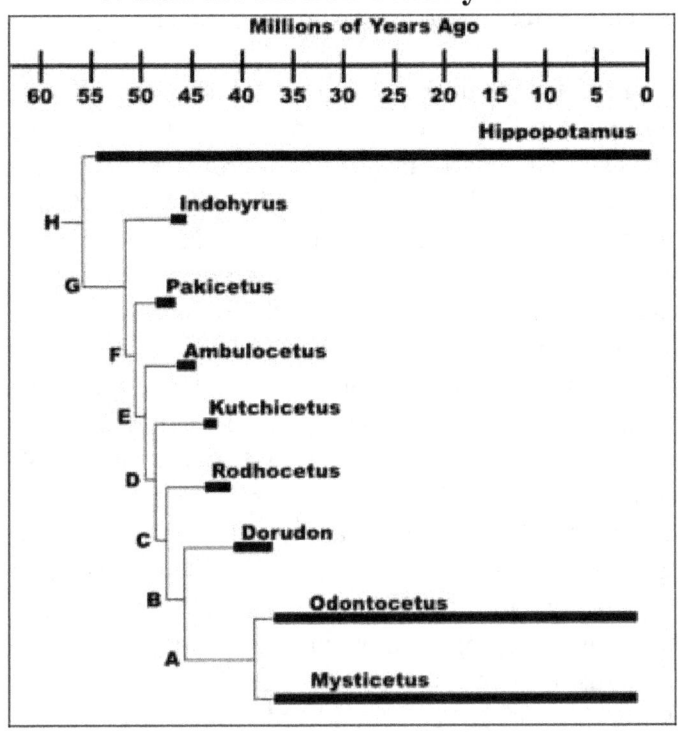

(Source of Chart Information: University of California—Berkeley and their wild imaginations.)

http://evolution.berkeley.edu/evolibrary/article/evograms_03

Look closely how Pakicetus is "related" to Ambulocetus. Pakicetus did not evolve directly into Ambulocetus. The thick horizontal lines show the time periods where actual fossils have been found. The thin horizontal lines are the time periods where there are no fossils. Those "ancestors" have never been found. The horizontal lines are connected to vertical lines in a branching fashion. The nodes at which the branchings occur are the supposed common ancestors of the species that follow them. But notice the vertical lines have no fossil evidence either. (They are thin lines.)

Starting at the present and going back in time, Mysticetus did not evolve from Odontocetus. Instead, they evolved from a common ancestor at "A." (Which has never been found.) "A" didn't evolve from Dorudon. Instead, "A" and Dorudon evolved from a common ancestor at "B." (Which has never been found.) Of course, "B" didn't evolve from Rodhocetus. Whale evolutionists say "B" and Rodhocetus evolved from a common ancestor at "C." (Which has never been found.) In the same fashion, "C" did not evolve from Kutchicetus. "C" and Kutchicetus had a common ancestor at "D." (Which has never been found.) You probably suspect "D" didn't evolve from Ambulocetus. You are right. "D" and Ambulocetus had a supposed common ancestor at "E." (Which has never been found.) Keeping up the tradition, "E" didn't evolve from Pakicetus. Keeping further with the tradition, "E" and Pakicetus evolved from a common ancestor at "F." (Which has never been found.) "F" didn't evolve from Indohyrus either. "F" and Indohyrus had a common ancestor at "G." (Which had never been found.) Finally, "G" did not evolve from the hippopotamus. (Which have been found.) Instead, "G" and hippos share a common "hippo-like" ancestor at "H." (Which has never been found.) None of these was an Actual Transition from what was before, to what came after. The fossils they found were Apparent Transitions from Apparent Common Ancestors for which there are no fossils. The "intermediates" are speculations-without-evidence. In case you think I am making this up, here is the very first comment made on the very same University of California—Berkeley Web Page that shows this Whale Evolution Family Tree.[16] (This is the same university where Dr. Padian teaches.):

"The first thing to notice on this evogram is that hippos are the closest living relatives of whales, but they are not the ancestors of whales. In fact, **none of the individual animals on the evogram is the direct ancestor of any other,** as far as we know. That's why each of them gets its own branch on the family tree." (emphasis mine)

Did you catch that? None of the species in this drawing is the direct ancestor of any other. That means none of these species evolved into any of the others. That means none of them is a real transition to any of the others. They are all "side branches" off the supposed Whale Evolution Family Tree. None of them is a true intermediate. That means you weren't blind or three days dead when you didn't see the intermediates. The supposed evolution of whales is not based on the real evidence they have; it is based on the speculative evidence they don't have. You have to "read-between-the-lines" to make it read what it doesn't say. This same truth applies to the evolution of other species; even man. Our "Human Evolutionary Tree" is filled by species connected to "common ancestors" for which there are no fossils. In fact, the entire "Evolutionary Tree of Life" is drawn mostly in "thin lines." Here's what some well-known evolutionists have said: (Truth in Advertising: Most of them favor Punctuated Equilibria over Darwinian Evolution.)

Colin Patterson, Director of the British Museum of Natural History:

"We have access to the tips of the tree; the tree itself is theory, and people who pretend to know about the tree and to describe what went on it—how the branches came off and the twigs came off—are, I think, telling stories."[17]

Gareth V. Nelson, American Museum of Natural History:

"It is a mistake to believe that even one fossil species or fossil 'group' can be demonstrated to have been ancestral to another. The ancestor-descendant relationship may only be assumed to have existed in the absence of evidence indicating otherwise."[18]

Stephen Jay Gould, Professor of Biology, Geology, and the History of Science at Harvard University:

"The extreme rarity of transitional forms in the fossil record persist as the trade secret of paleontology. The evolutionary trees that adorn our textbooks have data only at the tips and nodes of their branches; the rest is inference, however reasonable, not the evidence of fossils."[19]

A. H. Clark, Biologist, Smithsonian Institute, Washington, D.C.:

"No matter how far back we go in the fossil record of previous animal life upon earth, we find no trace of any animal forms which are intermediate between the various major groups of phyla."[20]

"Since we have not the slightest evidence, either among the living or the fossil animals, of any intergrading types following the major groups, it is a fair supposition that there never have been any such intergrading types."[21]

Richard B. Goldschmidt, Head of the Genetics Department, Kaiser Wilhelm Institute for Biology, Germany; Professor at the University of California, Berkeley:

"The facts of greatest importance are the following. When a new phylum, class, or order appears, there follows a quick explosive (in terms of geological time) diversification so that practically all orders or families known appear suddenly and without any apparent transitions."[22]

Lecomte du Nouy, Head of the Biophysics Division of the Pasteur Institute:

"In brief, each group, order, or family seems to be born suddenly and we hardly ever find the forms which link them to the preceding strain. When we discover them they are already completely differentiated. Not only do we find practically no transitional forms, but in general it is impossible to authentically connect a new group with an ancient one."[23]

Thomas S. Kemp, Curator of the Zoological Collections at the University of Oxford:

"In no single adequately documented case is it possible to trace a transition, species by species, from one genus to another."[24]

George Stuart Carter, Professor, Fellow of Corpus Christi College, Cambridge, England:

"We do not have any available fossil group which can categorically be claimed to be the ancestor of any other group.

We do not have in the fossil record any specific point of divergence of one life form for another, and generally each of the major life groups has retained its fundamental structural and physiological characteristics throughout its life history and has been conservative in habitat."[25]

Let's test Darwin's Hypotheses:

1.) He hypothesized the fossil record would reveal transitions in such small gradations, the differences between them couldn't be perceived. ("Insensibly Fine Gradations")

2.) He hypothesized the fossil record would reveal transitions in such great numbers, they couldn't be counted. ("Innumerable Transitional Forms")

3.) He hypothesized the fossil record would reveal so many fossils, with such small differences between them, it would be difficult to place them in the proper order. ("Nature in Confusion")

Did he get it right? No! Over 150 years after Darwin, we're still waiting to see those insensibly fine, innumerable transitional forms. The scientific observation is this: There are, at best, extremely few "transitional forms" in the fossil record; far too few to support Darwin's Theory of Evolution. Many of the "intermediates," like Rodhocetus, wind up on the garbage heap of evolutionary theory because other evolutionists prove they don't support the hype. The few remaining "intermediates" still reveal huge gaps—huge, huge gaps, between the species they're supposed to connect. There are no displays in any museum or university showing innumerable fossils with insensibly fine gradations between any two species. Usually, the museum displays and the textbook drawings show three, four, or five intermediates. Some might even show six or seven. None of them show innumerable intermediates. If Darwin was right, the fossil record should contain hundreds or even thousands of intermediates between EVERY taxonomic group. Darwin was wrong. The repeated scientific observations don't fit the theory. That disqualifies it as a scientific theory, and it shouldn't be taught in the science class. (Claiming that the innumerable transitions were there at one time, but have been destroyed by erosion and other natural forces, still leaves the theory outside of science. Lack of evidence cannot be used to defend a scientific theory. I could just as easily claim space-aliens came and stole those innumerable transitional fossils and took them back to the Planet Zuurtane. Thus, the missing fossils not only prove evolution happened, they prove there is a race of space-paleontologists living on Zuurtane.)

So, his hypothesis about the presence of innumerable transitional fossils, and his hypothesis about insensibly fine gradations, have been falsified by the fossil record. What about his hypothesis about the difficulty in detecting order in the fossil record? (All nature should be in, "confusion," due to vast numbers of fossils showing such small differences.) If his hypothesis is correct, then as more and more fossils were discovered, the task of ordering them chronologically would become more and more difficult. If he was right, then one-hundred and fifty years later, we shouldn't be able to place fossils in their correct order; or at least it would be a very difficult task. Is that what they discovered? No, they found the opposite situation. The Fossil Index System proved he was wrong. They kept finding the same kind of fossil, in the same kind of strata all over the world. Detecting the chronological order became an easier and easier task as more and more fossils were unearthed. It was so easy, any paleontologist could do it. Here is a comment from the *American Journal of Science* explaining how easy it had become:

"Each taxon represents a definite time unit and so provides an accurate even 'infallible' date. If you doubt it, bring in a suite of good index fossils, and the specialist, without asking where or in what order they were collected, will lay them out on the table in chronological order...."[26]

The ability to arrange fossils in their correct chronological order wasn't difficult after all. You didn't even need to reveal their geographical location or their geological age, and any paleontologist would instantly know from where they came and from when they were. Order COULD be detected; nature wasn't in confusion. The fossils have falsified Darwin's third hypothesis. You don't even need to be a paleontologist to show that. Ask an evolutionist to give you a copy of his or her favorite "Best-Proof-for-Evolution" Family Tree. Ask them for a copy, because you are going to take a pair of scissors to the Family Tree. Then with you scissors, cut out each species in the Family Tree. Place the individual pictures on a table and shuffle them. Now, ask the evolutionist if he or she can put them back in the correct order. They will be able to do so with ease. But when they do, point out to them that:

1.) There aren't innumerable transitions on the table—There are only a few.

2.) The gradations are not insensibly fine—They could easily tell a difference between each step.

3.) There was nothing confusing about it—They could easily sort them in the correct order.

Darwin's Hypotheses are false. The transitional fossils aren't innumerable. The gradations between fossils aren't insensibly fine. The chronological order of the fossils isn't in confusion. Atheistic Evolutionists apparently don't understand science very well because they don't understand scientific logic very well. When you destroy the hypotheses, you destroy the theory, no matter how much evidence you think you have. **Finding evidence FOR the Theory of Evolution does not PROVE the Theory of Evolution, but finding evidence FALSIFYING the Theory of Evolution does DISPROVE it**. The scientific evidence over the past one-hundred and fifty years has falsified Darwin's Theory. Darwin was wrong!

False Supposition 3: Natural Selection Caused Evolution

If Apparent Design is the evolutionists' counterfeit $100 bill, Natural Selection is their counterfeit $1,000,000 bill. There were other theories of evolution before Darwin, but he was the first to come up with a seemingly rational explanation for how life could evolve without a supernatural designer. Science and society of the 19th century were looking for a way to eliminate God from science and from their lives. Charles Darwin provided just what they wanted.

It was obvious to Darwin that all taxonomic groups consist of organisms with varying anatomical properties. There is a range of different characteristics that organisms can possess yet still belong to the same taxonomic group. This includes the taxonomic group we call, "Species." Not every individual in a species shares the exact same characteristics. There are Beagles, and Greyhounds, and Newfoundlands, and Chihuahuas, and although they have different characteristics, they are all still dogs. The same is true of horses. There are Clydesdales, and Thoroughbreds, and Arabians, and Appaloosas, but they are still horses.

In the 18th century, Swedish scientist Carolus Linnaeus devised a taxonomic classification system based on the similarity of physical traits. However, Linnaeus did not intend for his classification system to imply a physical kinship among living organisms. Yes, he put humans and apes in the same Kingdom, Phylum, Class, and Order, but he never thought humans and apes were physically related. He believed God created them similar in appearance but separate in nature. At that time, it was still easy to believe the taxonomic groups reflected the pattern of creation, not the pattern of evolution. (It wasn't unscientific to believe in God.)

Nevertheless, this classification system opened the door for Darwin's idea of descent with modification. Since everything in the Linnaean classification system was based on physical similarities, Darwin went one step further. Why not assume all similarities between all species were caused by physical descent? A man has red hair, and his son has red hair, and his grandson has red hair. This was because of physical descent. Why couldn't other characteristics be due to physical descent? Darwin proposed that physical similarities proved organisms evolved from one species to the next by physical descent. The more similarities two organisms shared, the more closely they were related. This gave rise to the expression, "homology implies relationship." In other words, physical similarities are an indication of physical kinship. I'll show you later why this idea fails, but let's stay focused on Natural Selection. To explain how Natural Selection works, let me borrow an excellent illustration Dr. Stephen Meyer created in his book *Signature in the Cell*.[27] I'll summarize his explanation of Natural Selection rather than quote it because it is several pages long.

Dr. Meyer Had a Sheep.
Its Fleece Was Short and Thin.
But Could its Wool Grow Long and Thick,
By Simple Mutation?

Dr. Meyer explained that if you were a sheep breeder and wanted to produce a line of sheep with longer and thicker wool, then you would keep selecting the sheep with the longest and thickest wool as your breeding stock. After several generations of this type of Artificial Selection, you would have sheep with longer and thicker wool. This kind of descent with modification was very familiar to plant and animal breeders. This kind of evolution was observable, testable, and repeatable. But, this kind of evolution also required intelligent agents making choices. Darwin didn't want that, and neither did society. The philosophy of science was changing in the 19th century. People didn't want an explanation for life that included a supernatural, moral agent. They wanted God out of the picture. (Just like the ancient Greeks—and for the same reason.) That's why they welcomed Darwin with open arms. Darwin proposed this same kind of change could occur over time without an intelligent agent. He said Natural Selection could bring about changes in heritable physical traits.

As Dr. Meyer explained in his book, a series of long, cold winters could accomplish the same thing the sheep breeder could, but without the need for a sheep breeder. It seemed reasonable to believe that in a long, cold winter, the sheep with longer and thicker wool would be more likely to survive. Sheep with thinner and shorter wool would more likely die from the cold. Sheep that die in the winter don't produce lambs in the spring. After enough long, cold winters, the only sheep remaining would be those with the longer and thicker wool. Over time, the sheep with the less-fit wool would be eliminated from the breeding stock. Thus, the physical characteristics of the sheep could change over time without an intelligent agent.

Darwin applied this kind of explanation to all physical characteristics, of all organisms, in all taxonomic groups. The Force of Natural Selection looked like it could do everything an Intelligent Agent could do. Here was a way of having "design" without a Designer. For those wanting to reject God, Natural Selection not only eliminated the need for God in science, it eliminated the need for God everywhere else. "Survival-of-The-Fittest," "Kill-or-Be-Killed," and "The-Law-of-the-Jungle," quickly became synonymous titles for the Theory of Evolution. If the Theory of

Evolution gave atheism a foothold in science, it gave immorality a stronghold in society. If we were created by the brute forces of nature, then we have every right to adopt a moral/behavioral standard and lifestyle based on the brute forces of nature. After all, the course of evolution was guided by millions of years of mindless violence and merciless killing... and the human race was its ultimate achievement. Millions of years of mindless violence and merciless killing was obviously a good thing. If Atheistic Evolution is true, then we are living in a mindless, merciless universe of brute forces (droughts, floods, earthquakes, fires, tsunamis, tornadoes, hurricanes, diseases, *etc.*) where only the fittest could survive.... No! I take that back. If Atheistic Evolution is true, then we are living in a mindless, merciless universe of brute forces (droughts, floods, earthquakes, fires, tsunamis, tornadoes, hurricanes, diseases, *etc.*) where only the fittest SHOULD survive. If evolution is true, the less-fit SHOULD die, so the more-fit can survive. According to the Theory of Evolution, death and destruction are good things. Unless the less-fit sheep die, the more-fit sheep can't evolve. So, let me ask you two questions:

Q.) Is the death of sheep good or bad?
A.) It depends on whether you are a less-fit sheep or a more-fit sheep.

Q.) Is the death of people good or bad?
A.) It depends on whether you are a less-fit person or a more-fit person.

Individual life and death become unimportant. What is important in evolution is for the less-fit people to die, so the more-fit people can live. (But what becomes the criteria for determining fitness... Physical strength? Economic status? Ethnicity? Race? Education? Political connections? Military strength? Religion? Whatever it is, if it helps the more-fit eliminate the less-fit, then evolutionists must admit it is a good thing.) This is what Atheistic Evolutionists must believe if they think we got here by Survival-of-the-Fittest. Without death, there would be no evolution, and since evolutionists believe evolution is good, they are forced to believe that death is good. Good and evil become meaningless words. If you die, or your child dies, or your spouse dies, or a hundred-thousand people die in a disaster, that's just tough luck. It's not morally right or morally wrong; morally good or morally evil. It's just what the brute forces do. In fact, if Atheistic Evolution is true, atheists should welcome disasters as nature's way of improving the species. **Unless conditions arise that can kill some members of a species, there is no selective pressure for improving the species.** If Atheistic Evolution is true, then a tsunami that wipes out a coastal city is a great way for evolution to select for those who are better able to swim for longer periods of time. If evolution eliminates the weak, then weak swimmers ought to die.

Now, consider this: According to evolutionists, the struggle for survival is against organisms which compete for the same resources. African lions are in no competition with honeybees. African lions are in competition with cheetahs, hyenas, jackals, and other carnivores. However, the greatest competition for African lions is from other African Lions. The greatest competition for cheetahs is from other cheetahs. If Atheistic Evolution is true, then intra-species competition shapes the course of evolution much more than inter-species competition. If Atheistic Evolution is true, then humans killing humans is the most efficient means of eliminating "less-fit" humans. If Atheistic Evolution is true, then the concept of moral good and moral evil is strictly a human invention. Morality, ethics, values, laws, virtues, and even religions are merely social conventions. These things might provide a benefit for human survival, but any benefit would depend on the local circumstances. Evolving a religion might be beneficial, but only if a rival religious group didn't kill you for not believing in their religion. In that case, evolving your religion would be a bad thing. If your religion is the one that kills people of other religions, then your religion is good; your religion perpetuates your selfish genes. No matter what your religion teaches and practices—murder, torture, racism, sexism, hatred, cruelty, prejudice, slavery, pedophilia, rape, or whatever—it is not bad if it helps promote your survival. **If Atheistic Evolution is true, the only thing that counts is survival.**

If Atheistic Evolution is true, there are no absolute, objective moral values. Good and bad are relative. Stealing a loaf of bread might get a peasant thrown into prison. That kind of stealing would be "bad" for society. However, seizing the homes and properties of entire towns would make a king rich and powerful, and that would be "good" for society. Whether stealing is good or bad depends on someone's definition of good and bad, and on whether they are powerful enough to get away with it. Darwinism provided the perfect excuse to live by force, not by faith. Oh, I know evolutionists will complain that "Brute Force Morality" is an incorrect supposition derived from Darwin's Theory, but by whose standard of morality do they complain? I find it quite telling that societies based on Survival-of-the-Fittest always practice brute force morality against the "less-fit." Nazism, Communism, racism, ethnic cleansing, abortion on demand, *etc.* are all examples of man's attempts to eliminate the people they consider less-fit.

Heredity and Environment

Darwin made another incorrect supposition. He supposed the environment played a major role in the evolution of heritable traits. (As in Dr. Meyer's illustration: Long cold winters caused long, thick wool in sheep.) Darwin believed Natural Selection was the force that caused new species to originate. That was why he named his book, *On the Origin of Species by Means of Natural Selection*. No one in Darwin's time knew what caused physical traits to pass from one generation to the next. There were a lot of opinions, but they were all wrong; including Darwin's. No one knew a biomolecular nano-computer system transmitted encoded instructions for physical traits. DNA wouldn't be discovered for nearly a century. At that time, the person who knew the most about heredity was Gregor Mendel. (1822-1884) Mendel was an Austrian monk, as well as one of the greatest scientists of all times... only no one knew about him until the 20th century because he was a Christian Creationist whose evidence contradicted evolution. 19th century "scientists" weren't interested in Mendel's research. 19th century evolutionists believed heritable traits were somehow created, shaped, formed, or modified by environmental factors. Again, long, cold winters produced long, thick wool in sheep. In a similar fashion, droughts caused fish to evolve into higher life forms. (Droughts were either "good" or "bad" depending on whether you could survive them.) As lakes dried up and became swamps and forests and deserts, the fish in them became amphibians and then reptiles and then mammals—that kind of thing. Change in the environment was one of the driving forces of evolution. Darwin believed a physical force outside of living organisms was responsible for evolution. That force was Natural Selection. Darwin believed Natural Selection created the variety and complexity of physical traits seen in the fossil record. Mendel proved Darwin was wrong. Mendel proved heritable traits were caused by something already inside the organism; not by environmental conditions. Even though Mendel published his findings in the scientific journals of his day, and even though Mendel sent copies to the top European scientists, (including Darwin) 19th century academia shunned him. The historical evidence is ironic. Although he had a copy of Mendel's work, Darwin didn't even read it.

Darwin said evolution had two driving forces: changes in heredity and changes in environment. The first force caused new physical traits to appear. Again, he didn't know how that happened. Today we know it is caused by mutations in DNA. The mutations necessary for evolution had to be random. (No guidance by divine hands.) Unfortunately, random mutations are almost always harmful. Random mutations alone would cause de-evolution rather than evolution. Random mutations alone would have eventually destroyed life instead of improving it. (Cosmos goes to chaos.) So, a second force was needed. Something was needed to eliminate the randomness of random mutations. The second force was any change in the environment that was either beneficial or harmful to the organisms struggling to survive. This enabled Natural Selection to remove less-fit organisms from the breeding stock. **(Very, very Important: Natural Selection does not create more-fit organisms; it can only eliminate less-fit ones.)** Without Natural Selection, new species would never arise. Without Natural Selection, there would be nothing to direct the course of evolution. Here are some quotes from evolutionists who confirm this idea:

Charles Darwin: "The main cause, however, of innumerable intermediate links not now occurring everywhere throughout nature depends on the very process of natural selection, through which new varieties continually take the places of and exterminate their parent-forms."[28]

J. B. S. Haldane: "No satisfactory cause of evolution other than the action of natural selection on fortuitous variations has ever been put forward."[29]

J. B. S. Haldane was a British geneticist and biologist who believed ultraviolet light shining on the gases in earth's first atmosphere created the organic molecules necessary for the primordial soup to produce life from non-life.

Stephen Jay Gould: "The essence of Darwinism lies in a single phrase: natural selection is the creative force of evolutionary change."[30]

Stephen Jay Gould was a Professor of Paleontology, Biology, Geology, and the History of Science at Harvard University.

Ernst Mayr: "The real core of Darwinism, however, is the theory of natural selection. This theory is so important for the Darwinian because it permits the explanation of adaptation, the 'design' of the natural theologian, by natural means, instead of by divine intervention."[31]

Ernst Mayr was a Professor of Zoology at Harvard University and the Director of its Museum of Comparative Zoology.

Douglas Futuyma: "The reason that natural selection is important is that it's the central idea, stemming from Charles Darwin and Alfred Russel Wallace, that explains design in nature. It is the one process that is responsible for the evolution of adaptations of organisms to their environment."[32]

Douglas Futuyma is a Professor of Ecology and Evolution at the State University of New York at Stony Brook, and the former President of the Society for the Study of Evolution, and the former President of the American Society of Naturalists.

T. Ryan Gregory: "Natural selection is one of the central mechanisms of evolutionary change and is the process responsible for the evolution of adaptive features."[33]

T. Ryan Gregory is a Professor in the Department of Integrative Biology at the University of Guelph, Guelph, Ontario, Canada.

Michael Ruse: "Natural selection allows the successes, but 'rubs out' the failures. Thus, selection creates complex order, without the need for a designing mind. All of the fancy arguments about a number of improbabilities, having to be swallowed at one gulp, are irrelevant. Selection makes the improbable actual."[34]

Michael Ruse is a Professor of the Philosophy of Science at Florida State University.

As you can see, Natural Selection is, "the main cause," "the one process responsible," "the central mechanism," "the real core," "the essence," and "the central idea" of evolution. Natural Selection is necessary for evolution because it supposedly removes randomness from evolution by directing the course of evolution. It, "makes the improbable actual." **Without Natural Selection, the Theory of Evolution cannot explain the origin of species.** (And Darwin knew that!) But, go back and reread the statements made by these evolutionists. You will see they conveniently leave out one little fact. They forget to mention that Natural Selection can't select for successes if DNA never creates the instructions for those successes. They mention, "new varieties," "fortuitous variations," "adaptations," and "successes," but they don't tell us how these things were created. They fail to tell us Natural Selection cannot create, "new varieties," "fortuitous variations," "adaptations," and "successes." DNA mutations do that. If the DNA doesn't create the, "new varieties," "fortuitous variations," "adaptations," and "successes," then there is nothing for Natural Selection to select. DNA mutations must create the new and beneficial traits BEFORE those traits can promote survival. Beneficial non-random DNA instructions must exist BEFORE they can be randomly selected for survival. New and beneficial traits can't evolve unless they already exist. **Natural Selection cannot explain the origin of a new species, because a new species must exist before it can be naturally selected.**

As scientists, we must now ask ourselves this question: If Natural Selection cannot cause random causes to produce non-random effects, is the Theory of Evolution a scientific fact? No; Natural Selection cannot do what evolutionists say it did. Natural Selection is a counterfeit cause. It has no power, force, guidance, control, or regulation over the very effect it is supposed to cause. It cannot cause non-randomness because it is itself random. The easiest way to explain this is to use Dr. Meyer's sheep illustration again. A very long series of very long and very cold winters would kill the sheep if the DNA mutations for longer and thicker wool didn't happen. The long, thick wool mutation is a good mutation for long, cold winters. At the same time, the long, cold winters are a good environment for the long, thick wool mutation. This means something must cause both the good mutations and the good environments for evolution to happen.

Without good environments, the Theory of Evolution cannot explain the origin of species.

Without good mutations, the Theory of Evolution cannot explain the origin of species.

According to evolutionists, Natural Selection is the cause of evolution, but it isn't true. Natural Selection neither mutates DNA, nor changes the environments.

Natural Selection does not cause changes in the DNA.

Natural Selection does not cause changes in the environment.

Since the "Driving Forces" of evolution were supposedly DNA changes and changes in the environments, we see how Natural Selection cannot be the "Driving Force" of evolution; it causes neither. **Evolution is not caused by Natural Selection.**

So, what causes the production of longer, thicker wool? It is caused by changes in the DNA instructions for wool. The DNA instructions must change from DNA instructions for shorter, thinner wool to DNA instructions for longer, thicker wool. Without changes in the DNA instructions, evolution could not happen. Natural Selection does not cause the changes in DNA. Natural Selection cannot select for longer, thicker wool if sheep never develop the DNA instructions for longer and thicker wool. Mutations in DNA are necessary for evolution to work, but mutations are random, and evolution requires some force that can remove randomness. Natural Selection supposedly eliminates randomness, but it works only if there are random changes in DNA and random changes in the environment.

How does the environment fit into this? Evolutionists agree that if sheep developed a mutation for longer and thicker wool, it would be advantageous only in a region that experienced longer, colder winters. Sheep living in a hot, arid region, like the Negev Desert of Israel, wouldn't benefit from a longer-thicker-wool mutation. In fact, it might even prove harmful. They might overheat. So, for the longer-thicker-wool mutation to become established in a sheep population, the sheep must live in a region where the winters continue to be longer and colder. Only if the winters continue to be longer and colder can mutations for longer and thicker wool become established as the new norm. If there was a mutation for longer and thicker wool in sheep, but it occurred in a niche where the winters were normal, then normal sheep wouldn't be selected against; they wouldn't be less-fit. In fact, they would be more-fit because they wouldn't expend valuable biologic energy on producing unneeded longer and thicker wool. In such an environment, the longer-thicker-wool mutation would provide a disadvantage, and the evolution to longer, thicker wool would never happen.

So, we need a very, very long period of longer and colder winters. What causes winters to be longer and colder? It is caused by weather patterns. What causes weather patterns? Weather patterns are caused by random forces. Random physical forces such as the sun, rain, cold, heat, wind, humidity, air pressure, volcanic eruptions, and even asteroid impacts bring about random changes in ecological niches. But, random physical forces causing random environmental changes do not eliminate randomness. Random weather patterns could not prevent a local environment from reversing a cold weather trend and become warmer. If the weather patterns are random, then any particular niche could just as easily become warmer again. If weather patterns are caused by random physical forces, then one would expect random warming and cooling fluctuations in any ecological niche. It would only be by chance that a longer, colder winter trend would continue long enough for sheep with longer, thicker wool to evolve. That means it would only be by chance that Natural Selection would work. And, if Natural Selection works only by chance, then Natural Selection is random. And, if Natural Selection is random, then evolution is random. And, if evolution is random, then evolution cannot create design. And, since design is an inherent and necessary quality of living organisms, Darwin didn't prove evolution. Darwin didn't prove his proposed mechanism for evolution, "descent with modification," caused evolution. He never explained the details of the mechanics necessary for the creation of new species. He merely assumed "descent with modification" COULD create new species, but he never proved "descent with modification" DID create new species. Darwin proved nothing.

E-Harmony?
(Evolution Harmony)

Two things must happen for the evolution of longer and thicker wool to happen:

1.) There must be a succession of DNA mutations that progressively cause increases in wool length and thickness. There can be no backward DNA mutations. Sheep with longer, thicker wool could never develop a mutation for shorter, thinner wool. If they did, evolution would stop. This is true of any trait that supposedly arose by the process of evolution. No matter how many thousands of slow, insensibly fine, gradual genetic steps it took for gills to evolve into lungs, the process could never reverse itself. The same can be said for the evolution of wings, eyes, opposable thumbs, and everything else. DNA changes must be irreversible or else evolution can't happen.

2.) There must be a succession of weather patterns that progressively cause longer and colder winters. There can never be a reversal of the weather pattern. The winters could never become warmer or shorter. If they did, then long, thick wool evolution would stop. And again, this is true for the conditions in any ecological niche supposedly causing any evolutionary change. A niche could only change in the new direction that favored the new trait; never back to what it was before.

The correct DNA changes and the correct environmental changes must occur at the same time, in the same place, in the same order, and for the same duration, or there would be no evolution of longer, thicker wool. The same thing must happen for every physical trait in every organism, in every niche. Imagine what must happen for fish to evolve into amphibians and then into reptiles. There must be simultaneous DNA instruction mutations that turn gills into lungs, fins into feet, fish scales into moist amphibian skin and then into thick, dry reptile hide, as well as all the other mutations needed for changes in the skeletal system, the muscular system, the cardiovascular system, and the nervous system. All the correct mutations must occur in insensibly fine gradations, and they all must occur at precisely the right time, and in the exact correct order. The environment also must change in insensibly fine gradations, also at the right time and in the right order. Gradually the lake must become a swamp, and gradually the swamp must become a forest, and gradually the forest must become a desert. The insensibly fine gradations in biologic changes must match the insensibly fine gradations in environmental changes perfectly. It wouldn't do a fish any good to evolve legs and thick hide if the lake became a desert before the fish had a chance to evolve lungs. Gills in a desert would be a bit of a disadvantage. Every step in the process must be precisely timed, perfectly tuned, and nothing can revert to a previous state. The desert can never become a forest, the forest can never become a swamp, the swamp can never become a lake, feet can never become fins, and lungs can never become gills. If any step in this evolution process stopped or reversed, there would be no fish to reptile evolution. For every trait, in every organism, in every ecological niche, everything that causes mutations and everything that causes environmental changes must act in this continuous, synchronous, finely-gradated, and non-reversing fashion. Both DNA changes and environmental changes must be irreversible.

The problem with this idea is that as soon as you prove they are irreversible, you prove they are non-random.

Irreversibility is a quality of evolution evolutionists don't like to publicize because they can't explain why random mutations can't reverse themselves or why random environmental conditions can't revert. Nevertheless, irreversibility is a necessity if evolution is to cause smaller, simpler organisms to become larger, more complex organisms. Here are some evolutionists who confirm this:

Louis Dollo: "An organism is unable to return, even partially, to a previous stage already realized in the ranks of its ancestors."[35]

Louis Dollo was a French-born, Belgian paleontologist (1857-1931) who co-developed the principles of paleobiology.

Salvador Edward Luria: "The modern theory of evolution, like all historical theories, is explanatory rather than predictive.... Evolution, like history, is not like coin tossing or a game of cards. It has another essential characteristic: irreversibility."[36]

Salvador Edward Luria was an Italian microbiologist (1912-1991) who won the Noble Prize in Medicine in 1969.

Bjorn Kurten: "Like other paleontological 'principles' of evolution, that of phyletic growth describes what usually or often happens, rather than what always happens. This holds to some extent even for the most nearly universal principle, that of the irreversibility of evolution, the fact that larger steps in evolution can never be retraced being aspect of the fact that history never repeats itself…"[37]

Bjorn Kurten (1924-1988) was a professor of paleontology at the University of Helsinki.

Henrique Teotónio: "The irreversibility of evolution is an extreme form of evolutionary constraint. It is the impossibility of return to evolutionary states that were once possible."[38]

Henrique Teotónio is a biologist, specialist in Experimental Evolutionary Biology, and Principal Investigator at Gulbenkian Institute of Science, Lisbon, Portugal.

If evolutionary changes are irreversible, then something non-random is causing them to be irreversible. If these changes are non-random, then something must cause them to be non-random. Since the forces of nature are random, something other than the forces of nature must be the cause of the continuous, synchronous, finely-gradated, perfectly timed, perfectly tuned, irreversible changes in DNA and environments required for evolution. If the natural, random forces can't do that, then what other force must be responsible? The only other choice is a supernatural, intelligent agent. This is what Theistic Evolutionists propose. Atheistic Evolutionists cannot allow that.

According to Atheistic Evolutionists, the causes of DNA changes and the causes of environmental changes must be the random physical forces. According to evolutionists, no intelligent agent is directing mutations and no intelligent agent is directing the weather. According to evolutionists, only the random forces of nature are directing the course of evolution. Yet they also insist Natural Selection directs the course of evolution by removing randomness. How can Natural Selection remove randomness if all the changes in DNA and all the changes in environment are random? Natural Selection cannot direct the course of evolution because **Natural Selection is a random effect, not a non-random cause.** As it turns out, changes in heredity and environment are caused by random forces. None of the supposed causes of evolution eliminates randomness. And that's fine if living organisms consist only of random biochemicals fashioned together into random patterns. But life requires more than random patterns; life requires intelligent instructions. **Random physical forces cannot create non-random, intelligent instructions.** Therefore, evolution did not create life; or improve life.

What evolution requires is for two independent forces, both of which are random, to direct the course of evolution so randomness is removed. This is the only way more-fit organisms could evolve. There would be no evolutionary winners if these two random forces couldn't have done that. Evolutionists admit the task seems daunting, but with enough time it would be bound to happen. Time becomes the trump card evolutionists throw down on the table. For evolution to win, it only needs enough time. What they don't understand is how time is the enemy of Natural Selection, not the ally. Let me explain with an illustration.

Evolution is A Craps Shoot

Suppose you want to win a billion dollars by playing the dice game Craps. (The name, "Craps," comes from either the French word *crapaud* meaning, "toad," or else the English word, "crabs," because the players traditionally squatted down on the ground to play. Personally, I think it's called, "Craps," because gamblers lose so much and yell, "crap," so often, that the name fits the game.) In this game, you roll two six-sided dice, each numbered one through six, and you bet on the outcome of your rolls. While you roll the dice together, each die is independent of the other in terms of what the numbers will be on each roll. Die One has no influence on Die Two. Die Two has no influence on Die One. The dice are independent, but whether you win or lose is dependent on the outcome of both dice together. The numbers must "fit" each other if you are to win. Likewise, the numbers on each roll have no influence on the numbers coming up in subsequent rolls, but unless your good rolls outnumber your bad rolls, you will lose more than you win. I won't go into detail about betting and winning because you probably know how this game works; but just to cite an example, you win if you roll a seven or an eleven on your first roll. The odds aren't in your favor, but you do have a chance, because it is a game of chance. If you roll two, three, or twelve on your first roll, you lose. Any other roll (four, five, six, eight, nine, and ten) becomes your, "point," the number you must repeat in a subsequent roll to win. This means there are some combination of rolls that are winners, some combinations of numbers that are losers, and some combinations of numbers that are neutral as far as winning or losing on the that particular roll. Whether a number is a winner or loser also depends on when it is rolled. A roll of seven on the first roll is a winner. However, if you roll something else on the first roll, and then roll a seven on a subsequent roll, you lose. Seven can be either a winning number or a losing number depending on when it is rolled.

Let's connect this to Natural Selection. Die One represents DNA Mutations and Die Two represents Environmental Changes. A DNA Mutation has no influence on selecting the environment, and Environmental Changes have no influence on selecting the order of nucleotides in the DNA. Each is independent of the other. For evolution to win, a random DNA Mutation must work in tandem with a random Environmental Change, so the combination allows for survivability. Some combinations help survivability, some combinations hurt survivability, and some combinations are neutral in terms of survivability. In the game of Craps, you are playing with two six-sided dice and the number of combinations is limited. With DNA Mutations and Environmental Changes, there are many, many more than six values for each factor. In fact, your "dice" would be many thousand-sided, and the combinations would be in the hundreds of millions. So, let us go back to the Craps Table to see how difficult it would be to win a billion dollars.

Actually, it wouldn't be difficult to win a billion dollars at the casino craps table if the casino let you bet a billion dollars at a time. To win a billion dollars by betting a billion dollars, all you need to do is be lucky on your first roll and win. One lucky win isn't probable, but it is possible. However, if you were trying to win a billion dollars at a casino with a betting limit of one-dollar, (insensibly fine gradations) then it would be impossible for it to happen. First, even if you experienced extreme luck and won every time you rolled, it would take you one billion rolls to win one billion dollars. (Assuming the payout was even.) That would take an extremely long time. If each roll could be completed in ten seconds, it would take you 317 years to make one billion rolls if you did it non-stop, without breaks, twenty-four hours a day, 365 days a year. I've not met any 317-year-old billionaires who made their fortunes at Craps. Now, back to evolution.

According to Darwin, evolution allows only "small bets" per roll. Remember, Natural Selection works in "insensibly fine gradations." In evolution, we are not dealing with six-sided dice, but "dice" with millions and millions of possible combinations. It would take trillions and trillions of years for Natural Selection to make this many "good rolls." It would take over $10^{40,858}$ times the age of the universe just to create the first minimally complex living cell. That's why so many evolutionists switched to Punctuated Equilibria. Punctuated Equilibria Evolution allows for some really "big bets" (large changes) between "rolls." The time factor becomes more favorable in Punctuated Equilibria Evolution, but the chance of repeatedly getting spurts of large numbers of good DNA Mutations and good Environmental Changes in the same "roll" becomes diminishingly small. The odds-factor is against Punctuated Equilibria Evolution, while the time-factor is against Darwinian Evolution. In either theory, the chances are impossible in our finite universe.

Evolutionists still insist all it takes is more time. But, that doesn't make sense. **MORE time makes random evolution LESS likely.** In the same way, the more time you spend playing Craps the more likely you are to lose money, the more time Natural Selection operates on life the more likely it is to destroy life. Ask any mathematician, statistician, casino operator, or professional gambler if this is not so. Unless you are playing a game where strategy is involved, such as Poker, you cannot win in the long run. If you spend too much time betting on games when the odds are greatly against you, you will lose. (If 99 out of 100 rolls of the dice caused you to lose, there isn't much hope of winning over time.) In the same way, if 99+% of mutations are harmful, there isn't much hope of evolving over time. In Poker, you might use strategy. You might keep a pair of Queens and throw in the other three cards hoping for another Queen or two, or another pair or triple, because you know that three Queens, or four Queens, or Two-Pair, or a Full-House will be better "Fitted-for-Gambling-Survival." That's strategy! In evolution, there can be no strategy. A DNA molecule can't decide to keep a pair of Cytosines and throw away a Guanine and an Adenine, hoping to get two more Cytosines because Cytosine might help make the sheep's wool grow longer and thicker. DNA can't do that because DNA can't decide anything. Then, even if it could, how would it know the next generation was going to experience longer and colder winters so that longer and thicker wool would be necessary? If the next generation of sheep experienced shorter, warmer winters, then the sheep with the DNA for longer, thicker wool would be selected against. And this is true for every hereditary trait. A trait that helps one generation may very well hurt the next generation. (Just like a seven might be good on one roll of the dice, but bad on another roll.) It would all depend on the random fluctuations in the environment. Exact timing would be necessary. It couldn't be left to chance. Nevertheless, everything about Natural Selection is chance—both the DNA changes and the environmental changes. Natural Selection doesn't cause evolution to happen. In fact, the term is self-contradicting. Nature cannot select for anything because nature has no ability to decide what to select, when to select, how to select, or why to select. When you select something, you base your choice on any number of factors your intelligence understands. Natural Selection cannot choose, because Natural Selection has no intelligence or understanding. **Natural Selection cannot select.** The more time you give Natural Selection, the less likely you are to get new and better organisms. If evolution could happen in giant, giant leaps, then evolution might have happened, but allowing the process of evolution to go on for hundreds of millions of years only decreases the chance anything would be alive today. Time is the enemy of evolution. The longer you gamble in a game of chance, the more likely you are to lose all your money. The longer Natural Selection operates, the more likely it is that all life becomes extinct.

Okay, you probably don't believe my opinion about the failure of Natural Selection. You probably think that, as a creationist, I don't even understand Natural Selection. (I've heard evolutionists say this about creationists.) Well, if you won't believe a creationist, will you believe these very prominent evolutionists? (With my emphasis added.)

Pierre-Paul Grassé: "The role assigned to natural selection in establishing adaptation, while speciously probable, is based on '**not one single sure datum**'. Paleontology (cf. the case of the transformation of the mandibular skeleton of the thecodont reptiles) **does not support it**; direct observation here and now of the genesis of a hereditary adaptation is **nonexistent**, except, as we have stated, in the case of bacteria and insects preadapted to resist viruses or drugs."[39]

Pierre-Paul Grassé was a Professor of Zoology at the Université de Clermont-Ferrand, France.

Arthur Koestler: "In the meantime, the educated public continues to believe that Darwin has provided all the relevant answers by the magic formula of random mutations plus natural selection—quite unaware of the fact that **random mutations have turned out to be irrelevant and natural selection a tautology**."[40]

Arthur Koestler was a Hungarian-born British journalist, author, and science editor.

Colin Patterson "**No one has ever produced a [new] species by mechanisms of natural selection**. No one has ever got near it and most of the current argument in neo-Darwinism is about this question."[41]

Colin Patterson was the Senior Paleontologist and Director of the British Museum of Natural History.

Roger Lewin: "It [natural selection] may have a stabilizing effect, but it does not promote speciation. **It is not a creative force**, as many people have suggested."[42]

Roger Lewin is the former News Editor of *Science* Magazine and a former staff member of *New Scientist* Magazine.

C. Loring Brace: "Readers of *American Scientist* may not realize the extent to which a major part of the field of biology and **almost all of paleontology has rejected Darwin's insights** concerning organic evolution. **Natural selection is dismissed as contributing nothing more than 'fine-tuning,'** and adaptation is largely ignored in practice."[43]

C. Loring Brace is a Professor of Anthropology at the University of Michigan.

William B. Provine: "**Natural selection does not act on anything, nor does it select (for, or against), force, maximize, create, modify, shape, operate, drive, favor, maintain, push or adjust. Natural selection does nothing. Natural selection as a natural force belongs in the insubstantial category already populated by the Necker/Stahl phlogiston or Newton's 'ether'... Having natural selection select is nifty because it excuses the necessity of talking about the actual causation of natural selection. Such talk was excusable for Charles Darwin, but is inexcusable for Darwinists now. Creationists have discovered our empty 'natural selection' language, and the 'actions' of natural selection make huge vulnerable targets.**"[44]

Dr. William B. Provine was Professor Emeritus of Biological Sciences, Cornell University, New York.

Without Natural Selection causing new species, evolution cannot happen; but Natural Selection does not exist as a cause. Natural selection causes nothing! It is a magician's Mumbo-Jumbo incantation meant to deceive and distract. Believe it if you want, but don't pretend you can believe it and be a scientist at the same time. Natural Selection is a religious belief of atheists.

Terminology Phenomenology

If you are an evolutionist, especially if you have been an evolutionist for many years, then what I just said sounds stupid. You know Natural Selection is a physical force. You know Natural Selection is not random. You know Natural Selection causes evolution. You know Natural Selection guides and directs evolution to eliminate randomness. Your belief in Natural Selection is so central to your thinking that you cannot imagine how anyone, especially an atheist professor of evolutionary biology, could say, "Natural selection as a natural force belongs in the insubstantial category already populated by the Necker/Stahl phlogiston or Newton's 'ether'...."

You think the same thing about evolution. You know it is true. You just cannot imagine how anyone could say evolution is not true. In your mind, evolution is so true, evolution is so proven, and evolution is so obvious, you cannot begin to process the thought that you are wrong.

I know you think this, because these were the thoughts I had when I was first confronted by a Christian who didn't believe in evolution. (I was in the Navy, and although I had been a Theistic Evolutionist for as long as I could remember, I had just recently become a Christian.) One day a shipmate and his wife told me they were raising their children in the truth—Creation was true, and Evolution was a lie. I didn't say anything because I didn't want to be rude... and because his wife often invited me over for meals with them, and she was a great cook. However, I did think to myself, "How quaint! How backward! How old-fashioned! How can anyone in the 20th century believe evolution isn't true?" I could not comprehend how anyone could think such thoughts.

At that time, I didn't realize how my belief in evolution rested entirely on 0° and 2° Perceptions. I had never looked for the 1° Perception Evidence required by science. I just believed the "experts." The names "Evolution" and "Natural Selection" were so ingrained in my mind, I thought they were actual physical forces. My 0° Perception was suffering from Terminology Phenomenology. This is a very common affliction in scientists. Terminology Phenomenology is when we come up with a name for some unexplained event or phenomenon. Then, the very fact we have a name for it, the name becomes the "proof" it exists as we think it does. We created the term "Natural Selection," and the idea became self-fulfilling. The same thing is true for the word "Evolution." We gave a name to a process we wanted to believe, and the name itself became our "proof." Every time we see, hear, read, or say these terms, they reinforce our own belief they are true. With enough time and enough self-reinforcement, our minds can't think otherwise.

Even now, if you are an evolutionist, you may be having a problem seeing how this works. That's why I like giving examples and illustrations. In this case, I will give a real-life example of Terminology Phenomenology. You have probably heard of El Niño. (Spanish for "Little Boy.") El Niño is a weather phenomenon that supposedly causes all kinds of strange and extreme weather events all over the world. Meteorologists often explain how a drought in one place was caused by El Niño, or how flooding in another place was caused by El Niño, or how an outbreak of tornadoes somewhere else was caused by El Niño. El Niño certainly seems to be a powerful force. But, does El Niño exist? Is there such a force as El Niño? To answer that, we need to find out what El Niño is. El Niño is defined as an area of warm water, warmer than normal, in the central and east-central equatorial Pacific Ocean.

It is a seasonal phenomenon, and it is counterbalanced by La Niña, (Spanish for "Little Girl.") which is described as an area of cool water, cooler than normal, over that same area of the Pacific. El Niño and La Niña have become such accepted terms in our vocabulary that we think of them as being the causes of weather patterns. We almost give them human qualities. (We talk about "Mother Nature" the same way.) In fact, I'll bet even now, you don't see why I'm using this illustration. I know you're telling yourself, "Certainly, El Niño and La Niña exist, and certainly El Niño and La Niña are the causes of world-wide weather events." Well, let's be real scientists and investigate to see if this is true.

What causes El Niño? If El Niño is an area of warm water in the Pacific, what causes it? The sun is the ultimate source of heat, of course, but the sun doesn't experience seasonal warming and cooling trends. That means something else must also be involved. Where does El Niño get its heat? The only way water in the Pacific could become warmer, is to absorb heat from warmer water and warmer air somewhere else. Likewise, what causes La Niña? Where does its heat go? The only way water in the Pacific could become cooler, is to lose heat to cooler water and cooler air somewhere else. It's called heat exchange. Heat energy is never created or destroyed in the process. So, if we blame El Niño for causing worldwide weather events, aren't we ultimately blaming whatever it is that causes El Niño? If we blame La Niña for causing worldwide weather events, aren't we blaming whatever it is that causes La Niña? Why don't those causes have names? And even if they did, couldn't we blame the causes that cause the causes that cause El Niño and La Niña? (Steven Dill's Law of Causes: The Cause of the Cause, is the Cause.) In the end, we discover we are blaming warmth for causing warmth. (In other words, we explain nothing.)

Yes, but still, we are so familiar with the names El Niño and La Niña that we can't divorce our minds from the idea they are real things that cause worldwide weather patterns. So, let me give an example of some "things" that don't have name familiarity. I think you will see why these "things" aren't the causes of weather events.

I live in Louisville, Kentucky. Louisville is in the Ohio River Valley, which runs in a southwest to northeast direction. Since the prevailing winds come from the west, most of our weather comes from the west and southwest as it moves up the Ohio Valley. Paducah, Kentucky is about 175 miles south and west of Louisville. This means the weather conditions Paducah experiences, are often experienced in Louisville a day or two later. I have noticed over the years, that when Paducah experiences warm weather, we experience warm weather the next day or two. When Paducah experiences cool weather, we experience cool weather the next day or two. Because of this, I have named the phenomenon of warm weather in Paducah, "El Gordo." (The Fat Man) I have also named the phenomenon of cool weather in Paducah, "La Gorda." (The Fat Lady) This means El Gordo causes Louisville to be warm; right? It also means La Gorda causes Louisville to be cool; right? Well, if El Niño and La Niña cause warming and cooling in other places, why can't El Gordo and La Gorda cause warming and cooling in Louisville?

Of course, I am setting you up with a trap. If you agree El Gordo and La Gorda cause weather patterns in Louisville, I will laugh at you, and tell you how wrong you are. El Gordo and La Gorda don't cause weather patterns in Louisville; El Alto and La Corta (The Tall Man and the Short Lady) do that. What are El Alto and La Corta? They are the names I give to the phenomena of warm and cool weather patterns over Owensboro, Kentucky. (Owensboro is located about half-way between Paducah and Louisville.) So, El Gordo and La Gorda cause El Alto and La Corta, which cause warmer and cooler weather in Louisville. Yes? No! El Alto and La Corta cause El Hombre Feliz (The Happy Man) and La Mujer Triste (The Sad Woman). El Hombre Feliz and La Mujer Triste are the names of warmer and cooler weather patterns over Hardinsburg, Kentucky. (Hardinsburg is about half-way between Owensboro and Louisville.) What names do I give the warmer and cooler weather patterns where I live? El Idioto and La Idiota, of course. (I won't tell you what they mean. I'm sure you can guess.)

Giving names to intermediary events and conditions doesn't explain the cause of anything. This is true of El Niño and La Niña, and it is true of Natural Selection. Natural Selection is a name we use to describe something we believe, but as Dr. Provine said, "Natural Selection does nothing."

Q: What is Natural Selection?
A: It is the Survival of the Fittest.

Q: What are the Fittest?
A: The Fittest are the organisms that survive.

Natural Selection is the name we give to the phenomenon of "The Survival of the Survivors," but that explains nothing. Do organisms survive because they are survivors, or are they survivors because they survive? Is it a cause or an effect?

The same thing is true for Evolution.

Q: What is Evolution?
A: Evolution is the development of new species caused by slow biological changes over time.

Q: What does Evolution do?
A: Evolution causes slow biological changes over time so that new species develop.

This means the slow change in species over time, is what causes species to change slowly over time. In other words, Evolution causes Evolution. Evolution becomes both the cause and the effect of evolution. The word "Evolution" sounds good, but it explains nothing. The terms "Natural Selection" and "Evolution" are stumbling blocks to the truth.

The point of all this is to show how our beliefs can be wrong, even when we are sure we are right. Sadly, 0° Perception can blind us to truth revealed by 1° Perception. So can 2° Perception. When our minds are blinded to the truth, we are unable to recognize the truth as the truth. We must train our minds to allow truth to stand on its own and not be molded to fit our presupposed beliefs. Too often we bend the facts to fit our beliefs, rather than bending our beliefs to fit the facts. Freeing ourselves from the presuppositions that have been hammered into our thinking is difficult. It won't come quickly, especially if you have been an evolutionist for a long time, but the only way to discover the truth is to let the truth be the truth. If you are an atheist, then what I am about to say will seem equally stupid. You cannot know the truth until you know THE TRUTH. The Bible tells us this. As an unbeliever, you are blinded to the truth.

John 8:32 "And you will know the truth, and the truth will set you free." (ESV)

John 16:13a "When the Spirit of truth comes, he will guide you into all the truth," (ESV)

2 Corinthians 4:4a "In their case the god of this world has blinded the minds of the unbelievers," (ESV)

John 18:37b "...For this purpose I was born and for this purpose I have come into the world—to bear witness to the truth. Everyone who is of the truth listens to my voice." (ESV)

1 Timothy 2:4 (God) "desires all people to be saved and to come to the knowledge of the truth." (ESV)

As I said in the first part of this book, I am not interested in winning arguments; I am interested in winning souls. Even if this book doesn't convince you evolution is a lie, I pray it convinces you Jesus Christ is the Way, the Truth, and the Life.

False Supposition 4: Evolution Permits Unlimited Change

Some evolutionists dismiss creationists when we demand an explanation for abiogenesis. They say evolution has nothing to do with abiogenesis. Instead, it deals only with the development of new species from the already-formed, first ancestral organism. Not all evolutionists feel that way; especially Atheistic Evolutionists. They know they must provide naturalistic answers for the origin of life, because if they don't, it allows for the supernatural creation of life. As a result of "believing-anything-but-God," they propose many different recipes for abiogenesis. Laughably, there are so many conflicting opinions that creationists can easily dispute any one of them. All we need to do is quote the other evolutionists who dispute them. There is no agreement on how the first ancestral organism got here. In fact, they can't even agree on what it was. (And remember, science must be able to prove what it was, not just what it might have been.) Some think the first lifeform consisted of amino acids, some say it was DNA. Some think it was lipids because lipids can form microspheres that superficially resemble simple cells. Many now believe RNA was the original form of life because RNA is simpler than DNA. (DNA is a double-stranded molecule, while RNA is single-stranded. Both DNA and RNA use the five-carbon sugar ribose in their structures, but DNA uses deoxyribose, which has one oxygen atom removed. Hence, the name "deoxy.")

RNA has some very interesting abilities. RNA can store instructions, RNA can act as a catalyst in some biochemical reactions, and some short RNA molecules can self-replicate. This makes RNA the ideal candidate for the first lifeform. Other evolutionists believe RNA is too complex and too fragile to have started the process by itself. They say TNA (Threose Nucleic Acid) was the first lifeform because it is simpler. (TNA uses a four-carbon sugar molecule.) Others think even TNA couldn't do it; so, they say it was GNA (Glycol Nucleic Acid) because it is even simpler—It uses a three-carbon sugar molecule. Another suggestion is PNA (Peptide Nucleic Acid—another three-carbon sugar molecule.) Of course, none of these hypotheses solve the problem. They don't explain the origin of the instructions, they have never been shown to create life, and they don't simulate the actual conditions and ingredients present in the primordial earth, atmosphere, or oceans. Self-Replicating RNA, TNA, GNA, and PNA are human-designed, artificially-produced nucleic acids, created under very specific conditions determined by their human creators. They were created by intelligent designers. Plus, there is no evidence they existed millions of years ago. Evolutionists are making an appeal to something that has never been observed in the past, to explain what they speculate happened in the past. This is not science because it uses unobserved causes as explanations for unobserved effects. Yes, there COULD HAVE BEEN molecules like them in the primordial ooze, but without observable evidence, COULD HAVE BEEN doesn't prove anything. It could have been the Zuurtanes.

In truth, it doesn't matter what chemical(s) you think started evolution because one way or another, it eventually had to reach the stage of the DNA-RNA-Ribosome-Amino Acid-Protein lifeforms of today. For the supposed ancestor of all life to evolve into the millions of different species today, it had to be able to evolve the billions of different biological organisms, systems, organs, tissues, cells, organelles, and biomolecules found in its supposed descendants. The only way this could happen is if its DNA instructions could mutate into all the instructions needed for all those new organisms, systems, organs, tissues, cells, organelles, and biomolecules. Just think about it. The first DNA life form had nothing at all resembling eyes, or skeletons, or wings, or opposable thumbs. Yet, from its simple DNA instructions, all the DNA instructions for everything living had to evolve. The quantity and quality of DNA instruction-changes had to be virtually unlimited to produce the virtually unlimited differences seen in the lifeforms today. If the mechanics of evolution limited the quantity and quality of DNA instruction-change, then evolution would have never happened.

So, let's test this idea with my own monkey-simulator. Just as the "Shakespearian Monkeys" had to type every piece of Shakespeare's works, my monkey-simulator must type all the books that have ever been printed. To make things easier, I'll not factor abiogenesis into my monkey-simulator. I will start with an intact and fully functional monkey-simulator. I will start my monkey-simulator with a very simple sentence (DNA instruction) already written. I will start with a very simple sentence because evolutionists assume our supposed ancestor was very simple. (They talk about how the first common ancestor consisted of simple biochemical monomers and polymers.) So, I'll let my "monkey" start with a correctly written, correctly spelled, grammatically correct sentence that qualifies as an instruction. What it instructs, how the instructions are understood and implemented, and how it replicates are irrelevant questions for the sake of this argument. Let's just assume it was possible.

What my "monkey" needs to do, starting from that one perfect sequence, is to re-type it over and over and over again until all the books in the world are created. The results are tested one word at a time. My monkey-simulator won't wait until thousands of bad sentences (bad DNA instructions) are generated before testing whether it is "fit to be read." That can't happen in real life. Reproducing the next generation depends on the survival of the current generation. So, in my monkey-simulator, the ability to re-type a new sentence depends on the old sentence being correctly written, correctly spelled, and grammatically correct; ("fit-to-be-read") otherwise, the simulation fails. If that happens, my "monkey" can't reproduce new "monkeys."

In my simulator, the words simulate the biomolecules, the sentences are the organelles, the paragraphs are the cells, the pages are the tissues, the chapters are the organs, the divisions are the systems, and the books are the organisms. Let me put this into a graph to make it easier.

"Words"   = Biomolecules
"Sentences" = Organelles
"Paragraphs" = Cells
"Pages"   = Tissues
"Chapters"   = Organs
"Divisions" = Systems
"Books"   = Organisms

What my "monkeys" must do, is change the "ancestral" sentence a word at a time, generation by generation, until all the books ever printed are created. Copy errors are certainly needed, but it must be done at the word level. "Monkey-Mutations" can alter a word, add a word, or remove a word, but it could happen only one word at a time. (Evolutionists speak in terms of mutations causing small changes in the nucleotides. This is why evolution moves in insensibly fine gradations from one generation to the next.) The more random errors my "monkey-simulator" makes per generation, the more unlikely the results will remain correctly written, correctly spelled, grammatically correct, and qualify as instructions. If my monkey-simulator makes more than a few mistakes per generation, the "book" won't be fit to be read. And if the "book" can't be read, it can't be replicated. (My "monkeys" would die.) Can my monkey-simulator accomplish this task? Of course not! If it took the Shakespearian Monkey-Simulator 2,737,850 million, billion, billion, billion simulated "monkey-years" to type four words, even without factoring in mutational death, (bad DNA sequences) there is no hope for my monkey-simulator to type millions of books within the entire energy-life span of the universe. So, while a few mistakes are necessary, my monkey-simulator proves the QUANTITY of DNA mutational changes is limited. In real life, evolution would end because life would end!

Evolutionists counter this argument by pointing out that errors in books don't necessarily make them unfit to read. If you picked up a book with the title, "*Little Red Riding Hood and the Big Bad Wof*," you would instantly recognize the typo in the title wouldn't make the book unreadable. That's true, but that's only because you filter the words through your intelligence, and mentally make the correction. DNA mutations can't do that. As biomolecules are constructed and assembled, the machinery in the cells can only follow the exact instructions from the DNA. The machinery can't intelligently reinterpret what the "sentences" are supposed to say. If I gave you a recipe for cookies, and it called for adding one cup of "suger," you would be able to make the cookies by correcting the error in my recipe. You would add one cup of sugar. That can't be done at the intracellular-machinery level. If the next step in building a biomolecule called for a suger molecule, the process would stop because it would never be able to find a suger molecule. There is no such thing as a suger molecule. The machinery can only follow orders; it can't reinterpret orders. This explains why 99+% of random mutations are harmful or fatal. A few very, very minor changes (insensibly fine) might slip by, but it wouldn't take much change before the process of evolution came to a screeching halt. The QUALITY of DNA mutational changes is limited.

My monkey-simulator shows how the mechanics of evolution would limit both the quantity and quality of allowable mutations. This puts evolution in a tough spot. Charles Darwin knew evolution required innumerable, insensibly fine changes between species. He also knew there was a limit to the changes Artificial Selection could produce. Human-caused changes were limited in both quantity and quality. Despite that, he believed the changes caused by Natural Selection were limitless. Random evolution could generate new Species, new Genera, new Families, new Orders, and on and on. Man couldn't do that. Randomness could do what intelligence couldn't.

If you stop to think about that concept, (randomness being able to do something intelligence can't) you will quickly realize how absurd it is. If you had ten dice and wanted to have all ten sitting on your desk with their one-side up, then your chance is 1 in 60,466,176 if you relied on randomly tossing the dice. Most likely, you would have to roll them millions of times before you would have a roll where all ten dice landed as ones. How long would it take? It would take years. (There are only about thirty-million seconds in a year.) But, what if I set a time limit of one minute? What are the odds you could randomly roll ten dice and get them to land all ones within one minute? Not very good!

Now, what are the odds you could take those ten dice and intentionally (intelligently) place them as all ones in less than one minute? It would be an easy task; a five-year old child could do it. An intelligent agent could easily accomplish what randomness couldn't. So, the idea random evolution could do what intelligent breeders couldn't do, is nonsense. No matter how many centuries man had been breeding sheep, and cows, and goats, and horses, and dogs; and no matter how many variations had been developed, breeders knew there was a limit to how much change was allowed. Sheep remained sheep. Cows remained cows. Horses remained horses. The same is true today. In spite of some wildly radical claims made by some wildly radical evolutionists, fruit flies, bacteria, soil nematodes, mice, and all the other organisms they have experimented with, have remained within their predesigned limits. The scientific observation is this: There is a limit to how far organisms can change. The underlying reason is because there is a limit to how far the DNA instructions for organisms can change. Too much change in the instructions, and the organisms die. The same is true for words, sentences, paragraphs, *etc.* in a book. Too many random changes, and the book is no longer fit to read. Science proves my monkey-simulator was correct; **there is a limit to the quantity and quality of allowable DNA mutations in real life.**

So, how can evolutionists claim there is no limit to the amount of good changes evolution can accomplish when almost all DNA changes (mutations) are fatal or harmful? It's easy. As Mary Poppins sang, "A spoonful of suger…" I mean, "sugar helps the medicine go down."[45] All you need is to add a little bit of truth and it makes swallowing the lie, oh-so-much easier. Actually, it takes two spoonfuls of sugar to swallow evolution's bitter pill. The first little bit of truth is the fact that mutations ARE seemingly unlimited. Oh yes, scientists can point to all kinds of strange and exotic mutations they have created in their laboratory experiments over the decades. Their favorite seems to be the fruit fly. (*Drosophila melanogaster*) There are mutant fruit flies with an extra set of wings. Some have no wings. Some have curly wings. Others have legs growing out of their heads where antennae should be. Some have orange eyes instead of the normal red. Some have white eyes. And some even have no eyes. By subjecting all kinds of plants and animals to a variety of mutagenic agents, scientists have created all kinds of mutations. Repeated observations prove there is seemingly no limit to the QUANTITY of mutations that can develop. But that has nothing to do with proving evolution happened. Evolution requires good (beneficial) mutations and these laboratory-induced mutations are overwhelmingly harmful.

Okay, that's the first "spoonful of sugar." What's the second? They try to convince us that beneficial mutations are easy to produce. Scientist now display the great number of Genetically Modified Organisms (GMO) they have created. They have created corn that produces more ears per stalk, rice that makes vitamin A, sugar beets that produce more sugar, and soybeans with greater resistant to insects. Since the DNA of these organisms is changed, they are technically mutations. However, unlike the harmful mutations that happen naturally, these are beneficial. We now have mutant bacteria that can produce human insulin. Human growth hormone can be produced in mice by a simple DNA insertion. These mutations are QUALITATIVE changes in DNA. Repeated observations seem to prove there is virtually no limit to the beneficial things scientists can do with DNA mutations. Since laboratory-produced beneficial mutations seem limitless, evolutionists want us to believe that naturally-produced beneficial mutations are limitless. But there is a difference! These beneficial mutations were intelligently selected; not naturally selected. They didn't come about by struggling to survive. This means they don't reproduce the conditions needed for evolution. Just as Stanley Miller's apparatus didn't reproduce the actual conditions of the past, these laboratory experiments don't reproduce the actual conditions of the past. This means they don't prove anything about the past.

Those are the two, "spoonfuls of sugar." What is the "medicine" they want you to swallow? They want you to believe large numbers of beneficial mutations are the same thing as evolution. All it takes is a large quantity of beneficial DNA mutations, and you prove evolution. Now, this is a logical argument if, and only if, a large quantity of beneficial mutations is the only factor involved in evolution. But large numbers of beneficial mutations aren't the only things needed for evolution. Large numbers of beneficial mutations are necessary for evolution, but large numbers of beneficial mutations are not sufficient for evolution. The reason they aren't sufficient for evolution is because mutations have no control over the environments that cause them to be beneficial. Longer, thicker wool on sheep doesn't cause the winters to become longer and colder. Again, the longer and thicker wool mutation would not benefit sheep unless, by chance, the winters were longer and colder. Since DNA mutations don't control the weather, a mutation for longer and thicker wool would be harmful if the weather got warmer. It doesn't matter how many beneficial mutations you generate. Beneficial mutations are beneficial only if the environments remain favorable. To create a new species, there would have to be a succession of many beneficial mutations, for many different biological components, coupled with a succession of beneficial environments favorable to all those mutations, without any reversals in the process, for a long enough period of time. What are the chances you can get a large number of successive finely-gradated beneficial mutations, and finely-gradated beneficial environmental changes for long periods of time? Not very good; natural mutations are almost always harmful, and environments are always changing.

Laboratory-caused mutations are beneficial only because they are created by design. Naturally-caused mutations are harmful because they are created by chance. It is only because intelligent scientists can decode and select beneficial DNA instructions, that they can create beneficial DNA mutations. They use intelligence every step of the way. It is only because intelligent scientists create and control the environments that their beneficial DNA mutations can survive. They don't have to struggle to survive. Without the intelligent control of both the mutations and the environments, their organisms wouldn't survive. Again, it screams out, "Intelligence is required!" I have yet to see a GMO project that relies solely on random mutations and random conditions. (I don't think I would want to eat what it produced.) The repeated observation is this: It takes INTELLIGENCE to create beneficial DNA mutations. It takes INTELLIGENCE to control the environments needed for those beneficial DNA mutations.

Evolutionists won't agree with this. They say the problem is solved because there were unlimited numbers of random mutations in the past. With an unlimited number of random mutations in the past, some beneficial mutations would be bound to happen. This idea is unworkable in real life. Unlimited random mutations can happen only if there is an unlimited amount of resources available. If your Petri dish has only enough growth medium to grow ten generations of bacteria, there is no chance for your experiment to produce a new species of bacteria if it takes 10,000 generations to do it. How many generations would it take for the bacteria to evolve into elephants? It's easy to say, "It's easy to evolve bacteria into elephants." It isn't so easy when you stop to think about what would be required in terms of time, space, matter, and energy. I'll believe in evolution when scientists inoculate Petri dishes with bacteria and they grow into elephants. You can't have unlimited beneficial mutations if you don't have unlimited time, space, matter, and energy. There has not been enough time, space, matter, and energy in this universe to evolve elephants from bacteria. The "Petri dish" is too small. That was why so many atheists hated the idea of the Big Bang. It limited the amount of available time, space, matter, and energy to an infinitesimal fraction of an infinitesimal fraction of an infinitesimal fraction of what was needed.

If unlimited numbers of random mutations could produce unlimited changes, they would overwhelmingly produce unlimited harmful changes. This is exactly what is observed when random mutations occur in nature; they are harmful. Unlimited harmful changes would lead to species death, not species evolution. If random mutations were beneficial, there would be no warnings about x-rays, cosmic rays, asbestos, lead, formaldehyde, chloroform, benzene, and a whole host of other chemicals found in our environment. Why don't evolutionists tell their children to play down at the abandoned chemical plant or the nuclear reactor? If random mutations could produce unlimited benefits, it would be good for their children to expose themselves to mutagens. Thankfully, there aren't any scientists telling their children to do that, so I'm going to assume they don't believe there are good mutagens in nature.

Ignoring these scientific facts about mutations, evolutionists today still suppose there is no limit to the beneficial changes that occur over time. Today we know this supposition is contradicted by repeated scientific observations. No scientist has observed the development of a new and better species by a long series of insensibly fine, beneficial, random mutations. Scientific observations don't fit the theory. In the old days, back before the philosophy and definition of science changed, this would have put the Theory of Evolution into the realm of philosophy or faith; not science.

False Supposition 5: Randomness Causes Evolution

Above all else, Darwin's disciples must exclude any intelligent agent from the mechanics of evolution. They need something to be the cause(s) of DNA mutations and something to be the cause(s) of environmental changes. They need something to direct evolution from small and simple organisms to large and complex organisms in an irreversible fashion. However, they can't let an Intelligent Agent be involved anywhere in the process. That is why they appeal to Natural Selection. They believe Natural Selection is the random force that eliminates randomness. How randomness eliminates randomness is never explored. They don't want you to worry about that little detail.

They also don't want you to worry about another little detail: **If the Theory of Evolution depends on randomness, it must be excluded as a scientific theory.** If the Theory of Evolution depends on randomness, it shouldn't be taught in the science class. Why not? It's because there is no scientific test for randomness. You can't scientifically prove a phenomenon or event was random, without observing the cause. Evolutionists say the changes in the DNA and the changes in the environment were random; no intelligent agent caused them. Otherwise, they would have to agree there was an Intelligent Designer. The problem is you can't test for randomness. Randomness can't be falsified. Randomness can't be measured. Randomness is not a force. Randomness is not an object. Randomness has no mass. It has no size. It has no charge. It does not occupy space. It has no units of measure. Science can't explain something it can't measure. (How much do five units of randomness weigh? How much energy do they contain? What color are they?) No scientific test can prove an effect was randomly caused if it can't observe the cause. Even if it appears random, that is not proof it was random. (An Intelligent Agent could intentionally make it appear random.) On the other hand, if it appears designed, then the rules of probability and statistics can provide a way of testing for design. Randomness can't be tested, but design can. Here is an illustration of this:

Let's say I lifted a scarf off a table to reveal a single, six-sided die (like from our Craps Table) sitting on the table-top. The number on the top of the die is three. Now, tell me if the number is three because I randomly rolled the die and got a three, or if I intentionally placed the die with the three-side up? Since you didn't observe the cause, you can't prove the cause. All you can see is the effect. It wouldn't be much less scientific to claim it was random than to claim it was designed. It is frightfully easy for a random roll of a die to land as a three. The chance of randomly rolling a three with one die is 1 in 6. (The chance an intelligent agent could place one die with the three-side up is 1 in 1, if that's what he wants to do.) But, what if I lifted the scarf to reveal two dice, and both were threes? Would you be able to tell how they got that way? Would you be able to falsify the theory I intentionally placed two dice, three-side up? (Again, you did not witness how the dice got that way.) No, you couldn't do that. The only clue you have, is that it is less likely to roll two threes with two dice, than it is to roll one three with one die. The chance of rolling two threes with two dice is 1 in 36. (The chance an intelligent agent could place two dice, both with their three-side up, is 1 in 1, if that is what he wanted to do.) Now, what if there were three dice, all with their three-side up? Well, it's not impossible for a random toss of three dice to land all threes; the chance is 1 in 216. (The chance an intelligent agent could place three dice, all with their three-side up, is also 1 in 1, if that is what he wanted to do.) However, it would be less likely to happen unless I had made multiple tosses of the dice, which could have been possible because you weren't a witness of how the three dice were caused to be threes. It might have been random, but the odds are greater that I placed them that way. What if there were four dice and all four were threes? The chance would be 1 in 1,296 they got that way by a random toss. You still wouldn't know if it was random, but logic tells you the arrangement of the dice was more likely designed. It begins to look designed. If I lifted the scarf to reveal five dice that were all threes, the odds would be 1 in 7,776 a random toss caused it. If I used six dice, the odds would be 1 in 45,656 that randomness caused it. It looks even more like design. If I used ten dice, the odds would be 1 in 60,466,176. If all ten dice were threes, it would certainly appear more like design than luck. We begin to see a trend: **The less likely an unlikely event can happen by randomness, the more likely it can happen only by design.** Now, what if I revealed one-hundred dice, all with their three-side up? The chance of that happening by a random roll is 1 in 6.5×10^{77}. This arrangement of one-hundred dice looks so designed, you'd be a fool to believe it was random. The only sensible way you might consider randomness as the cause, is to assume I made lots and lots of rolls of the one-hundred dice until I finally got all one-hundred to land as threes and then stopped. But how long would it have taken me? If I started when the universe began, and I could make 10^{43} rolls per second, (one roll per Planck Time) then I would just now be on my $5 \times 10^{60\text{th}}$ roll. That means I have more than 10^{17} times the age of the universe to go. (Evolutionists say they know a way the process could be hastened. Simply roll all one-hundred dice, pick out the dice that don't land as a three, and then keep re-rolling them until they are threes. Their rule is: When a die lands as a three, it is selected to remain in a "safe place" where it is never rolled again. This would certainly speed things up, but it wouldn't simulate the evolutionary process of DNA mutations in living organisms. Since mutations are random, there is no way previous good DNA sequences could be protected from later bad mutations. Good nucleotides couldn't be set aside in a "safe place" while waiting for the rest of the good nucleotides to mutate.)

Which cause is more reasonable: The one-hundred dice are due to randomness, or the one-hundred dice are due to design? One-hundred dice sitting on a table with all of them being threes certainly looks designed. But, remember Francis Crick's advice: You must always keep in mind that what you see is not designed. No matter how designed it appears, you just must keep believing it is Apparent Design. To believe what you want to believe, you need to ignore the mathematical test (probability and statistics) of this event. (Which is what evolutionists did to Fred Hoyle.) Mathematics would prove the one-hundred dice got that way by design. Design is testable. In this case, what appears so obviously designed, is designed. If this is true for one hundred dice that appear designed, how much more so for the six billion nucleotides in our DNA that clearly appear designed?

To prove an effect is random, you must prove a non-random (intelligent) agent couldn't cause the same effect. Remember, science requires that statements must be falsifiable. You must prove an intelligent agent couldn't place one-hundred dice, all with their three-side up. You couldn't prove that. But, here is why randomness can't be tested: What if I lifted the scarf and the one-hundred dice were not all threes? Instead, what if they were more-or-less evenly divided ones through sixes? Would it be random? It would look random, but could you prove it was random? You could prove it was random only if you could prove it was impossible for me to place each die with the number I wanted. In this case, if I had wanted to place the dice in the exact locations, with the exact numbers you now see, I could have intentionally placed them that way. It would look random, but it wouldn't be. You can't prove something is random just because it looks random. There is always a chance an intelligent agent can cause the appearance of randomness. An intelligent agent can cause Apparent Randomness. (For example, a coded message that appears to be random but actually contains intelligence.) Not being able to detect intelligence in a message is not proof the message is random. Even if you can't detect the intelligence, it doesn't mean there is no intelligence. The Navajo Code-Talkers who transmitted military information during World War II, transmitted radio messages in their native tongue. This was no mere code. This was an entirely different language the Japanese couldn't translate. The Japanese cryptographers couldn't identify the intelligence that was transmitted. To them, it was nothing but unintelligible syllables. They missed the intelligence, but the intelligence was there. Not recognizing design is not proof design doesn't exist. This means evolutionists cannot prove evolution was random. Since the Theory of Evolution absolutely requires evolution to be random, (Evolutionists can't allow intelligence to be a factor.) the Theory of Evolution depends on a mechanism that cannot be scientifically tested.

Look again at what Francis Crick said about design:

"Biologists must constantly keep in mind that what they see was not designed...."

Let me counter his statement with my statement about randomness:

"Biologists must constantly keep in mind that what they see was not random...."

How can you scientifically determine which one of these two statements is true? You can't prove the first statement is true! No matter how un-designed something may appear, it doesn't prove it is truly un-designed. No matter how unarranged something may seem, you can't prove some intelligent agent didn't arrange it that way for a reason or purpose unknown to you. Which one of these sets of six letters is not random?

WUITKZ	ABYJBF	VNWHCG
QNFIXC	BPBSCP	KOYFCW
PQBOJZ	ZVKCXV	GWTNRK
VQKCSH	PFFTVK	JIRRVR
QEBSPQ	COVIOG	EXHQWV
MMUCFD	HWLIVO	YBLQYV
LCUFBR	VNETZJ	UTROWV
IZCVXC	ARMCET	LPEWJZ

Can't tell? Okay, what if I told you my father's name was **B**ert, my mother's name was **P**eggy, my older brother's name is **B**ert, my name is **S**teven, my younger brother's name is **C**lifford, and my sister's name is **P**atricia? Now can you tell which set of six letters I typed by design? It certainly seems easier to believe an intelligent agent could create the appearance of randomness, than it is for a random force to create the appearance of design. This is especially true when the apparent design contains the actual instructions for creating actual, living organisms.

Do you remember my Domino Universe? If you didn't witness the dominoes as they fell, you couldn't prove from their arrangement whether they fell that way, or I intentionally arranged them that way. **Unless you were an eyewitness to the creation of life, you have no way of proving whether the chemicals of life were randomly arranged to create life or intelligently arranged to create life.** Science can't prove the necessary DNA changes were random.

So, while it is impossible to prove randomness, it is possible to prove design. Design can be tested. Instead of a straight line of a hundred "fallen-down" dominoes, imagine there were three thousand "fallen-down" dominoes arranged in cursive fashion that spelled:

inthebeginninggodcreatedtheheavenandtheearth

Obviously, this arrangement of fallen-dominoes would not be random; it reveals intelligent information. Even if the dominoes fell according to the laws of gravity and motion, so that the 1st domino knocked down the 2nd domino, which knocked down the 3rd domino, and on and on until the 2,999th domino knocked down the 3,000th domino, it is apparent the laws of gravity and motion didn't arrange the dominoes in the first place. Such an arrangement of dominoes would prove it was caused by an intelligent agent; it contains intelligence.

An intelligent agent could line up a hundred dominoes in a straight line that contains no intelligence. (A design intended not to contain intelligence, such as a false-code designed to throw off a cryptographer.) An intelligent agent could line up three thousand dominoes in a cursive line that spelled Genesis 1:1. Francis Crick would look at this long cursive line of dominoes and tell us we must constantly keep in mind it was not designed. Francis Crick wasn't concerned with the truth.

The sad truth for evolutionists is that life is a much longer line of "dominoes" (nucleotides) than the letters in, "In the beginning God created the heavens and the earth." Randomness cannot do what evolutionists say it did, and even if it could, it would still be a scientifically untestable event. The Theory of Evolution is not science, and it should not be taught in the science class.

False Supposition 6: Homology Implies Relationship

"Homology Implies Relationship," is another standard argument for the Theory of Evolution that fails scientific testability. Homologies are similarities in physical structures seen in the different taxonomic groups. Homologies can also consist of similarities of biochemicals, such as proteins and DNA sequences. An example of homologous structures is the five sets of bones in the wings of a bat, the flippers of a whale, and the hands of apes and men. Because they are physically similar, evolutionists believe these species are historically evolved. The pattern of five sets of bones supposedly arose millions of years ago in an ancestor common to bats, whales, apes, and men. Since that time, however, the descendants of the supposed common ancestor have evolved into different species. The differences between these species are caused by the accumulation of mutations over the years. Thus, the more time that has elapsed since the common ancestor, the more mutational differences there would be. The similarities that remain are the indicators of a common heritage. Species which share many homologies are thought to be more closely related than species sharing only a few homologies. We share some features with whales and bats, but we share many more homologies with apes. Because of this, apes and man are considered more closely related to each other than they are to whales and bats. Darwin believed a classification based on homologous structures was a classification based on physical kinship.

Evolutionists believe all organisms are physically related. They believe the first species changed into other species over time. Those species changed into other species over time, and those species changed into other species over time. They believe the degree of physical similarity between organisms is an indication of evolutionary descent. They assume evolution is true. From this they conclude that homologies should be found in the fossil record. Remember, this is what Darwin predicted. So, when they find homologies in the fossil record, they claim it proves evolution. **In fact, of all the beliefs of evolutionists, this is the most foundational and the most mentally entrenched conviction.** It is believed by all evolutionists; no exceptions. It is so ingrained in their thought process, they just can't imagine how we creationists miss this point. Surely, we are blind or three days dead (or evil) not to grasp this most obvious of clues. To them it is the most self-evident and self-reinforcing of all the tenets of evolution. Simply ask an evolutionist for evidence for evolution, and 99% of the time you will be bombarded with examples of homologous physical structures, homologous gene sequences, and homologous biochemicals. They think homologies prove evolution. They believe this so much that every time they see examples of homologies, it reinforces their belief in evolution. They automatically assume evolution caused the homologies. But, does finding homologies in the fossil record prove their assumption? No; they want you to think it does, but it's another counterfeit claim. "Homology implies relationship," sounds very scientific, but if you are familiar with logic, philosophy, epistemology, or debate, you will instantly recognize this as cyclic reasoning. They are using their conclusion to "prove" their assumption. The rationale of evolutionists is this:

1.) If evolution is true, then homologies should exist.
2.) Homologies do exist.
3.) Therefore, evolution is true.

Let me show you why you can't use a conclusion to prove your assumption. There are some evolutionary scientists who reject Darwinian Evolution and believe space-aliens came to earth and purposely planted life here. This is called The Directed Panspermia Theory. Francis Crick and Fred Hoyle were two good examples of evolutionists who believed this theory. The claim is made that a race of superior beings from another planet brought all the different species, or at least species-types, to earth at the exact time and place where they appeared in the geologic record. They brought Ordovician-Type organisms here during the Ordovician Period; they brought Jurassic-Type organisms here during the Jurassic Period; and they brought Cretaceous-Type organisms here during the Cretaceous Period. Thus, they have been controlling or directing the history of life on this planet. This theory fits the geologic record even better than the Punctuated Equilibria Theory. In fact, it fits the fossil record perfectly. There are no contradictions between The Directed Panspermia Theory and the fossil evidence in the Geologic Column. The Directed Panspermia Theory also proposes the space-aliens make periodic visits to tinker with the life forms they had brought before. They remove some of the old ones and bring in some new ones. (I hope they aren't planning on removing humans at their next visit.) If this is true, then this theory may explain the periods of mass extinctions the earth seems to have experienced. Maybe the space-aliens caused the giant asteroid that wiped out the dinosaurs sixty-five million years ago. If space-aliens brought in new species and killed off old species over long periods of time, then the homologies seen in the fossil record would not be due to evolution. Instead, those homologies would be the result of space-aliens bringing physically similar organisms to earth. The rationale of Directed Panspermia evolutionists is:

1.) If space-aliens brought life to earth, then homologies should exist.
2.) Homologies do exist.
3.) Therefore, space-aliens brought life to earth.

If I assume space-aliens planted earth's lifeforms, then I could conclude that there should be homologies in the fossil record. (Maybe I should write a book entitled: *The Origin of Species, by Means of Space-Alien Selection*.) DOES FINDING HOMOLOGIES IN THE FOSSIL RECORD PROVE SPACE-ALIENS WERE THE CAUSE? I sure hope you don't think so. If you do, then you are confusing the EFFECT for the CAUSE. This is exactly what evolutionists do when they say homology implies relationship. They think seeing the supposed EFFECT of evolution is the same as seeing the actual CAUSE of evolution. But, observing a past EFFECT is not the same as observing a past CAUSE. This sleight-of-hand maneuver is contrary to the Scientific Method. This means:

The presence of homologies does not prove homologies were caused by evolution.

The presence of homologies does not prove homologies were caused by space-aliens.

The presence of homologies does not prove homologies were caused by God.

The presence of homologies does not prove HOW those homologies came to be. This means fossils CAN'T prove evolution. Shock of all shocks! FOSSIL HOMOLOGIES DON'T PROVE ANYTHING ABOUT THEIR CAUSE. Neither do protein homologies or DNA homologies. **DNA similarities don't prove hereditary relationship if the similarities** are the result of **CREATION** rather than **PROCREATION**. (The DNA is the same; only the cause is different.) Similarities in structures and biochemicals don't prove evolution unless you first prove evolution, and only evolution, caused the similarities seen in homologous structures and biochemicals. This will be a tough job since virtually all the evidence for evolution is based on the similarities seen in homologous structures or biochemicals. You can't use your conclusion as proof for your assumption and still claim to be a scientist. You need to be religious to do that! **The effect of homologies doesn't prove the cause of homologies.** Even if you find innumerable transitional fossils with insensibly fine gradations, it doesn't prove God couldn't have created life by means of innumerable, insensibly fine acts of creation. (Theistic Evolution) It wouldn't prove space-aliens couldn't have brought innumerable, insensibly fine variations of species over time. (Directed Panspermia) As it turns out, fossils don't prove evolution. So much for the displays in our museums!

"Homology Implies Relationship" is a cyclic argument. To believe homology implies relationship, you must believe in evolution. Yet to believe in evolution, you must believe homology implies relationship. The only independent evidence that could validate this cyclic argument is eyewitness testimony to the actual cause of homologies. The effect of homologies is in the present, but the cause of homologies was in the past. Unless you were an eyewitness to the cause of homologies in the past, you can't prove evolution was the cause. Let me give an example to clear this up a little.

The Two-Universe Model

Imagine there are two separate universes. I know "uni" means "one," and it's logically impossible to have two universes, but humor me long enough to make this point. Matter, energy, and the physical forces of nature are eternal and uncreated in Universe One. No God is present in Universe One. In Universe Two there is no matter, there is no energy, and there are no physical forces. However, there is a God capable of creating them. This God possesses great intelligence and power and is able to create and manipulate matter, energy, and the physical forces of nature. You are a multi-dimensional, multi-temporal observer, and can freely travel back and forth between the two universes. You are fascinated by watching Universe One go through endless cycles of Big-Bangs, expansions, contractions, and then Big-Crunches... and then Big-Bangs again. During some of those cycles, intelligent beings arise from the way the fundamental forces randomly act on the fundamental particles. In some of those cycles, evolution happens.

TIME = 0
UNIVERSE ONE

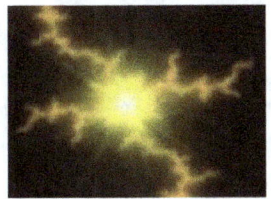

(Artwork: Courtesy of Thomas Dill, Louisville, KY)

1. NO GOD
2. ETERNAL MATTER
3. ETERNAL ENERGY
4. ETERNAL PHYSICAL FORCES

TIME = 0
UNIVERSE TWO

(Artwork: Courtesy of Thomas Dill, Louisville, KY)

1. ETERNAL GOD
2. NO MATTER
3. NO ENERGY
4. NO PHYSICAL FORCES

One day you visit the God of Universe Two to see if He knows about Universe One. It's been about 14,000,000,000 years since the last Big-Bang in Universe One, and there is a particularly interesting planet inhabited by creatures who call themselves, "humans." The God of Universe Two isn't impressed. "Any half-omnipotent being could make those," He says. You challenge His statement, so the God of Universe Two looks over at Universe One and duplicates it exactly. His duplication is perfect, right down to the last quark, photon, neutrino, Higgs boson, and quantum string. Even all the atheists and evolutionists are perfectly duplicated.

TIME = 14,000,000,000 Years
UNIVERSE ONE

(Artwork: Courtesy of Thomas Dill, Louisville, KY)

1. NO GOD
2. ETERNAL MATTER
3. ETERNAL ENERGY
4. ETERNAL PHYSICAL FORCES

TIME = 14,000,000,000 Years
UNIVERSE TWO

(Artwork: Courtesy of Thomas Dill, Louisville, KY)

1. ETERNAL GOD
2. CREATED MATTER
3. CREATED ENERGY
4. CREATED PHYSICAL FORCES

You, as an independent observer, have watched evolution take place in Universe One over the last 14,000,000,000 years. The people there are correct when they believe homology implies relationship. Their homologies are due to hundreds of millions of years of evolution. However, people in Universe Two, who were created less than five minutes ago, are incorrect to believe homology implies relationship. Their homologies are due to an intelligent creative act, and not to years of evolution. They were created with intact homologies. For them, homology implies a Creator who created homologies. Only your knowledge of what occurred BEFORE the creation allows you to know the difference between the origins of species in the two universes. Since science cannot observe, measure, or detect anything before time and space came into existence, science cannot detect a difference between these two universes. The two universes are exactly identical. They have the exact same organisms with the exact same homologies, and the exact same fossils in the exact same strata. No matter what physical results you got from whatever physical experiment or observation you made in Universe One, you would get the exact same physical results from the exact same physical experiment or observation in Universe Two. This is why homology doesn't necessarily imply an evolutionary relationship. Assuming homology implies relationship is valid if and only if evolution is true to begin with. You can't use homologies as proof of evolution unless you first prove evolution, and only evolution, created those homologies.

You Need to Know Which Universe You are in Before You Can Use Homologies as Evidence for Evolution

The people in Universe Two have homologies with the cows and fish of Universe Two. The people of Universe One have those exact same homologies with the cows and fish of Universe One. Evolution caused the homologies in Universe One, but an Intelligent Being created them in Universe Two. The existence of homologies doesn't prove how those homologies came to be. USING HOMOLOGIES AS PROOF FOR EVOLUTION, PRESUPPOSES EVOLUTION IS TRUE. It's a cyclic argument! You must first prove evolution is the only possible cause for homologous structures, homologous biochemicals, and homologous DNA in your universe. You must falsify The Directed Panspermia Theory. You must falsify The Special Creation Theory. You must falsify the "It-Just-Popped-Into Existence-This-Way-Five-Minutes-Ago Theory." Only then can you use homology as a basis for classifying organisms into evolutionary family trees.

This means homologies can't be used as proof for evolution. This means fossils can't be used as proof for evolution. No matter how many you dig up, regardless of how many fossils you discover, and however you want to arrange them, fossils can't be used to prove your argument unless you first prove your argument. Similarities between fossils don't prove evolution until you first prove evolution caused those similarities. In fact, if I assume a creator-being caused homologous structures, then I can say, "Homology implies a creator-being," and use the very same fossils, laid out in the very same order, as proof. I could make the same statement about space-aliens if I assumed space-aliens caused homologous structures. I could make the same claim about our universe popping into existence, exactly as it now is, only five minutes ago. All the homologies popped into existence five minutes ago; therefore, homologies are proof we popped into existence five minutes ago. After all, if we really did pop into existence five minutes ago with all these homologies as they now are, then we would expect to see all these homologies as they now are... and we do see them as they now are! Does the presence of homologies prove we popped into existence five minutes? No! "Homology Implies Relationship," is a counterfeit claim.

False Supposition 7: Evolution is Simple

When we creationists point out the extreme improbability for evolution to create the complex forms and functions of living organisms, evolutionists just laugh at us. "It's not complex at all," they tell us. "Abiogenesis and evolution are ever so simple. All it takes is the right chemicals." Here is a well-known and highly-respected pro-evolution Web Page that espouses this view.

www.talkorigins.org: The Talk Origins Web Site describes itself this way:

"What is the Talk.Origins Archive?—The Talk.Origins Archive is a collection of articles and essays that explore the creationism/evolution controversy from a mainstream scientific perspective. In other words, the authors of most of the articles in this archive accept the prevailing scientific view that the earth is ancient, that there was no global flood, and that evolution is responsible for the earth's present biodiversity."[46]

This is an organization of scientists who are Pro-Evolution and Anti-Bible. Here is one of their articles:

"Lies, Damned Lies, Statistics, and Probability of Abiogenesis Calculations

By Ian Musgrave

A Primordial Protoplasmic Globule

So the calculation goes that the probability of forming a given 300 amino acid long protein (say an enzyme like carboxypeptidase) randomly is $(1/20)^{300}$ or 1 chance in

2.04 x 10^{390}, which is astoundingly, mind-beggaringly improbable. This is then cranked up by adding on the probabilities of generating 400 or so similar enzymes until a figure is reached that is so huge that merely contemplating it causes your brain to dribble out your ears. This gives the impression that the formation of even the smallest organism seems totally impossible. However, this is completely incorrect.

Firstly, the formation of biological polymers from monomers is a function of the laws of chemistry and biochemistry, and these are decidedly *not* random.

Secondly, the entire premise is incorrect to start off with, because in modern abiogenesis theories the first '*living things*' would be much simpler, not even a protobacteria, or a preprotobacteria (what Oparin called a protobiont and Woese calls a progenote), but one or more simple molecules probably not more than 30-40 subunits long. These simple molecules then slowly evolved into more cooperative self-replicating systems, then finally into simple organisms."[47]

    Ian Musgrave sounds convincing, but now for some real science:

    Firstly, notice the italicized words are his emphasis, not mine. He uses, "*living things*," instead of saying they were living things. Not only does he put the words in italics, he puts them in quotes. This is his way of trying to make his readers believe he is talking about living things when he knows he is talking nonsense. He knows they aren't living things. Living things require instructions, and these "*living things*" would have had no instructions.

Secondly, he says evolution is possible because the laws of chemistry and biochemistry are not random. Is he right? Are the laws of chemistry and biochemistry not random? I guess it depends on what you mean by "random," and by what you think randomness can accomplish. What laws of chemistry and biochemistry govern the formation of biological polymers from monomers? If Fred Hoyle were alive, he would tell you the laws of chemistry and biochemistry comply with the Laws of Thermodynamics. He would explain how electromagnetism operates in accordance to those Laws. (Electromagnetism is the force that binds the atoms and molecules together, so they can form biological monomers and polymers.) Yes, Hoyle would agree the force of electromagnetism does not operate in a random fashion—positive charges always attract negative charges; negative charges always attract positive charges; positive charges always repel positive charges; and negative charges always repel negative charges. They never act randomly. However, that does not make the undirected electromagnetic force a cause for creating instructions. The electromagnetic force, in accordance to the Laws of Thermodynamics, can cause forest fires to destroy trees and whole forests. Forest fires never act non-randomly when it comes to what happens to the trees. The carbon in the trees is always bound to the oxygen in the air, and the results are always disastrous. Trees are always destroyed, and forests are always damaged. Forest fires turn living trees into dead ash. Electromagnetic energy in the form of forest fires never turns living trees into fine walnut cabinets, maple tables, oak chairs, or teak jewelry boxes. However, electromagnetic energy directed by a skillful, intelligent agent (a carpenter) can turn trees into those beautiful items. Fred Hoyle didn't need to know much about biology to know the forces of chemistry and biochemistry can't create biological instructions unless they are directed by a skillful, intelligent agent. Ian Musgrave, like all evolutionists, uses arguments that work only if you don't know much about biology... or chemistry... or physics... or mathematics.

So, can the non-random physical forces of nature create a specific string of biological monomers and polymers that would come to life? Let's turn to a mental exercise to evaluate this concept. Think about the Kentucky Lotto® Game. You know how it works. There is a big, transparent drum full of Ping-Pong balls being tumbled to make sure their distribution is random. Each Ping-Pong ball has a different number on it. That means the numbers on the Ping-Pong balls are not random. Next to the spinning drum stands a beautiful lady ready to proceed with the drawing. The fact she is beautiful is not random either, but that has nothing to do with the subject at hand. When the drawing is ready, the drum stops spinning and the pre-specified number of Ping-Pong balls are allowed to drop down through a clear plastic tube and into their final resting place. The number of Ping-Pong balls allowed to drop is not random either. Then the beautiful, not-random, lady turns each Ping-Pong ball in a not-random fashion, so the television audience can see the numbers. There! The numbers have been drawn. The sequence has been created.

Was it random? According to the way evolutionists think, the answer is, "no." Why do they think that? It's because the Force of Gravity caused the Ping-Pong balls to drop DOWN the tube. The Law of Gravity is just like the Laws of Chemistry and Biochemistry. It is not random. Like all the Laws of Physics, it always operates in a specific way. It never acts randomly. When the drum stops spinning and the entrance to the clear plastic tube is opened, the Ping-Pong balls will always drop down the tube. They will never float in mid-air or move up toward the top of the drum. Their movement is not random because the Law of Gravity is not random.

So, while the Ping-Pong balls falling down the clear plastic tube was, "decidedly not random," does this mean the sequence of Ping-Pong balls was not random? (After all, the Physical Law that governed the movement of the Ping-Pong balls was not random.) No! The sequence of Ping-Pong balls was completely random because the Force of Gravity had no ability to control which Ping-Pong balls would drop down the tube. The Force of Gravity moved the Ping-Pong balls in a specific way, (down) but it couldn't move the Ping-Pong balls into a specific sequence. The specific sequence of numbers was a random event. Let's say the numbers were: 12-27-4-45-38. The Force of Gravity could not intentionally select this specific sequence. This sequence was random. (Assuming the beautiful lady wasn't secretly bribed to switch the Ping-Pong balls with another set of rigged numbers.) The sequence was random because gravity cannot prefer one Ping-Pong ball over another.

The same is true for the Laws of Chemistry and Biochemistry. The Fundamental Physical Force that determines the Laws of Chemistry and Biochemistry is the Force of Electromagnetism. The Force of Electromagnetism always operates in specific ways. It is not random. Oxygen atoms always bind to hydrogen atoms in specific ways. Chlorine atoms always interact with sodium atoms according to the Laws of Chemistry. Water reacts with carbon dioxide during the process of photosynthesis according to the Laws of Biochemistry so that plants produce sugar molecules, and not Ping-Pong balls with numbers on them. So, while the Laws of Chemistry and Biochemistry can non-randomly connect nucleic acids and deoxyribose-phosphate molecules together into long Double-Helix strings of DNA, (provided the ingredients and the conditions are right) they can never select the specific sequences of nucleotides needed for life. Those sequences contain instructions, so those sequences require instructions. Just as 12-27-4-45-38 would be a random sequence of Ping-Pong balls, A-G-G-T-C-A would be a random sequence of nucleotides. But such a sequence would do nothing because it doesn't contain instructions. Yes, as Musgrave said, the Laws of Chemistry and Biochemistry are non-random. They non-randomly govern the movement of the molecules, but the sequence of the molecules is not selected by those laws. The fact the Laws of Chemistry and Biochemistry are not random has no bearing on the specific arrangement of nucleotide sequences in the instructions found in DNA. Musgrave's smokescreen is blown away by the facts.

The *"living things"* he is talking about are not even bacteria. The smallest, simplest, autonomous living organism is the bacterium *Mycoplasma hominis*. It contains about six hundred different proteins, and many of those proteins are made up of hundreds of amino acids each. The simplest living thing contains 600,000 nucleotides in its genome. 600,000 biomolecular subunits in a real living thing is quite a bit larger than the 40 biomolecular subunits of his imaginary *"living thing."* *Mycoplasma hominis* has 50% more biomolecular subunits than all the letters and spaces contained in this book you are now reading. That means it would be easier for monkeys to type this book randomly than for the Electromagnetic Force to create the DNA instructions in *Mycoplasma hominis* randomly... and that's the smallest, simplest, autonomous living organism. Musgrave wants you to believe that randomly generating forty letters is the same as randomly generating an entire book.

Evolutionists appeal to an undiscovered category of simpler *"living things"* called, "protobacteria." (Not to be confused with Proteobacteria, which are a group of gram-negative bacteria that includes *E. coli, Salmonella,* and other true bacteria.) Musgrave is not talking about bacteria. Musgrave is not talking about protobacteria, a hypothetical precursor to bacteria. Musgrave is not even talking about pre-protobacteria, a hypothetically hypothetical precursor to protobacteria. He knows even pre-protobacteria would be too complex for the undirected forces of nature to create. Those *"living things"* haven't been seen either. No, Musgrave is talking about *"living things"* that would have to be even simpler than pre-protobacteria. Now, if science has never discovered protobacteria, and science has never discovered pre-protobacteria, why is it scientific to use even simpler *"living things"* to defend the Theory of Evolution? They've never been seen! His *"living things"* were only 30-40 subunits long. This is much too simple to be a living thing, unless you consider a lug nut a Lamborghini[tm]. (Licensed Trademark of *Automobili Lamborghini* S.p.A., Bolognese, Italy)

What class of monomers is he talking about? If he is talking about amino acid monomers, then forty amino acids in a peptide isn't as simple and easy as he wants you to believe. We will assume the twenty different amino acids necessary for life were in the "primordial soup" in high concentrations with no impurities. (Unlike Stanley Miller's Apparatus.) Since any one of the amino acids could fit into any one of those forty spaces of his *"living thing,"* there would be 40^{20} possible arrangements. That's:

$$109,951,162,777,600,000,000,000,000,000,000$$

different ways. In addition, all the amino acid monomers in his *"living thing"* had to have the correct chirality.

Chirality is a quality in biochemical molecules that is sometimes referred to as, "handedness." You see, these molecules can be arranged as mirror images of themselves; the atoms are the same, but their physical organization is reversed. (Think of the difference between a right glove and a left glove.) All but one of those twenty different amino acids have a "right-handed" and a "left-handed" form. Only the "left-handed" form is used in living things. The amino acid Glycine is the smallest of amino acids. It is so simple, it has only one form. Since we have no idea if the first *"living thing"* would even contain Glycine, we can't determine the exact odds for this *"living thing"* to form randomly. However, if the other amino acids were allowed to bond randomly, the odds of getting forty left-handed ones in a peptide would be 1 in 2^{40}. That's 1 in 1,099,511,627,776—less than one in a trillion. Putting these two numbers together, we see the chance of getting the forty correct amino acids, all with the correct chirality, into all the right places, would be less than 1 in 1.20×10^{44}. That's 1 with forty-four zeros following it. Get one amino acid monomer wrong and his *"living thing"* would become a dead thing. Musgrave thinks overcoming the odds of one chance in 120 million, trillion, trillion, trillion is a simple thing... well, he at least wants you to think it is a simple thing. Even if you could randomly create his perfect forty-amino acid *"living thing"* it wouldn't be able to replicate; therefore, it could never evolve. Musgrave loses again.

Randomly combining biologic monomers could never produce life. An explosion in a print shop might put ink onto paper, but it could never print the letters, spaces, and punctuation found in the instruction book for building the Space Shuttle. There is no random force in the universe that can do that. An explosion in a print shop could never create the instructions for building a tricycle, and then have subsequent explosions in subsequent print shops gradually change those instructions into instructions for the Space Shuttle. There is no random force in the universe that can cause biological monomers and polymers to interact in such ways as to create the instructions necessary for the first living thing. There are no random forces that could evolve those simple instructions into more complex instructions. Evolutionists want us to believe things about mathematics that aren't true. Fred Hoyle's mathematics about Darwinism was right. It didn't happen because it couldn't happen!

But wait! There is more!

Once what-couldn't-happen, supposedly happened, all that had to happen was for it to evolve slowly until it evolved into the Beautiful Lotto Lady. Look again at Musgrave's last sentence:

"These simple molecules then slowly evolved into more cooperative self-replicating systems, then finally into simple organisms."

Oops! I think I just called the Beautiful Lotto Lady, "a simple organism." Sorry, Beautiful Lotto Lady. I didn't mean it that way. (Rats! There goes my chance at getting a date with the Beautiful Lotto Lady... as well as my chance to rig the Kentucky Lotto Game.®)

According to evolutionists, all that was required for evolution is for simple molecules to evolve.

In order for life to evolve, all life had to do was evolve.

Yes, that sounds easy, but it is non-explanatory. It is a tautology, as Arthur Koestler revealed earlier. It is devoid of proof. Unfortunately, they don't need proof. Their belief is their "proof." No explanation is needed because they all "know" life evolved. But how did it evolve? What caused it? What were the mechanics? How did living organisms arise from non-life, and how did they become self-replicating instead of just duplicating? Self-Replication is vastly different from mere duplication. Duplication would require only another explosion in another print shop, creating another instruction book for building the Space Shuttle. Self-Replication would require the explosion to create an instruction book not only for building the Space Shuttle, but for building a new print shop, along with the instructions for building an explosive device that when exploded would create an instruction book for building a new print shop, along with the instructions for building another Space Shuttle, along with instructions for building an explosive device that when exploded would... repeat, repeat, repeat.... Oh, and it would also require instructions for how the printing presses would be reconfigured by the explosions, so they would become machines that could take in raw materials and build new printing presses and everything else needed in the new print shops. Evolutionists hope you have the gullibility of a four-year-old child. They have no scientific answers; just imaginary stories with anthropomorphic overtones. What is meant by, "more cooperative?" Must oxygen atoms first agree to bind with hydrogen atoms? What if the hydrogen atoms decide they don't want to cooperate? Then, where does evolution take you? This is the same as saying all you need to evolve a Space Shuttle is to have some simple pieces of metal slowly change over time until they finally become a Space Shuttle. All iron has to do is cooperate with copper, and with aluminum, and with gold, and with silver, and with zinc, and with…. This is the exact same argument... only making the Space Shuttle would be easier.

All evolution had to do was evolve homologous structures, and we can use homologous structures as proof for evolution.

All evolution had to do is evolve DNA instructions, and we can use DNA instructions as proof for evolution.

All evolution had to do was cause Natural Selection to cause evolution, and we can use Natural Selection as proof for evolution.

All evolution had to do was create living organism in one of the infinite universes, and we can use living organisms as proof for infinite universes.

All evolution had to do was utilize the pagan's Impersonal First Principle of Order, and we can use the existence of order as proof for evolution… and as proof for pagan morality.

Simple? Yes! Science? No! Why not? Let's think back to the supposed story of whale evolution. Ian Musgrave makes it sound like all you need to evolve a dog-like animal into a whale is to take the dog-like animal and make it bigger and change a few structures until it becomes a whale. He wants you to think it is as simple as a child using modeling clay to make animals. Just add more clay to make it bigger, shape the legs into fins, flatten the tail so it is fluked, and bingo; you've got a whale. He doesn't want you to think about what would be required in real life. It's not enough to make the "whale" bigger; all its systems, organs, tissues, and cells must remain functional and interactive the whole time. This means they all must experience the same "good" mutations in super-harmony. Evolution could make a whale from a dog only if mutations in the DNA instructions for all the systems, and all the organs, and all the tissues, and all the cells, and all the organelles, and all the biochemicals changed in exactly the right way, in the exactly correct sequence, and for exactly the right length of time. It wouldn't help the whale to mutate DNA instructions for a different skeletal system if the DNA instructions for all the muscles in the muscular system didn't also mutate correctly at the same time. Having the bones of a dog's tail gradually mutate into the bones of a whale's tail wouldn't help if the muscles, tendons, ligaments, cartilage, nerves, arteries, veins, and epithelium of the dog's tail didn't also gradually mutate into the muscles, tendons, ligaments, cartilage, nerves, arteries, veins, and epithelium of the whale's tail. If the DNA instructions that code for all the parts of the heart didn't mutate in just the right way, the poor creature couldn't pump enough blood to live. That means the DNA instructions for the ventricular and atrial muscles, the heart valves, the Purkinje fibers, the endocardium, the coronary artery, and all the other heart-parts were mutated in the correct beneficial fashion, all precisely at the right time. But, that means the DNA instructions for the production of the aortic arch, the aorta, the vena cava, and the pulmonary arteries and veins would also have to experience the same beneficial DNA mutations. In addition, the nerves of the sinoatrial node would have to be reprogrammed by a series of perfect beneficial DNA mutations to allow for the required change in heart rate. A whale with the heart rate of a dog couldn't live. But that would require a whole set of beneficial mutations involving the parasympathetic nervous system and the brain. Of course, that wouldn't help unless all the parts of the lungs; the alveoli, the bronchioles, the main stem bronchi, the trachea, *etc.* all experienced their own beneficial mutations at the same time. Unfortunately, a whale with a new respiratory system wouldn't survive unless the kidneys, the liver, and the digestive tract also mutated in the proper, beneficial way. A whale with dog kidneys would die of uremic poisoning. A whale with a dog pancreas would die of diabetes. A whale with a dog digestive tract wouldn't be able to digest food. The entire gastrointestinal system would have to mutate along with all the other parts of the whale at the same time. On top of that, all the DNA instructions for all the nerves of the nervous system would have to mutate properly so they would still connect to all the parts, so they would still function. That means all the nerve roots of the spinal cord and all the foramen (holes in the bones where nerves and vessels pass through) would have to be changed in just the precise way and in just the precise places. If all these mutations didn't happen at the same time, to the same degree, in the same individual organism, then a dog-like animal could never evolve into a whale.

Plus, evolutionists must explain how the changes in the environment naturally selected each one of these DNA mutations to be beneficial. What kind of environment selects for changes in the Purkinje Fibers? Does it have to get hotter or colder to change the size and shape of the Foramen Magnum, so the nerves of the spinal cord can pass through safely? Does the extent of cloud-cover have an influence on changes in the glomerular filtration mechanism of the kidneys? If so, then how does it do that? Every one of these finely-gradated changes in anatomy must be caused by finely-gradated changes in DNA instructions coupled with finely-gradated changes in the environment. This would be the true mechanics of evolution, but it is never explained how it worked. **It's easy to say that all evolution has to do is evolve, but it doesn't explain anything. And since it doesn't explain anything, it doesn't prove anything.**

False Supposition 8: All It Takes is Infinite Time, Space, Matter, and Energy

As I mentioned before, there are a number of evolutionists who have gone over to the dark side... I mean the exotic side of science. They believe billions of universes pop into existence every second. (And you thought my Two-Universe Model was a stretch of the imagination.) They use the Multiverse Theory in an attempt to do an end-run around the scientific evidence presented by people like Fred Hoyle when they show it is mathematically impossible for life to have arisen without an intelligent agent; "a superintellect," as he called it. Their problem with Fred Hoyle's Directed Panspermia Theory is it includes the existence of intelligent agents. And while they are not supernatural agents, the very idea allows Intelligent Design and Special Creation a place at the science table. To eliminate all forms of intelligence as a means of causing life, evolutionists get around all the impossible odds by saying there are an infinite number of universes. With an infinite number of universes, every possibility is guaranteed. This means there will be universes where life arises and evolves by chance alone. (And we're just lucky to live in one.) Actually, this is a not a scientific theory; it is a belief without physical evidence. (In other words, it is a faith-based religion.) It is a creation in the minds of people needing an excuse for not believing in creation. In fact, there is one extreme form of this religion that says a new universe pops into existence at every quantum event.

If there are:

1 X 10^{81} Fundamental Quantum Particles in the Universe, and

1 X 10^{43} Fundamental Quantum units of time per second (Planck Time), and

4 X 10^{195} Fundamental Quantum units of space (Planck Volume) in the universe.

Then:

4 X 10^{319} Quantum Events happen every second.

Disciples of this religion-without-a-God believe a new universe pops into existence with every Quantum Event. This makes every possible permutation of matter-energy-space-time events, happen somewhere in one of those universes. Every universe that CAN exist, MUST exist. This eliminates all the creationists' arguments about the Fine Tuning of the Universe, and the mathematical improbability for life happening by chance. This means 4 X 10^{319} new universes come out of our universe every second. (And 4 X 10^{319} new universes come out of each one of those new universes every second, and 4 X 10^{319} new universes come out of each one of those new universes every second, and 4 X 10^{319} new universes come out of each one of those new universes every second, *ad infinitum*.) With this many universes possible, ours just happens to be one where life came into existence by the process of evolution. This idea really does come from the dark side, but it is passed off as science. It is not science because it is not observable, and it is not falsifiable. Therefore, it should not be taught in the science class either.

Infinite Universes Don't Help

Evolutionists think the Infinite Universes Hypothesis is an exquisite argument that makes the Theory of Evolution scientific. In truth, it renders it completely unscientific. For the same reason science cannot observe, measure, test, or repeat randomness, science cannot observe, measure, test, or repeat anything infinite. Any theory that relies on any necessary factor being infinite, is a theory that must be disqualified as a scientific theory. Science can't handle the infinite.

Let's say I propose a new chemical "theory" concerning an, as-of-yet, unknown reaction between sodium and chlorine. We know under normal circumstances that sodium atoms react with chlorine atoms in such a way they give off a great amount of heat energy and produce sodium chloride; table salt. But, what if I said an infinite amount of sodium combined with an infinite amount of chlorine will produce yappy Chihuahuas instead of salt. (And only an infinite amount of sodium and chlorine can create yappy Chihuahuas.) Such a "theory" would be rejected because it relies on observing and testing an infinite quantity of sodium and chlorine. Science can't do that. This "theory" is not scientific because it cannot be falsified. Scientists around the world would instantly recognize my "theory" as not only non-science, but nonsense. They would not permit my "Yappy Chihuahua Theory" to be taught in the science class.

Okay, if an infinite amount of sodium and chlorine can't do it, what if I added an infinite amount of carbon and hydrogen? Will that create yappy Chihuahuas? No! Well, what if I throw in an infinite amount of oxygen, nitrogen, and potassium? Will that work? No? In that case, let me add an infinite amount of copper, iron, calcium, phosphorus, magnesium, selenium, and sulfur. Will infinite amounts of these fourteen elements create yappy Chihuahuas? Never! So, let me add an infinite amount of all the elements on the Periodic Table. Can an infinite amount of all the elements create yappy Chihuahuas?

Do you see the foolishness of evolutionists? According to the Theory of Evolution, all you need is an infinite amount of the elements, and it will produce yappy Chihuahuas. But no scientist has ever observed it. No one has ever seen infinite universes create life. No one has ever tested infinite universes to see if they can create life. No one can falsify the Infinite Universes Theory. Infinity cannot be used in any scientific statement and remain scientifically valid.

Evolutionists say there are an infinite number of universes; therefore, all possible universes must exist. This supposedly eliminates all the Fine-Tuning Arguments for life. This may sound scientific, but using infinity in any scientific hypothesis, theory, or law creates contradictory conclusions. If there are an infinite number of universes, then a universe exactly like ours must exist. But, if there are an infinite number of universes, then more than one universe exactly like ours must exist. In fact, if there are an infinite number of universes, then an infinite number of universes exactly like ours must exist. But, it also means an infinite number of universes not like ours must exist. This means an infinite number of universes like ours, and an infinite number of universes not like ours both exist and don't exist at the same time. This removes the Theory of Evolution from the realm of science, and puts it in its proper place—A Man Made Religion full of contradictory nonsense without any scientific support.

Atheists have no explanation for the existence of the universe. There are only two possibilities:

1.) An infinite regression of natural causes and effects.

2.) An eternal and uncaused Supernatural cause.

Atheists are quick to point out that science can't accept the latter explanation because science can't observe, measure, or test the supernatural. **However, they fail to recognize that science can't observe, measure, or test an infinite regression either.** Infinity is an abstract concept, not a measurable quantity. No infinite units of anything can be observed, measured, or tested. Where would a scientist store an infinite amount of H_2O if his experiment needed an infinite amount of water? If an infinite amount of energy was needed to cause a particular chemical reaction, then wouldn't the scientists involved in the study of that reaction need to cease to exist since their existence subtracts from all available energy in the universe? When would a scientist be able to finish her research if she studied the infinite past? Even if she could invent a time machine and directly observe the infinite past, how long would it take her to finish her project? It would take an infinite amount of time. What if she could observe the infinite past at one-million times normal speed? It would still take infinite years to finish her observations. What if she could observe the infinite past at one-trillion times normal speed? It would still take infinite years to finish her observations. What if she could observe the infinite past at $10^{10,000,000}$ times normal speed? It would still take infinite years to finish her observations. No explanation for the origin of the universe that relies on anything being infinite (time, space, matter, or energy) can ever be a scientific statement.

No explanation for the origin of life that relies on anything being infinite can ever be a scientific statement.

None of the Infinite Universe Theories helps, and there are multiple Multiverse Theories: Bubble Universes, Parallel Universes, Daughter Universes, Infinite Ensemble Universes, Black Hole Universes, and others. (The Black Hole Universe Theory says our universe is inside a black hole of another universe, which is inside a black hole of another universe, which is inside a black hole of another universe, on and on to infinity. Oh, and of course all the black holes in our universe contain universes with black holes that contain universes with black holes that contain universes with black holes that....) ALL THE MULTIVERSE THEORIES ARE UNSCIENTIFIC BECAUSE THEY RELY ON PROVING THE EXISTENCE OF INFINITE AMOUNTS OF TIME, SPACE, MATTER, AND ENERGY. Science can't prove that time, space, matter, and energy are infinite. Science can't test whether time, space, matter, and energy are infinite. No one can observe, measure, or test an infinite amount of time, space, matter, or energy. Since the atheists' explanation of the infinite universe is scientifically untestable, it falls out of the realm of science and into the realms of philosophy and theology. Realistically, it falls into the realm of lunacy. Atheistic Evolutionists are not scientists at all; they are religious fanatics dressed in scientists' clothing.

But, I have some questions for those who are members of the Infinite Universes Cult. How does the Multiverse Theory prove ALL the universes weren't created by God? How does the Multiverse Theory prove OUR universe wasn't created by God? If ALL possible universes MUST exist, then one possible universe is a universe where a Super-Powerful, Superintellect called,

"God," took clay, formed it into a man, breathed life into him, caused him to fall into a deep sleep, removed one of his ribs, made a woman out of the rib, placed them both in a beautiful garden, gave them the right to eat the fruit of any tree in the garden except for one tree, commanded them not to eat of that tree lest they die... (Parenthetical Break: In this parenthetical break, all the events of the Old Testament, New Testament, and all of history just happen to happen.) ...He returns to judge His creatures, saves those who put their faith in Jesus Christ, and damns those who reject Jesus to an infinite number of years in the Lake of Fire.

If all possible universes WILL happen somewhere in one of the infinite universes, then the universe described in the Bible MUST exist somewhere. How do you know you are not in the universe the Bible describes? If what atheists say about infinite universes is true, then there MUST be a universe exactly like the universe the Bible describes. How do you know you are not in the universe where God prepared an eternal Lake of Fire for all those who reject His Son? What are the chances you are in a universe that only APPARENTLY looks like the one described in the Bible?

The Multiverse Hypothesis doesn't offer a way of escaping the teachings of the Bible. The Hebrew of Genesis 1:1 does not say, "In the beginning God created the heaven and the earth." The actual word for "heaven" is *SHAMAYIM*, and it is in the plural. Genesis 1:1 literally says, "In the beginning God created the HEAVENS and the earth." Let atheists prove there are multiple "heavens," and I will remind them of the accuracy of the Bible when it said God created the "heavens."

False Supposition 9: The Mind is Matter

There is an old story about a floor painter who starts painting before he starts thinking. He doesn't pay attention to what he is doing and soon realizes he painted himself into a corner. He must sit there looking rather foolish since he has no way of escaping his own shoddy work. This is what evolutionists have done. They have "painted" elaborate explanations for how the universe came to be, and how life arose on this planet. Only they didn't pay close attention to what they were "painting," and now they find themselves stuck by shoddy arguments.

One shoddy argument is the argument for Scientific Materialism. Scientific Materialism is the belief that the only things that exist are time, space, matter, and energy. According to Scientific Materialists, everything that exists is composed of matter and energy; everything! This includes the mind. All thoughts, ideas, perceptions, awareness, beliefs, emotions, memories, values, knowledge, judgments, and intentions are nothing more than the physical products of the physical brain.

Earlier in this book I mentioned how ancient Greek philosophers, like Xenophanes, thought of thought as something other than material. They thought of the mind as an immaterial phenomenon capable of interacting with and acting on material, without itself being material. That's why they believed in an afterlife. (A life without a material body.) Now, what I said was true, but there was more to the story. You see, there were other Greek philosophers who rejected that notion. The idea of strict materialism didn't start with Darwin. Greek philosophers, such as Thales of Miletus (6th century B.C.), Leucippus of Miletus (5th century B.C.), and Democritus of Thrace (Late 5th century to early 4th century B.C.) believed nothing existed except matter and energy. To them, the mind consisted only of matter and energy. They also believed time and space were infinite. Modern-day evolutionists must align themselves with these materialistic pagan philosophers. Again, if you allow for the existence of anything non-material, then you open the door for belief in a non-material Agent capable of creating the universe. (The Unmoved-Mover begins to look like a Who rather than a what.) Evolutionists know you can't keep God out of the science class if you allow the mind to be immaterial. After all, this would be an admission that something immaterial (the mind) defines science itself. If they allow the mind to be immaterial, it would be an admission that Strict Materialism is self-contradictory. How can the immaterial mind claim that nothing immaterial exists? The atheists' logic is founded on the premise the mind is strictly material; just like Thales, Leucippus, and Democritus taught. A good example of this modern-day ancient thinking can be heard by going to the Discovery Institute's webpage,

    http://www.discovery.org/v/1761

and clicking on the Audio Player to hear a debate between Dr. Stephen Meyer and Dr. Peter Atkins: (Dr. Atkins is an atheist and proponent of evolution.) Here is a transcript of a portion of that debate. The numbers in parentheses are the approximate time (in minutes and seconds) into the debate when these things were said. (Note: The ..." marks at the end of the sentences indicate when the speakers cut each other off in mid-sentence.)

<u>Speakers:</u>
Stephen Meyer, Intelligent Design
Peter Atkins, Atheistic Evolution
Produced by Premier Radio UK
January 16, 2010

(28:04) Meyer: "But for us, we regard the activity of mind as explanatory. If you're looking at the Rosetta Stone, you can look in vain if you limit yourself to materialistic explanations of wind and erosion and the like, and don't open yourself to the possibility that mind played a role in the organization…"

(28:20) Atkins: "But see, we accept. We think of mind…"

(28:22) Meyer: "of those characters."

(28:23) Atkins: "But mind is…"

(28:24) Meyer: "Mind is a reality."

(28:25) Atkins: "Mind is material. Mind is an activity of the brain, and the brain is solely material."

There you have it! Dr. Peter Atkins is a brilliant man. He is professor-emeritus of chemistry at Oxford where he taught for forty years. He authored many of the chemistry textbooks used in British universities. He hasn't been idle in his retirement either. He is one of evolution's strongest advocates and has written numerous books and articles defending it. He has spoken and debated on numerous occasions in an attempt to eradicate religion from the world. He believes nothing exists except the material. That's why he is always trying to show how matter and energy can create life without Divine intelligence. Simple chemicals just evolved; that's how it happened. (Just like how the Space Shuttle evolved from simple metals.) Dr. Atkins rejects the notion of an immaterial mind because he knows if immaterial minds can exist, then the immaterial Mind of an immaterial God might exist. Dr. Atkins doesn't want that. Dr. Atkins isn't alone.

Atheistic Evolutionists around the world agree with him.

According to Atheistic Evolutionists, the mind is material. Dr. Atkins said, "Mind is material," and he gave two reasons: 1.) "the brain is solely material." and 2.) "Mind is an activity of the brain." I agree to a certain point. The brain is material, but is the brain the same thing as the mind? Is the activity of something the same thing as the thing producing the activity? That's what he wants you to believe. But that's like saying a car is the same thing as driving. Driving is the activity of the car, but driving is not the car itself. Dr. Atkins' mind is trying to fool our minds. Let's see if we can use our brains to engage in an activity that can determine whether the mind is material or immaterial.

Can science determine if the activity of the brain is immaterial? I think it can. If what Dr. Atkins says is true, then all intelligence, information, instructions, thoughts, beliefs, ideas, perceptions, understandings, awareness, emotions, memories, values, knowledge, judgments, and intentions are material. If they are material, then there ought to be a way to detect or observe them materially. If they are material, there should be some sort of material unit (mass and/or energy) by which they can be measured. By using The Scientific Method, I can actually provide a scientific test that falsifies Dr. Atkins' belief.

According to the Laws of Physics, matter and energy cannot be created or destroyed. They can take on other forms, and each one can be transformed into the other. Matter can become energy, and energy can become matter, but there can be no absolute gain or loss in the process. So far, Dr. Atkins' position isn't shaken. He would say that if I have a thought, then that thought is the activity of my brain, and the activity of my brain is generated by the electro-chemical activity of the neurons of the brain, which in turn depends on the energy provided by the food I eat. Therefore, energy becomes thought. This sounds reasonable if you don't think about it... Let's think about it.

Energy does not become thought. What he doesn't want you to understand is that energy is used to create thought, but energy is not thought itself. Gasoline may be used to drive the car, but gasoline is not the same thing as the drive. The question I ask is this: Can thoughts, ideas, information, or instructions exist independently of matter and energy? Can thoughts, ideas, information, or instructions exist in a form that can't be materially measured? Because if they can, then they are not material!

Imagine I took a blank sheet of paper and wrote a set of instructions on it with a pencil. The paper now contains something it didn't have before; it contains a set of instructions. Peter Atkins wouldn't be impressed. "True," he would say, "But your paper also has something it didn't have before. It now has fine graphite lines. When you added instructions to your paper, you added carbon atoms to your paper. You also expended energy to write them. Therefore, your instructions are material."

So far, it looks pretty bad for my side. My example does not seem to prove instructions are independent of matter and energy. But, let's continue my example. What if I wrote a longer set of instructions on a bigger sheet of paper? Peter Atkins still wouldn't be convinced. What if I wrote out two sets of instructions on two sheets of paper? Dr. Atkins would simply point out how the more instructions I wrote, the more matter and energy would be required. Peter Atkins would be grinning ear-to-ear at this point. My example seems to prove his belief... and I knew it would. So, let's try another example. What if I created a set of instructions using a particular medium, in this case paper and pencil, but then used the same medium to create gibberish? Let's go back to our John 3:16 example of instructions. (Instructions are a subset of intelligent information.) Remember, we compared the specific sequence of letters and spaces between these two sentences.

"For God so loved the world that he gave his only begotten Son that whosoever believeth in him should not perish but have everlasting life."

"hserl moroh hibtnh gwg vdsl eitev sF nevte wnol tduat hlaar hveis oleoey aveGs leun tveh endlh ngdot oeo ebioht poios hiht etrao bf rSeti."

These two sentences are identical in terms of the specific letters used and the number of spaces they contain. You could reproduce these sentences with any material you wanted; paper and pencil, symbols pressed into clay tablets, chalk on a chalkboard, Scrabble® tiles on a table, or huge stone letters the size of the blocks at Stonehenge. The quantity of matter and energy required would be the same for each sentence in its respective material. Sentence One in Scrabble® tiles would have the same amount of energy and matter as Sentence Two in Scrabble® tiles. It would take the same amount of chalk to write Sentence One as it would take to write Sentence Two. Sentence One in Stonehenge-sized letters would have the same amount of energy and matter as Sentence Two in Stonehenge-sized letters. In spite of this, Sentence One contains something not found in Sentence Two. Sentence One contains instructions. Sentence Two doesn't contain instructions; it doesn't tell you how to have everlasting life. No matter what material you used to create these sentences, the matter and energy of Sentence One would be the same as the matter and energy of Sentence Two. Regardless of the quantity of matter and energy used, Sentence One would contain non-material instructions while Sentence Two wouldn't. Sentence One contains something more than Sentence Two. And, since Sentence One doesn't contain any more matter and energy than Sentence Two, the instructions it contains are immaterial.

If you wrote Sentence One on a slip of paper, and Sentence Two on another slip of paper, there is no way you could determine if either contained instructions simply by measuring their matter and energy. You could measure their physical mass by weighing them on a scale, but that wouldn't tell you if they contained instructions. You could measure their physical energy by burning them in a Bomb Calorimeter, but that wouldn't tell you if they contained instructions. Measuring the physical mass and the physical energy could not determine if, how many, and what kind of instructions were contained on those slips of paper. It takes intelligence to do that. The simple test is this: Without using intelligence, prove there is no intelligence on the slip of paper with John 3:16 correctly written. You see what a corner they have painted themselves into. They need intelligence to reject intelligence.

Furthermore, the quantity and quality of the instructions would be the same regardless of the quantity and quality of material used. Non-material instructions are independent of the material used to store them. Reproducing John 3:16 in Stonehenge Blocks would require much more matter and energy than reproducing it on a slip of paper using a pencil. Yet, the quantity and quality of the instructions are the same for both systems. The heavy stones would convey no more instructions than the fine graphite lines on paper. The quantity and quality of matter and energy used to create the instructions is independent of the quantity and quality of the instructions themselves. If the quantity of instructions was dependent on the quantity of matter, then there would be more instructions created if Stonehenge-sized blocks are used. There would be less instructions if graphite lines on paper are used. But this isn't the case; the quantity of matter and energy doesn't dictate the quantity of instructions. **Instructions are independent of matter and energy; therefore, they are immaterial**. From this, we can rightly conclude that Dr. Atkins' belief is scientifically false. Yes, the brain requires matter and energy to process instructions, but the instructions themselves are not material. The mind is immaterial. This brings up three disturbing thoughts that must weigh heavy on the minds of atheists.

1.) If the human mind is immaterial, how can they reject the notion the immaterial exists?

2.) If the immaterial exists, how can they disprove the existence of an immaterial God?

3.) If the human mind is immaterial, how can they insist it is limited by or restricted to the material realm? **What happens to it when the material part of man dies?** (You need to be thinking about your destiny right now, not just your origin.)

They don't want to think about these things, so they create exotic and elaborate pseudo-scientific arguments. Insisting the mind is material, is an extension of their belief only the material exists. They must believe this, or else their entire argument against an immaterial Creator fails. They will NOT budge from their corner.

But, what happens if they are right? If they are right, then there is no non-material, non-physical component of man. Man is the sum-total of his physical parts. His entirety is made up of his anatomy and physiology. What makes us, us?

Whatever makes us, us, is what determines what we know.

Whatever makes us, us, is what determines what we think.

Whatever makes us, us, is what determines what we believe.

Whatever makes us, us, is what determines what we say.

Whatever makes us, us, is what determines what we do.

Whatever makes us, us, is what determines what we are.

So, what makes us, us? According to atheists, it is our subatomic particles. Let's compare the two thoughts.

1.) The Christian says, "You are what you think."

2.) The Atheist says, "You think what you are."

If the materialists are right, there is no human volition. We make no true choices. No one can make a decision based on anything other than what his subatomic particles cause him to choose. (That's because our subatomic particles cause us to believe what we believe.) But choices require knowledge, and the only knowledge we can have is what our subatomic particles cause us to know. Any beliefs we think we have, are not the strict activity of our brain, they are the strict activity of the subatomic particles that make up our brain. If you had different subatomic particles, or if they were arranged in a different way, you would have different beliefs and make different choices. Remember, Peter Atkins believes the mind is strictly the activity of the brain, and the brain is strictly material. You have no choice to think and believe, except what your subatomic particles cause you to think and believe. Of course, subatomic particles have no choice in where they are, what they are, or what they do. Subatomic particles are caused by the fundamental particles and forces of nature; but they make no choices either. They have no choice in the matter because they are just matter. You have no choice in the matter because you are just matter. You have no more ability to choose what to do, than the rocks of an avalanche can choose what to do when moved by that first little stone. Remember, this is a universe of causes-and-effects. If nothing but the material exists, then you are the product of a long chain of material causes and effects—nothing more. Ultimately the events of Big Bang pre-determined what you are, what you think, and what you believe. You can't change yourself because:

1.) You can't change your subatomic particles.
2.) You can't change the fundamental forces.
3.) You can't change the properties of the fundamental particles.

You are what you are because that's what you are. Your life is pre-determined and there is no way you can change it. Every good thing you have done is meaningless because "you" didn't do it. Your subatomic particles did it. Every bad thing done to you by others is meaningless because "they" didn't do them. Their subatomic particles did them. Every disaster, every death, every moment of pain, suffering, and sorrow are nothing more than what the subatomic particles cause. In a strictly material universe, good and bad mean nothing. Is the sun good because it sustains life, or is it bad because it causes cancer and death? Death means nothing! It's just something the subatomic particles cause. But, if death means nothing, then life means nothing. And, if life means nothing, atheists can't get mad about disasters, diseases, violence, *etc.* when they cause death.

This also means love means nothing. Love does not come from "us." It comes from our subatomic particles. What we call "love" is not love; it is only Apparent Love. (It looks like love, but since subatomic particles cannot love, it cannot be Actual Love.) It is only a function of our subatomic particles over which we have no control. It is erroneous to think we have control over our subatomic particles, since it is our subatomic particles that give us our ability to control anything. This means we can't control love. We can't control to whom we give love, and we can't control from whom we receive love. It is all the inter-workings of mindless, inanimate subatomic particles.

The same thing applies to joy, hope, pride, courage, knowledge, wisdom, friendship, loyalty, honesty, kindness, dependability, patriotism, devotion, and every other emotion, value, or standard we love. Oops, I forgot. We can't love these things; we only think we love them. Oops, I forgot again. How can we think we love them if we can't think?

Even worse, we must apply the same beliefs to the emotions, values, and standards we say we hate. Anger, racism, bigotry, hate, fear, envy, lust, greed, injustice, cruelty, and violence are all nothing more than the works of subatomic particles. Pain and suffering are meaningless concepts. If these things are the sum-total of our material components, then they are nothing more than the interactions of mindless, merciless subatomic particles. No one is to blame for anything they say, think, or do. No person is responsible for evil because there is no such thing as evil, and there are no such things as persons.

According to materialism, there is no such thing as WHO we are; there is only WHAT we are. According to materialism, life is meaningless. It has no value and it has no purpose. It's only the activity of a bunch of mindless subatomic particles that give "us" the illusion of perception that life has meaning, value, and purpose. If Peter Atkins is right, then Peter Atkins and his beliefs are the meaningless activities of his subatomic particles. He has no meaning, value, or purpose. Teaching Chemistry at Oxford for forty years was meaningless. Writing Chemistry textbooks was meaningless. Any feelings of self-fulfillment, accomplishment, pride, or success are merely the activities of the mindless subatomic particles that make up his brain. Dedicating his life to stamping out Christianity is also meaningless. At best, he is claiming his subatomic particles disagree with our subatomic particles. In the end, he doesn't prove he is right and he doesn't prove we are wrong. If he is right, he only proves his subatomic particles make him reject God, and our subatomic particles make us believe in God. According to his belief, his ultimate source of knowledge are his subatomic particles. Why should we trust his subatomic particles? What do they know about how they came into existence? What a useless life Peter Atkins has lived if he is right! If he is right, no one can make free choices. To make a free choice a person would have to choose his own subatomic particles, and no one can do that.

No one except Jesus, that is! In eternity past, Jesus fully planned His Advent on earth. In the beginning, He created the fundamental particles that would make up His body for every Planck unit of time He would live on the earth. He designed all the forces to be what they are, and do what they do. Fundamental particles and forces have no control over Jesus because He controls them. He created them, and He sustains them. In the beginning, He created every fundamental unit of matter and energy, and He has been sustaining their existence ever since. Yes, all the fundamental particles and forces need to be sustained every Planck Unit of time. None of them exist without God continually causing them to exist. Neither does the framework of time and space into which He places them. As awesome as creating and sustaining the universe is, it is "Finger-Work" for Him. (Psalms 8:3) There is something even more awesome that Jesus did with His absolute and perfect control over time, space, matter, and energy; He created you.

The Bible rejects materialism because it says God made us in His image and likeness. He made a body (the material) and then He breathed the breath of life (the immaterial) into that body so that we became a living-soul. (A combination of the material and immaterial.) The Bible rejects materialism because it says God loves us. Jesus did not come to die on the Cross to save your subatomic particles. He could save those in a jar. He died on the Cross to save your soul. He loves your soul. He died to save you because you are not a mindless cloud of subatomic particles. You mean something to Him. You are valuable to Him. He has a purpose for you. You have meaning and value and purpose because God has given you meaning and value and purpose. They don't come FROM you; they are given TO you. The Bible rejects materialism because it says we have meaning, value, and purpose that come from the immaterial God. If you want to discover your meaning, value, and purpose, you must repent of your sins, put your faith in Jesus Christ, and then dedicate your life to studying and obeying His Word.

Well, I won't pretend to deceive myself. In the first part of this book I said I doubted formal debates would change the minds of many atheists. I doubt this book will change their minds either. At least not if they are die-hard atheists who take the approach that belief in anything is better than belief in God. But, I pray if you were unsure, or merely leaning toward the atheistic view, that you will have been convinced by my evidence that belief in God IS scientifically valid. If you still find yourself rejecting God, it may be because there is another corner you have painted yourself into. Atheists make another claim in an effort to reject the truth. They say God doesn't exist because they have never seen Him. They say they refuse to believe anything they can't see. How many times have you read or heard atheists say they would believe in God if He would just reveal Himself to them? This is a dodge for three reasons.

First, the very fact they say they have never seen God, proves they already know (or think they know) something about God. What if, by chance, we Christians are wrong about God and the Eastern Pantheistic Religions are right. In Pantheism, God is the universe and the universe is God. That means everything in the universe is God, and God is everything in the universe. That would mean when you see a tree, you see God. When you see the moon, you see God. When you see a bird, you see God. If Pantheism is true, then the atheist sees God everywhere he looks. For an atheist to claim he has never seen God, he must know Pantheism is false. But, how does he know God doesn't exist as a tree, or the moon, or a bird? Atheists stand as mortal specks of dust, living on a speck of dust, making claims about what God can and cannot be.

Second, some people wouldn't believe in God even if He did a monkey-dance on their heads. God HAS revealed Himself to many people, on many occasions, for many reasons, in many ways, and in many places, but they still refused to believe in Him. Pharaoh of Egypt experienced all ten plagues God sent against him, but he still hardened his heart and refused to believe in God. For forty years, the Jews were led by a Pillar of Cloud by day and a Pillar of Fire by night. God was in that Pillar. It was a forty-year miracle. They saw it every day. They experienced it every night. They received miraculous food (manna) for that same forty-year period. God gave them physical evidence every morning. Still, millions of them refused to believe in the God they had seen and experienced. Judas Iscariot witnessed every miracle performed by Jesus during His ministry, including the raising of the dead. Yet, he still refused to believe the physical evidence that Jesus is God. Seeing God doesn't guarantee faith in God. Experiencing His miracles won't change your mind if you hate Him. Those who refuse to believe in God, refuse to accept God in spite of the revelations He gives them.

The third reason this claim is bogus is because they DO believe in things they cannot see. If they refuse to believe everything they cannot see, they must also refuse to believe science. Science is based on forces that cannot be seen. Let me explain. If I hold a rock in my hand and let it go, what happens to the rock? It falls to the ground. Why? The answer is easy; it's because of gravity. Now for the tough question: Have you ever seen gravity? Your first inclination is to say you see gravity all around you. Ahhh, but think about what you actually see and do not see. You see the EFFECTS of gravity. You do not see gravity itself. The Force of Gravity is invisible. The only way we can detect the Force of Gravity is by what it CAUSES. You see its effects and you feel its effects. There would be no way to detect the Force of Gravity if we couldn't measure its effects. So, while you can't see gravity, you still believe in it. You still believe an invisible force causes rocks to fall and planets to orbit the sun. You believe a CAUSE you cannot see causes the EFFECTS you can see.

You believe the same thing about the other fundamental forces of nature. No one can see the Strong Nuclear Force, or the Weak Nuclear Force, or the Electromagnetic Force. All we can see are the effects those forces cause. The forces themselves are invisible. "But what about light," you ask? "Don't we see electromagnetic energy when light strikes the pigmented retinal cells in the back of our eyes? No. When photons strike the light-sensitive molecules in the retina, the electromagnetic energy causes those molecules to alter their shape. This starts a chemo-electrical cascade of events that sends signals to the brain, where they are interpreted. It's similar to what happens when a brick falls on your toe. You don't feel gravity; you feel the effects of gravity. We don't see light; we detect and interpret (in our minds) the effects of light. So, if you believe in forces you cannot see, why don't you believe in the God you cannot see?

I could formulate a new concept of "physics" by saying there are no fundamental physical forces. God Himself directly acts on the fundamental particles to make them do what they do. Gravity doesn't cause rocks to fall; God does that directly. Atomic nuclei are not held together by the Strong Nuclear Force; God is holding them together. (And if you split one, God gets mad and releases energy according to the formula: $e=mc^2$.) Photons aren't emitted from stars by the Electromagnetic Force. God is doing that. What scientific observation can you use to prove my "physics" is wrong? According to my "physics," all the scientific observations would look the same, all the scientific measurements would be the same, and all the scientific experiments would yield the same results. The only difference would be whether we attributed the causes to an invisible personal God or to invisible impersonal forces. If I could get all the politicians to believe in my "physics," we could write laws making it illegal to teach that the four fundamental physical forces exist. We could keep them from being taught in the science class. We could flunk students who believed in them. We could fire teachers and professors who taught them. With enough time, less than ten-percent of Nobel-Prize-Winning scientists would be atheists.

Neither God nor the four fundamental physical forces themselves are directly observable according to science. How can you prove the four fundamental natural forces exist, other than my observing their effects? Then, even when you observe their effects, how do you prove they are/were caused by natural forces? What if I claimed there were four supernatural forces that cause those natural effects? How could you disprove that, by relying on natural observations alone? You couldn't. In fact, I have the same amount of evidence God exists, that atheists have that the physical force of gravity exists. They say they know gravity exists because they see rocks fall. I say I know God exists because I see rocks fall. In both cases, we are basing our beliefs on the $0°$ Perceptions of what we think causes rocks to fall. What causes rocks to fall? What causes the cause of rocks to fall? Gravity is not eternal; it came into existence at the Big Bang. What caused it to come into existence? What existed before time, space, matter, and energy that could cause time, space, matter, and energy? The physical forces are not self-caused, they are not self-existent, and they are not eternal. The Founding Fathers of modern science were more than willing to accept the belief that fundamental physical forces existed. However, they believed those fundamental physical forces were caused by an eternal, self-existent, omnipotent, omniscient, omnipresent, immutable, supernatural, personal God. They believed God wrote the Laws of nature that governed the existence and behavior of nature. This belief does not, in any way, contradict the true definition of science. It only contradicts the modern, distorted definition of science.

Atheists reject the idea of an ultimate supernatural cause. They don't believe in a fundamental supernatural force. Yet, they believe in fundamental physical forces. Why are the fundamental forces easy for atheists to believe, while belief in God is not? The reason goes back thousands of years: **Impersonal forces are not moral forces.** If the universe itself is governed by impersonal physical forces, then there are no absolute values or morals that must be obeyed. The ancient Greeks knew that. So, do modern evolutionists. In truth, it is not science that shapes the opinions of atheists and evolutionists; it is their rejection of an absolute moral authority. That's why they redefined science. It is no less scientific to include an invisible God as a causal force, than it is to include invisible physical forces as causal forces. In both cases, we cannot see the causes; we can see only the effects. We CAN observe the effects of God. The effects of God ARE observable and measurable and testable. The Bible told us this thousands of years ago. Let me rephrase Psalms 111:2 in a slightly different way:

Psalms 111:2 "Great are the **effects** of the Lord, **observable** by all who take pleasure therein."

False Supposition 10: The Universe was Caused by Nothing

Here's where another shoddy argument comes into focus. Evolutionists now insist the universe was uncaused. They say this because they have been confronted by the illogic of their previous arguments that can't eliminate the necessity of a Creator. You see, logic tells us if something exists, then it either has existed eternally, or else it began to exist at some point in time. There are no other options. The ancient pagan philosophers recognized the significance of this long before science was science. Something (or Someone) had to exist eternally. Either the universe was eternal (an infinite regression of causes and effects) or else there was an eternal Uncaused-Cause/Unmoved-Mover. They opted for an eternal universe governed by an Impersonal Principle of Order. Otherwise, they would have to believe the Unknown and Unknowable God (The Eternal, Omnipotent, Omniscient, Omnipresent, Immutable, Personal, Moral, Self-Existing God) created the universe. They didn't want that God peeking into their bedrooms. So, for millennia, God-haters said the universe was eternal. However, with the discovery of the Big-Bang, science proved them wrong. Since time, space, matter, and energy (nature) began to exist fourteen billion years ago, they were not eternal. This means they had to be caused. But since a cause must exist before the effect, something had to exist before the cause of the universe. Whatever that cause was, it had to be "other than," "outside of," and "beyond" nature. It had to transcend time, space, matter, and energy. It had to be immaterial and eternal. It had to be supernatural. So, in the light of the scientific evidence for the Big Bang, how do atheists explain how the universe came into existence without a supernatural Creator? "That's easy," they say. "The universe was caused by nothing. Nothing created everything."

Oh, I wish Aristotle were alive today. Arguably, he was the greatest of all the ancient philosophers, and he would laugh at this suggestion. He knew that nothing is nothing. He knew that nothing can do nothing. He knew that nothing is not a force. He knew that nothing cannot cause movement. He knew that nothing cannot cause anything. He knew that nothing cannot change anything. He said, "Nothing is what rocks dream of." Since the Second Law of Thermodynamics proves there is no Impersonal Principle of Order governing the universe, how can atheists today say, "Nothing created the universe?" The answer is simple. They redefine the word "nothing" by giving it an altogether different meaning. Their "nothing" is not the same as the classic definition of "nothing." Their "nothing" is something called, "The Quantum Vacuum."

What is the Quantum Vacuum? Supposedly, it was a "sea" of fluctuating energy fields at the lowest possible energy level that produced virtual waves and virtual particles which ceased to exist as soon as they came into existence. If these "things" popped in and out of existence within one Planck Unit of time, then no net matter/energy gain was accomplished, and the Quantum Vacuum continued to be "nothing." What happened, they speculate, is that fourteen billion years ago, the Quantum Vacuum popped gazillions of virtual waves and particles into existence, and then for some unknown reason they got "stuck" and didn't pop back out of existence. Since each virtual wave or particle is supposed to pop back out of existence as quickly as it pops into existence, it defies the odds that 10^{81} fundamental particles have all managed to remain for fourteen billion years instead of for only 10^{-43} seconds. Each second the universe continues to exist, it defies 1 in 10^{124} odds. Not even the Kentucky Lotto Lady could rig those numbers. Their "nothing" is not nothing. Their "nothing" IS something (a minimum energy field) that DOES something (creates and destroys virtual waves and particles). Real nothing IS nothing that DOES nothing. Real nothing cannot, "force, maximize, create, modify, shape, operate, drive, favor, maintain, push or adjust," anything. These evolutionists are playing fast and loose with the definition of the word "nothing." They are giving an explanation they think we can't disprove. They say we can't prove the Quantum Vacuum didn't do it, because we can't observe, measure, test, or verify anything that existed before the Big Bang. Since the Quantum Vacuum existed before the Big Bang, we can't prove the Quantum Vacuum didn't cause the Big Bang.

On the contrary, I think we can prove the Quantum Vacuum couldn't have caused the Big Bang; at least, not by itself. Something (or Someone) had to cause the Quantum Vacuum to cause the Big Bang. The reason I can say this is by using the logical principles of cause and effect. If a cause causes an effect, then there are only two ways it can do so. The cause either eternally exists, or else the cause begins to exist. If it is eternal, then it is eternally causing the effect. (Unless something else acted upon the cause to change it from not-causing-the-universe, to causing-the-universe. In that case, however, the cause is not the ultimate cause of the effect—something else caused the cause to cause the effect. The cause would only be an intermediary cause. Remember El Gordo, La Gorda, El Alto, La Corta, *etc.*?) So, if a cause is an ultimate cause and has been eternally causing an effect, then the effect has been caused for eternity. This means if the Quantum Vacuum is the ultimate and eternal cause of causing the universe to come into existence, then the universe has been caused to exist for eternity. Science proves this is not so. The universe was caused about fourteen billion years ago.

The Quantum Vacuum cannot be an ultimate and eternal cause. At best, it might be an intermediary cause of the universe, but it cannot be the ultimate and eternal cause. It might be the boulders of the avalanche that smashed the house, but it is not the tiny pebble that started the avalanche. Calling it, "the cause," of the universe is merely an example of Terminology Phenomenology. The ultimate cause of the universe must be an eternal, uncaused cause, not dependent on any outside/other-than force.

So, what can be an ultimate and eternal cause that neither changes, nor eternally causes an effect? It must be able to change what it causes without being changed itself. The only way a cause can remain an eternally unchanged cause is if it is an eternal and immaterial mind capable of making decisions about what it will or will not cause. Do you remember what the Greek philosophers taught? An immaterial mind is the only force that can cause an effect without having to be caused (changed/moved) to do so by some outside/other cause. This means the ultimate cause of the universe was an eternal and immaterial mind capable of making decisions, and it decided to cause the universe fourteen billion years ago. (And it did so without itself being changed. It decided to change what it DID, not what it WAS.)

In the end, evolutionists knew that as long as they struggled to find a cause for the universe, they would be doomed in their attempts to eliminate God from being that cause. Even their attempt at defining the Quantum Vacuum as, "nothing," failed. The Quantum Vacuum was not nothing. It was something, but it was something that couldn't cause the universe in-and-of itself. So, they shifted theories. They theorized that the universe was not cause by anything. It was truly uncaused. It just popped into existence fourteen billion years ago without a cause. Why do they believe this?

If matter and energy and space and time were caused to come into existence at the Big Bang, then what was the cause? Since there was no nature before the Big Bang, the cause had to be something "other than" nature; it had to be Supernatural. Atheistic Evolutionists reject this, but one must be an observer before the event to know the cause of the event. (Recall my Domino Universe illustration. You wouldn't know who pushed the first domino unless you were there before the first domino was pushed.) They want you to believe the Big Bang didn't have a cause, because if it had a cause, then the Cause existed before time, space, matter, and energy. Something had to exist before the Big Bang. Whatever the Cause of the Big Bang was, it wasn't time, space, matter, or energy, *i.e.*, it wasn't something natural. Again, this would mean the Cause was Supernatural. In an effort to flee the possibility of a Supernatural Cause, they run toward the idea the universe came into existence without a cause. They tell us the Laws of Cause and Effect apply only to the physical realm. They say the Scientific Laws didn't apply to the Pre-Big Bang "universe." Let me ask them, "Is that a Scientific Law?" How do they know the Laws of Cause and Effect didn't operate before the Big Bang? How many Pre-Big Bang "universes" have they observed and tested? Scientists can make these claims, but as soon as they make them, they become priests. Still, they insisted the universe was uncaused.

That only landed them in another shoddy philosophical, theological, scientific corner. The instant they "prove" causes aren't necessary for effects, they remove the necessity of causes. This destroys the foundation of science itself. Science is based on the idea this is a universe of causes and effects. We can observe, test, measure, and repeat the causes and effects so well, we can devise natural laws explaining nature. Things fall because gravity is a natural cause. The sun emits light because thermonuclear fusion is a natural cause. Atomic nuclei exist because the Strong Nuclear Force is a natural cause. How do you prove the sum-of-all-natural-effects (the universe) can be un-caused? How do you observe, test, measure, and repeat "un-causes?" What Laws of "nothing" (nothing existed before the Big Bang) have they provided to explain how natural things are un-caused? How many "nothings" did it take to create the universe? Was one "nothing" enough, or did it take two? Can only square "nothings" create universes, or can triangular "nothings" do it too? What color was the "nothing" that created the Big Bang? I'm sure only green "nothings" can do it, because purple "nothings" can only create yappy Chihuahuas. (Provided they have an infinite amount of sodium and chlorine.) If nothing existed before the Big Bang, how could nothing change to something? There was nothing to change and no way it could change. "Change," means something was something at one time, and then something else at a later time. But, if time didn't exist, there could be no such thing as "later." If there was no such thing as "later," then nothing couldn't change from nothing to something. If you remove the necessity of causes, you remove the necessity of effects. If you remove the necessity of effects, you remove the necessity of science. If you remove the necessity of science, you remove the Theory of Evolution as a scientific explanation for the origin of species.

False Supposition 11: The Universe is Nothing

Atheistic evolutionists have one last desperate avenue of escape from the possibility of a Supernatural Cause. They forget about the cause and redefine the effect. Today, atheists say the universe has no cause because the universe doesn't truly exist! The effect is illusory. There is no need for a cause because there is no effect. You see how far they've come down Ludicrous Lane. At first, the universe had no cause because it was eternal and infinite. Then, when science proved that was wrong, they switched to the idea the universe had no cause because it came out of nothing without a cause. (Nothing created everything.) But, science must reject that idea if science itself is to remain a basis for proving anything. If they allow the idea of uncaused-effects, they must reject the idea that even life was a caused effect. They can't insist evolution CAUSED life because they can't prove life was caused. The universe may have popped into existence this way five minutes ago. Life, homologous structures, and everything else just popped into existence without a cause. But, that leaves the Theory of Evolution without any scientific foundation. Again, since they can't prove life was caused, they can't insist evolution caused it. They must reject the very notion that natural phenomena can be explained by scientific hypotheses, theories, or laws. The idea nature can be defined by scientific statements requires that natural effects be caused by natural causes. Science becomes Un-Science if effects don't require causes. If this idea is true, then they must reject science itself. So, to get around this little epistemological problem, they now proclaim nothing exists. (Nothing created nothing.)

Oh surely, you think I am out of my mind when I say this. To say nothing exists is nonsense. It directly contradicts strict materialists, like Dr. Peter Atkins, who insist matter and energy are the only things that exist. Don't blame me for this idea! Naturally, I don't believe nothing exists; I believe I exist. I believe you exist. Nevertheless, brilliant Atheistic Evolutionists now say matter and energy don't exist. Let me quote a brilliant Atheistic Evolutionist who believes this. Let me quote Dr. Peter Atkins. Dr. Peter Atkins is a brilliant man. He is professor-emeritus of chemistry at Oxford where he taught for forty years. He authored many of the chemistry textbooks used in British universities. He hasn't been idle in his retirement either… wait; I think I said this already.

Here is an excerpt from a debate between Dr. William Lane Craig and Dr. Peter Atkins. (Dr. Craig is a Christian Creationist. He earned his PhD in Philosophy at the University of Birmingham, and his Doctorate of Theology at the University of Munich. Dr. Atkins is the same Dr. Atkins we met before in his debate with Dr. Stephen Meyer.) The title of this debate was, "What is the Evidence For/Against the Existence of God?" It was held at The Carter Presidential Center in Atlanta, Georgia on April 3, 1998. Here is what Dr. Atkins said about the existence of matter and energy: (with my emphasis)[48]

"Science can already show that a Creator had less to do than perhaps meets the eye. Let me present one tiny technical argument this evening. How much electric charge is there in the universe?" (He pauses) "The answer is none. We know experimentally that there is an equal amount of positive and negative charge. Which, if summed together gives zero charge overall. At the creation, no-charge separated into opposite charges. **Nothing separated into opposites.** Secondly, and more pertinently, how much material is there in the universe? Another way to answer this question is to ask, 'How much energy is there in the universe?' For Einstein showed that mass and energy are equivalent. When the sum is done, and that involves adding together all the masses of all the protons, all the people, all the priests, all the planets, all the stars, and all the galaxies, as well as the gravitational attraction between them. The answer is close to zero. I suspect that as observations are refined, the total will approach zero. **There is no energy in the universe. Nothing did indeed come from nothing. Science shows that the universe is in fact, a big confidence-trick. There is truly nothing here.**"

Let me get this straight. Dr. Atkins is a strict materialist; he believes only matter and energy exist. (Strict materialists believe this because if anything immaterial exists, it destroys the modern definition of science and allows for the existence of an immaterial God.) Yet, Dr. Atkins also believes there is truly nothing here. He asks, "How much material is there in the universe?" According to Dr. Atkins, there is none! This is why he calls the universe, "a big confidence-trick." According to Dr. Atkins, matter and energy don't exist; the material is not here. But, if there is no material, then in what other category can we place the universe? It can't be denied that we perceive the universe. (We all perceive perceptions.) So, if what we perceive is not material, what is it? The only other choice is it is immaterial. If the universe is not material, then what appears to material is not material; it is immaterial. This means we can perceive something immaterial. Dr. Peter Atkins, the strict materialist thinks the universe is immaterial. This must mean he thinks Dr. Peter Atkins is immaterial. In the other debate, he said there was nothing but the material. In this debate, he said there is no material.

Dr. Atkins believes two contradictory beliefs about the universe. He claims to be a strict materialist, but he also claims matter doesn't exist. If there is no matter, then what he perceives as material is immaterial. But, if the universe is immaterial, how can he eliminate the possibility of the existence of the immaterial? If the immaterial exists, how can he eliminate the possibility of an immaterial God? What scientific observations of the immaterial has he conducted? What scientific experiments can he perform on the immaterial? What instruments has he used to test the immaterial? What are the Laws governing the properties of the immaterial? What scientific predictions can he make about the actions of the immaterial? Since science can only test things that truly exist, what scientific experiments can test the belief nothing truly exists? Dr. Atkins can't use science to prove his belief. It must be his religion.

Do matter and energy exist, or don't they? Evolutionists want it both ways because they try to use each argument in a way to disprove God. (And they will believe in anything but God, no matter how impossible, ridiculous, or contradictory they are.)

Romans 1:22 "Professing themselves to be wise, they became fools," (KJV)

I won't continue the scientific arguments any longer. The reason is because we have made a full circle and have come back to, "Who gets to decide the correct definition of science?" Each of these positions, "Matter and Energy Exist" and "Matter and Energy Don't Exist," can be defended "scientifically" depending on your definition of science. If you try to argue against one position, they will use the other definition. That's how the same Dr. Peter Atkins can insist on two different beliefs about matter and energy, in two different debates, with two different people, at two different times, in two different locations. (Of course, it is possible that one was the positive Peter Atkins and the other was the negative Peter Atkins.)

No, it would be a waste of time to continue refuting their "science." They are playing by their rules of science, and they change the rules as needed to make sure they win the game. That's why creationist students are flunked out of classes and refused admission to graduate schools. That's why creationist teachers, instructors, and professors lose their jobs, their grants, and their tenure. They don't play by the rules. For every scientific argument I could present against the Theory of Evolution, they can present a pseudo-scientific argument for it. Again, it boils down to the real definition of science. In terms of philosophy and science, there may be not a way to discover WHAT is truthful, but there is a way to discover WHO is truthful.

How do you know if someone is telling the truth? When it comes to science, I won't insist that scientists tell the absolute truth, 100% of the time. We all are ignorant, we all make mistakes, and new discoveries often change old scientific "truths." But, I would like some assurance "scientists" aren't intentionally lying. Can we trust what they tell us? Recall what I said about $2°$ Perception: "When someone tells us something is true, we know it's true only if we first know they are truthful and knowledgeable sources of truth and knowledge." I think it is evident Atheistic Evolutionists aren't truthful and knowledgeable sources of truth and knowledge.

At the beginning of this book, I presented my first foundational statement upon which I thought we all could agree. (This was in the section dealing with epistemology.) That foundational statement was: "We all perceive perceptions." Now, as I conclude this book, let me present my second foundational statement: (And I think we can all agree on this, too.)

Second Foundational Statement: It is dangerous to trust the words of a hypocrite.

Atheists accuse Christians of being hypocrites. They claim the Church is full of hypocrites. That's one way they try to nullify the work of the Church in our culture. They ask, "Why believe a bunch of hypocrites?" They are right, of course, but only partially right. The Church IS full of hypocrites. But, so are college campuses. So are factories. So are businesses. So are hospitals. So are science laboratories. So are the halls of Congress. So are the entertainment industry, the sports industry, the automotive industry, the education industry, the military industry, and on and on and on. Hypocrites are everywhere, in every walk of life, including among atheists. They demand we Christians practice our beliefs. They accuse us of hypocrisy if we don't. Why can't we demand the same from them? Why can't we demand the same thing from all philosophers, of all philosophies that deny the truth of the Bible? If they don't live what they say they believe, why should we believe them? I will lay one final charge against these evangelists of evolution. **If they truly believe nothing truly exists, why don't they truly live as if they truly believe it?**

If you say you believe something, but don't put it into practice, then you are a hypocrite. If Peter Atkins says he believes nothing exists, then he must live his life as if he believes nothing exists. When he steps into the street and an oncoming bus honks its horn, he must not act as if he believes the bus exists. If he jumps back onto the sidewalk, he demonstrates he doesn't practice his beliefs. That makes him a hypocrite. If he becomes ill and goes to the doctor, that makes him a hypocrite; diseases don't exist. When he goes to the bank to collect his retirement check or the royalties from his books, he has no right to complain if the banker tells him his money doesn't exist. Above all else, if he believes nothing exists, then he needs to quit writing and speaking and trying to convince people (who don't exist) that evolution (which never happened) caused (but never did) all the forms of life (which are not here). No, I think if anything is a confidence-trick, it's the Theory of Evolution.

As soon as Dr. Atkins said he didn't believe anything existed, Dr. Craig could have gone over, hit him on the head, stolen his wallet, watch, and car keys, and defended his action on the basis that wallets, watches, and car keys don't exist. Of course, Dr. Craig wouldn't do that because he is a true Christian. Dr. Craig wouldn't do that because he truly loves Dr. Atkins. Dr. Craig believes Peter Atkins exists. Dr. Craig also believes heaven and hell exist. Dr. Craig believes Peter Atkins has an immaterial, immortal soul. Dr. Craig believes Peter Atkins will spend eternity either in heaven or hell depending on what he believes about our God and Creator, The Lord Jesus Christ. Dr. Craig also believes Jesus loves Peter Atkins enough to go to the Cross and die for his sins. Dear reader, I believe the same thing about you.

John 1:10-12 "He was in the world, and the world was made by Him, and the world didn't know Him. He came unto His own, and His own did not receive him; but as many as received Him, to them He gave the power to become the sons of God, even to them that believe on His name:"

Conclusion

The ancient pagans believed the Creator-God was unknown and unknowable. They believed the Creator-God was outside of knowledge; outside of science. This is WHAT they believed. The Bible reveals WHY they believed it. They had to exclude the Creator-God, or else they had to accept His morality. Above all else, they didn't want that. Rather than acknowledge God as Creator, they created their own "god," the impersonal First Principle of Natural Order. This "god" made no moral demands on them. Modern evolutionists take the same approach. Above all else, the Creator must be excluded; not just from science, but from all aspects of life. So, rather than acknowledge God as Creator, they created their own impersonal "creator"—evolution. This "creator" makes no moral demands on them either.

The counterfeiter's greatest trick is to make his bills seem so real that people won't give them more than a quick glance. Most people, even people untrained by the Treasury Department, can recognize counterfeit bills if they scrutinize them carefully. Evolutionists don't want you scrutinizing their "science" carefully. If you do, you will quickly notice some things are not-quite-right about their "science."

Did you notice that most of their "evidence" was presented in the form of: "IT-COULD-HAVE," instead of "IT-DID?" Life COULD-HAVE started by a mixture of methane and ammonia gases. It COULD-HAVE been DNA. It COULD-HAVE been RNA. It COULD-HAVE happened in hyperthermal ocean-floor vents. It COULD-HAVE happened in outer space. Simple monomers COULD-HAVE evolved into more complex life. Evolution COULD-HAVE happened in insensibly fine gradations. Evolution COULD-HAVE happened in giant leaps. Random chemical reactions COULD-

HAVE generated intelligent DNA Instructions. Whales COULD-HAVE evolved from dog-like ancestors. Whales COULD-HAVE evolved from hippopotamus-like ancestors. Natural Selection COULD-HAVE caused evolution. Evolution COULD-HAVE caused Natural Selection. Evolution COULD-HAVE been caused by innumerable, perfectly sequenced, perfectly timed, and perfectly written mutations perfectly coupled with innumerable, perfectly sequenced, perfectly timed, and perfectly conditioned environments for extremely long periods of time. Did you notice they never presented the actual, observable, testable, falsifiable evidence it DID happen in outer space? They never presented the actual chemicals from millions-of-year-old strata that DID create intelligent DNA Instructions. All these "Could-Have Arguments" are designed to make you think evolution is true. Their arguments are meant to satisfy the mind, without providing truth. Like I said, evolutionists aren't interested in truth. Assuming the Material Universe is the Real Universe, REAL science must explain REALITY, not just the "could-have-should-have-would-have." **Evolutionists fail to explain your origin. Why do you trust them with your destiny?**

Your Destiny is More
Important than Your Origin

If you are a Christian, I hope this book strengthens your trust in Jesus Christ and His Word. I hope this book helps you see why the Theory of Evolution is a lie, and why it is so dangerous. The Theory of Evolution is based on pagan philosophy, man-made theology, and unobservable and untestable "science."

If you are not a Christian, I hope this book helps you see your true condition. You, the real you, your soul, your mind, your essence; whatever you want to call it, is non-material. Your body and your brain are material, but YOU exist as a non-material being. I think I have given you ample evidence the mind is non-material. This means YOU won't cease to exist when you die. Right now, that non-material being lives inside a material body, but it won't always be that way. When you die, your soul will continue to exist apart from your body. How and where you exist for eternity depends on one thing: **Do you trust Jesus Christ for your salvation?** It does not depend on your deeds. You will not be accepted by God because of your good deeds. You will not be rejected by God because of your bad deeds. Your salvation depends on what you think **(Remember, you are what you think.)** of Jesus Christ.

"For all have sinned and fall short of the glory of God," (Romans 3:23 NIV)

"For the wages of sin is death;" (Romans 6:23a NIV)

"For God so loved the world that he gave his one and only Son, that whoever believes in him shall not perish but have eternal life." (John 3:16 NIV)

"Whoever believes in the Son has eternal life, but whoever rejects the Son will not see life, for God's wrath remains on him." (John 3:36 NIV)

Jesus Christ paid for your sins when He went to the Cross. He was your substitute for your eternal death. He died so you could live. Now, the only way to have His substitutionary death apply to your life is by repenting of your sins and by putting your trust in Him.

"Believe in the Lord Jesus Christ, and you will be saved." (Acts 16:31b NIV)

PLEASE, MY DEAR FRIEND,
PLEASE, DO THAT TODAY!

Index

Ambulocetus, 160, 163, 164
Aratus of Soli, 47
Atkins, Peter, 260, 261, 262, 263, 266, 267, 270, 284, 285, 286, 287, 288, 289
Axe, Douglas, 53
Berta, Annalisa, 17, 19
Brace, C. Loring, 196
Carter, George, 167
Clark, Austin H., 166
Craig, William Lane, 284, 289
Crick, Francis, 94, 136, 220, 221, 223, 227
Darwin, Charles, 16, 22, 51, 93, 113, 134, 135, 145, 152, 153, 158, 159, 168, 170, 171, 172, 173, 174, 177, 178, 179, 180, 181, 182, 185, 192, 195, 196, 209, 217, 225, 226, 259, 299
Dawkins, Richard, 136
Democritus of Thrace, 259
Directed Panspermia, 25, 227, 229, 251
Dollo, Louis, 126, 188
Dorudon, 160, 164
du Nouy, Lecomte, 167
Einstein, Albert, 49, 285
First Degree Perception, 30
Futuyma, Douglas, 181
Gingerich, Phil, 15, 16, 17, 18
Glycol Nucleic Acid, 205
Goldschmidt, Richard, 166
Gould, Stephen Jay, 166, 180
Grassé, Pierre-Paul, 195
Gregory, T. Ryan, 181
Haeckel, Ernst, 126
Haldane, J. B. S., 180
Henderson, Bobby, 128
Herschel, John, 93
Hoyle, Fred, 50, 51, 53, 113, 136, 220, 227, 239, 245, 251, 299
Hubble, Edwin, 49
Humason, Milton, 49
Jastrow, Robert, 136
Kemp, Thomas, 167
Koestler, Arthur, 195, 245
Kurten, Bjorn, 188
Kutchicetus, 160, 164
Leucippus of Miletus, 259
Lewin, Roger, 195
Luria, Salvador Edward, 188
Mayr, Ernst, 180
Mendel, Gregor, 92, 178, 179
Meyer, Stephen, 53, 173, 174, 178, 182, 260, 261, 284
Miller, Stanley, 139, 145, 146, 147, 148, 149, 150, 151, 211, 243
Multiverse Theory, 25, 35, 251, 256, 257
Musgrave. Ian, 237, 238, 240, 242, 243, 244, 245, 247
Mysticetus, 162, 164
Nelson, Gareth V., 166
Odontocetus, 162, 164
Padian, Kevin, 17, 19, 164
Pakicetus, 160, 163, 164
Patterson. Colin, 165, 195
Paul, the Apostle, 46, 47, 48, 103, 129, 130

Penzias, Arno, 50, 96, 97
Peptide Nucleic Acid, 205
Provine, William, 196, 201
Punctuated Equilibria, 159, 165, 192, 227
Quantum Vacuum, 278, 279, 280
Rodhocetus, 15, 17, 18, 160, 164, 168
Ruse, Michael, 181
Sagan, Carl, 85
Scientific Materialism, 89, 259
Second Degree Perception, 32
Teotónio, Henrique, 188
Thales of Miletus, 259
The Flying Spaghetti Monster, 128, 129, 134
The Monkey Shakespeare Simulator Project, 120
Threose Nucleic Acid, 205
Watson, James, 94
Webster, Noah, 38
Wilson, Robert, 50
Xenophanes, 45, 259, 299
Zero Degree Perception, 30

Bible References

(KJV) = Scriptures quoted from the HOLY BIBLE, *KING JAMES VERSION*. Public Domain.

(NIV) = Scriptures taken from the HOLY BIBLE, *NEW INTERNATIONAL VERSION*, Copyright © 1973, 1978, 1984 International Bible Society. Used by permission.

(ESV) = Scripture quoted from the HOLY BIBLE, *ENGLISH STANDARD VERSION*, Copyright © 2001, 2007 by Crossway Bibles, a ministry of the Good News Publishers of Wheaton, IL. Used by permission.

References

1.) Carl Werner, *Evolution: The Grand Experiment*
Audio Visual Consultants, Inc. Copyright © 2009
http://thegrandexperiment.com

2.) OxfordDictionary.com
http://oxforddictionaries.com/definition/english/science?q=science
Oxford University Press. Copyright © 2013

3.) Dictionary.com
http://dictionary.reference.com/browse/science?s=t
Dictionary.com, LLC. Copyright © 2013

4.) Wiktionary
http://en.wiktionary.org/wiki/science?rdfrom=Science
Wiktionary.org, Copyright © 2013

5.) http://1828.mshaffer.com/d/word/science
Noah Webster's Dictionary of the English Language, 1828 (Public Domain)

6.) Encyclopedia.com
http://www.encyclopedia.com/topic/Xenophanes.aspx
Encyclopedia.com, Copyright © 2013, HighBeam™ Research, Inc.

7.) Sir Fred Hoyle, as quoted by Lee Elliot Major, "Big Enough to Bury Darwin"
Guardian (UK), Thursday, August 23, 2001

8.) Stephen C. Meyer, *Signature in the Cell*
New York: Harper Collins, June 2009

9.) Stephen C. Meyer, *Signature in the Cell*, page 213
New York: Harper Collins, June 2009

10.) Francis Crick, *What Mad Pursuit: A Personal View of Scientific Discovery*, Page 138
New York: Basic Books, July 1990

11.) Richard Dawkins, *The Blind Watchmaker: Why the Evidence Reveals a Universe Without Design*, Page 1
New York: W. W. Norton & Company, 1996

12.) Robert Jastrow, *God and the Astronomers*,
New York: W. W. Norton and Company, 1978

13.) Fred Hoyle, "The Universe: Past and Present Reflections." *Engineering and Science*, Page 12
Pasadena, California: The California Institute of Technology, November, 1981

14.) Charles Darwin, *On the Origin of Species*, First Edition, Page 171
London: John Murray, 1859

15.) Over The Rainbow taken from *In The Beginnings*, by Steven E. Dill, copyright 2007, 2010, 2018, Steven E. Dill

16.) University of California—Berkeley
http://evolution.berkeley.edu/evolibrary/article/evograms_03

17.) Brian Leith, *The Listener*, Vol. 106, No. 390 (1981)

18.) Gareth V. Nelson, "Origin and Diversification of Teleostean Fishes," *Annals of the New York Academy of Sciences*, Page 22 (1971)

19.) Stephen Jay Gould, *Natural History*, Vol. 86, No. 5 (1977)

20.) Austin H. Clark, *The New Evolution; Zoogenesis,* Williams and Wilkins, Baltimore, Page 189 (1930)

21.) Austin H. Clark, *The New Evolution; Zoogenesis,* Williams and Wilkins, Baltimore, Page 196 (1930)

22.) Richard B. Goldschmidt, *American Scientist*, Vol. 40, No. 97 (1952)

23.) Lecomte du Nouy, *Human Destiny*, The New American Library, New York, Page 63 (1947)

24.) Thomas S. Kemp, *Mammal-Like Reptiles and the Origin of Mammals*, Academic Press, New York, Page 319 (1982)

25.) George Stuart Carter, *Structure and Habit in Vertebrate Evolution*. University of Washington Press, 1967

26.) J. E. O'Rourke, "Pragmatism versus Materialism in Stratigraphy," *American Journal of Science*, vol. 276 (January 1976), pp. 51-52.

27.) Stephen C. Meyer, *Signature in the Cell* New York: Harper Collins, June 2009

28.) Charles Darwin. *On the Origin of Species*, First Edition, Page 279
London: John Murray, 1859

29.) J. B. S. Haldane, *Possible Worlds*, Page 43
London: Chatto & Windus, 1928

30.) Stephen Jay Gould, "The Return of Hopeful Monsters," *Natural History*, Vol. 86, 1977, Page 28

31.) Ernst Mayr, In the Foreword to *Darwinism Defended*, by Michael Ruse, Pages xi-xii
New York: Addison-Wesley, 1982

32.) Douglas J. Futuyma, "Natural Selection: How Evolution Works"
ActionBioscience, December 2004,
http://www.actionbioscience.org/evolution/futuyma.html

33.) T. Ryan Gregory, "Understanding Natural Selection: Essential Concepts and Common Misconceptions,"
Evolution: Education and Outreach, June 2009, Volume 2, Issue 2
http://link.springer.com/article/10.1007/s12052-009-0128-1/fulltext.html

34.) Michael Ruse, *Darwinism Defended*, Page 308
Reading, MA: Addison-Wesley Publishing Co., Inc., 1982

35.) Louis Dollo, *Les lois de l'évolution. Bull. Soc. Belge Geol. Pal. Hydr*, VII:164-166, 1893

36.) Salvador Edward Luria, *Life: the Unfinished Experiment*, Souvenir Press Limited, 1973

37.) Bjorn Kurten, *On Evolution and Fossil Mammals*, Columbia University Press, March 1988

38.) Henrique Teotónio, *Evolutionary Genetics*, Universidade de Lisboa, Lisboa, Copyright Instituto Gulbenkian de Ciência , 2007

39.) Pierre-Paul Grassé, *Evolution of Living Organisms*, Page 170
New York: Academic Press, 1977

40.) Arthur Koestler, *Janus: A Summing Up*, Page 185
New York, Vintage Books, 1978

41.) Colin Patterson, "Cladistics," *BBC*
Interview with Brian Leek and Peter Franz,
4 March 1982

42.) Roger Lewin, *Science*, 1982, No. 217, Pages 1239-1240

43.) C. Loring Brace, *American Scientist*, Vol. 82, September/October 1994, Pages 484-486

44.) William B. Provine, *The Origins of Theoretical Population Genetics*, Pages 199-200
University of Chicago Press, 2001

45.) "A Spoonful of Sugar" by Robert B. Sherman and Richard M. Sherman.
From the Walt Disney film *Mary Poppins*. Copyright 1964, Walt Disney Studios, Burbank, California

46.) Talk.Origins
http://www.talkorigins.org

47.) Talk.Origins
http://www.talkorigins.org/faqs/abioprob/abioprob.html

48.) ReasonableFaith
www.reasonablefaith.org/media/craig-vs-atkins-carter-center-atlanta

www.ingramcontent.com/pod-product-compliance
Lightning Source LLC
Chambersburg PA
CBHW052014070526
44584CB00016B/1743